Challenging the Qualitative–Quantitative Divide

Explorations in Case-focused Causal Analysis

Barry Cooper, Judith Glaesser, Roger Gomm and Martyn Hammersley

continuum

Continuum International Publishing Group

The Tower Building   80 Maiden Lane
11 York Road   Suite 704
London SE1 7NX   New York NY 10038

www.continuumbooks.com

British Library Cataloguing-in-Publication Data
A catalogue record for this book is available from the British Library.

ISBN: 978-1-4411-1439-6 (paperback)
      978-1-4411-7144-3 (hardcover)

Library of Congress Cataloging-in-Publication Data
Challenging the qualitative-quantitative divide: explorations in case-focused causal analysis / Barry Cooper . . . [et al.].
    p. cm.
Includes index.
ISBN 978-1-4411-7144-3 (hbk.) – ISBN 978-1-4411-1439-6 (pbk.) – ISBN 978-1-4411-4220-7 (ePub.) – ISBN 978-1-4411-0063-4 (PDF)
1. Qualitative research. 2. Quantitative research. 3. Causation. 4. Social sciences – Methodology. I. Cooper, Barry, 1950- II. Title.

H62.C4466 2012
001.4′2–dc23
                                        2011024276

Typeset by Newgen Imaging Systems Pvt Ltd, Chennai, India
Printed and bound in India

Contents

Acknowledgements

Chapter 2 was first given as a paper at a symposium on Methodological Issues in Research on Social Class, Education and Social Mobility, British Educational Research Association annual conference, Manchester, September 2009. A revised version was given at the annual British Sociological Association, London School of Economics, April, 2011.

An earlier version of Chapter 6 was presented at the European Consortium for Sociological Research Conference, *Analysing Education, Family, Work and Welfare in Modern Societies: Methodological Approaches and Empirical Evidence*, in Bamberg in 2010. The chapter, and that paper, were developed from a shorter paper that appeared in *Methodological Innovations Online* in 2010.

Chapter 7 is a revised and expanded version (adding a new comparison of fsQCA and cluster analysis) of a paper that previously appeared in the *International Journal of Social Research Methodology* (Cooper and Glaesser 2011).

Introduction: The Qualitative–Quantitative Divide

During the course of the twentieth century there emerged a methodological divide between qualitative and quantitative approaches in many areas of Western social science (Bryman 1988). It came to shape the work of individual researchers, affecting which kinds of data and forms of analysis they used; and it became institutionalized within research communities – for example in the editorial policies of journals, with some journals being explicitly committed to either quantitative or qualitative work, as well as in the planning of conferences and patterns of participation in them. The divide also came to be embedded in the structure of research methods courses and in methodology textbooks, where it is now routinely used as an organizing principle. In broader terms, the qualitative–quantitative distinction has come to be employed by researchers, both novice and more experienced, as a means of navigating, and locating themselves within, the very large and complex field that is social science today, where specialization in terms of substantive topic is frequently entwined with, or subordinated to, the adoption of particular methodological and theoretical approaches.[1] Large numbers of social scientists identify themselves as either quantitative or qualitative researchers, though of course there are some who would claim 'dual nationality', or even citizenship in a 'third paradigm' of mixed methods (Tashakkori and Teddlie 2003; Johnson and Onwuegbuzie 2004; see also Cresswell and Plano Clark 2007; Teddlie and Tashakkori 2009).

As a result of this process of institutionalization, the distinction between quantitative and qualitative approaches has now come to be largely taken for granted in some form or another. Yet its conceptualization has shifted in fundamental ways over time, reflecting changes on both sides of the divide, but especially in qualitative research. Over the course of the twentieth century, the fortunes of quantitative and qualitative approaches waxed and waned relative to one another. In many fields, the broad pattern was of the growing dominance of quantitative research up to and beyond the middle of the century, followed by revival in the fortunes of qualitative approaches, to the point of marginalizing quantitative research in some fields in some countries. Furthermore, rather than a single coherent tradition of qualitative research prevailing, what emerged instead was a plethora of competing approaches across, and even within, particular fields.

Early in the twentieth century, the distinction between quantitative and qualitative approaches generally revolved around positive and negative attitudes towards the use of 'statistical method', as against the study of individual cases. In some forms, this was itself a substantial modification of a nineteenth-century contrast between nomothetic and idiographic approaches: whereas the latter treated the socio-historical sciences as concerned with documenting the unique character of particular events and situations, some early advocates of case study in US sociology, notably Znaniecki, argued that this method (and only this method), which he called analytic induction (AI), could discover universal laws (Znaniecki 1934; see also Hammersley 1989).

---

1 Even the more specific concepts employed in methodological navigation tend to adhere to one side of the divide or the other – 'experimental method' and 'ethnography', for example, are now viewed as *essentially* quantitative and qualitative, respectively, even though not all experimental work in the past was quantitative (see, for example, some of the experiments of Piaget) and mid-twentieth-century anthropological ethnography often drew on quantitative as well as qualitative data. Labels that apparently span the divide – such as 'content analysis' and 'case study' – tend to split into competing versions that lie on opposite sides of it: thus, 'qualitative content analysis' and 'qualitative case study' mark themselves off from their quantitative cousins.

He dismissed statistical method as only producing probabilistic generalizations and therefore as unscientific.

Despite such arguments, up to the middle of the twentieth century, quantitative research gradually became dominant in US sociology, and in many other social science fields. There was a strong emphasis on the need for rigorous measurement and sophisticated statistical analysis. This commitment was shaped by nineteenth-century philosophy of science and also by early twentieth-century ideas like behaviourism, operationism and logical positivism. It is worth noting the quite radical character of these latter positions. For instance, many logical positivists rejected the concept of causality as metaphysical, while operationism involved a constructivist attitude towards the process of measurement, in which there was denial of either the existence or the accessibility of any social reality existing 'behind' the measurements.[2] Over time, this philosophical radicalism was tempered considerably, under the impact of various sorts of criticism, so that quantitative researchers subsequently came to adopt a largely taken-for-granted realist position; though they continued to insist on the importance of numerical data in measuring variation in social phenomena, and to emphasize the need for statistical analysis in documenting probable causal relationships and in providing for effective generalization.

From the 1960s onwards, however, the claims of quantitative method came under growing attack, particularly within sociology, and applied fields like education, partly on the grounds that it had not delivered what it promised but also because of changes in philosophical ideas about scientific method and about what is required in order to understand human social action. The qualitative–quantitative divide often came to be reinterpreted as a contrast between positivism and an alternative approach that was more in line with nineteenth-century German arguments about *Geisteswissenschaften* (Hammersley 1989). 'Interpretive' approaches emerged that championed qualitative work as investigation of the social meanings that shape how people

---

2 On the 'metaphysical' character of causation, see Pearson 1892; Russell 1912. Russell famously wrote: 'The law of causation . . . is a relic of a bygone age, surviving, like the monarchy, only because it is erroneously supposed to do no harm' (1992, p. 193). On operationism, see Bridgman 1927 and 1938, and the article on operationalism in the *Stanford Encyclopedia of Philosophy*, at (accessed 3.2.11): http://plato.stanford.edu/entries/operationalism/. On behaviourism see Thyer 1999 and the article in the *Stanford Encyclopedia of Philosophy*, at (accessed 3.2.11): http://plato.stanford.edu/entries/behaviorism/

experience the world, their actions and the social institutions that develop out of these. This was contrasted with quantitative researchers' emphasis on the observable, their concern with causal explanation and their appeal to fixed, standardized methods for collecting and interpreting data. Advocacy of interpretative approaches drew on symbolic interactionism within sociology and on the philosophical resources of pragmatism, phenomenology and hermeneutics – albeit rather selectively.

The development and proliferation of qualitative approaches continued rapidly during the 1970s, with some older forms of qualitative work now being dismissed as positivist along with quantitative method; and as part of this there was a major shift of emphasis in how the qualitative–quantitative divide was conceptualized by many qualitative researchers. What now came to be rejected as positivist was any claim to study phenomena existing independently of human action, and perhaps even independently of the research process itself. And the central task of qualitative work was taken to be to show how all phenomena are socially constructed, including even the phenomena which natural science claims to have discovered (see, for example, Woolgar 1988). One of the major signs of this shift was the growth of discourse and narrative analysis, but constructionism also came to shape how older forms of qualitative research were understood and practised, including ethnography and life history. Constructionism has taken a variety of forms, from moderate to radical, perhaps with a tendency for methodological statements to be more extreme than practical research strategies; so that only a few writers have taken constructionism to its 'logical' conclusion (for an example see Ashmore 1989). Constructionism, in its different forms, has drawn on many of the same sources as interpretivism but also often on ethnomethodology and post-structuralism.

Equally important in shaping ideas about the difference between quantitative and qualitative approaches in the second half of the twentieth century, frequently in combination with interpretive and constructionist ideas, was advocacy of a 'critical' orientation, modelled loosely on Marxism and Critical Theory.[3] This takes an oppositional stance to some aspects of the socio-political status quo, and calls for research to adopt an activist orientation, being designed to feed into 'emancipatory' political action. Within qualitative social science today we find several varieties of 'critical' work,

---

3 For assessments of the concept of 'critical' research, see Hammersley 1995: ch2 and 2005a.

including those inspired by feminism, anti-racism, queer theory, and disability activism, alongside and sometimes integrated with multiple versions of 'action research'. There are also influential ethical conceptions of research, notably that it must 'give voice' to marginalized groups, perhaps involving them as co-participants in the research process. These developments reflect the impact of 'new social movements', as well as the influence of that complex and confused mixture of French intellectual sources labelled 'postmodernism'. One of the effects of the latter has been to reinforce existing tendencies within interpretative and 'critical' qualitative research towards sustained scepticism about the categories used to understand society, both those characteristic of common sense *and* those used by social science itself.

As a result of these complex developments, by the beginning of the twenty-first century, across much of social science, qualitative research had become an extremely heterogeneous field, and there were now paradigm wars occurring among various positions within it as much as across the qualitative–quantitative divide. For instance, many specific types of qualitative research came themselves to be fragmented into competing approaches that relied upon sharply discrepant assumptions, and employed different methods designed to produce distinctive sorts of product. An illuminating example is discourse analysis, where there are versions coming out of philosophy and linguistics which are not only at odds with one another but also with those developed in sociology and psychology; and some of the latter are fundamentally at variance with others, for instance conversation analysis with 'critical' and Foucauldian approaches. As a result, there is now very little that is shared in common by all discourse analysts beyond an interest in analysing one or another kind of textual data; and in some cases they differ even in the sorts of text they typically analyse (see Wetherell et al. 2001).

During the latter decades of the twentieth century the predominant attitude of quantitative researchers in many fields was a defensive one that recognized the value of qualitative work, albeit usually in a secondary role; and this fed into the development of the mixed methods movement. However, around the turn of the twenty-first century, some advocates of quantitative method moved to being more critical of qualitative research, and especially of its dominance. The most striking example of this development were arguments – notably in the study of health, education, social policy, and crime – about the need for research to serve evidence-based policymaking and practice, along with advocacy of randomized controlled trials as the gold standard for determining 'what works' (see, for example, Oakley 2001; Chalmers 2003; see also

Hammersley 2005b). It is worth noting, however, that this challenged the rationale for non-experimental quantitative research as well as that for qualitative work; and initially radical versions of the argument were later qualified, acknowledging a complementary, if again usually subordinate, role for qualitative research in producing evidence for policymaking and practice.

The current status of the qualitative–quantitative divide

In light of these developments, it is hardly surprising that the various methodological ideas that now shape the work of social scientists no longer fall neatly into two internally coherent, and clearly differentiated, positions; if they ever did. Instead, there is a complex and shifting set of contrasts whose assigned priority varies across fields and over time.

If we take the items usually included in standard lists of the contrasting features of qualitative and quantitative research (see, for example, Cook and Reichardt 1979: 10; Bryman 1988: 94) we find that many of them are equivocal. One example is the opposition between 'inductive' or 'emergent' and 'hypothetico-deductive' or 'confirmatory' modes of inference.[4] It is true that qualitative research usually begins from relatively broad and open-ended research problems, and is committed to developing descriptive and theoretical ideas through the collection and analysis of data, but such research is also 'progressively focused' so as to check some of the ideas developed. It is also true that an influential model for much quantitative research is the testing of closely defined hypotheses. However, it by no means always takes this form; there is often a considerable amount of data exploration, including that where the hypothesis-testing involved concerns statistical hypotheses about the likelihood of sampling error rather than theoretically derived hypotheses. These complexities highlight a point that has long been recognized: that all research necessarily involves both 'inductive' and 'deductive' modes of inference. Any difference between quantitative and qualitative approaches in this respect is a matter of degree. And the predominance of one form of inference

---

4 Some of these terms are misleading because their core meanings refer, in the case of 'induction', to inference from empirical regularities to universal laws, and in the case of 'deduction' to strict logical inference of implications from premises. Neither form of inference is exclusive to either quantitative or qualitative research.

over the other should perhaps usually reflect the phase of development of the field in which research is being carried out.

Another common contrast cited between quantitative and qualitative work is between a reliance on numbers or on words. Here, again, there is a clear difference in tendency, in that qualitative researchers typically do not use numerical data or techniques of analysis, or they employ them only in a subordinate way. But of course they *do* use words to refer to variation in frequency and degree ('often', 'to a large extent', etc.). Equally important, quantitative research reports make considerable use of words, of course, and this can include both non-numerical data and verbal forms of analysis.

Another frequently used contrast suggests that qualitative research is subjective in orientation whereas quantitative work is committed to objectivity. This is an issue that is more problematic than the other two contrasts already discussed. While it is true that some qualitative researchers explicitly embrace 'subjectivity', and that quantitative researchers routinely assume that their research must be 'objective', these terms are fraught with ambiguities and problems (Hammersley 2011a). Moreover, there are qualitative approaches, such as ethnomethodology, that reject any claim to document the 'subjective', and therefore renounce the aim of accessing the subjectivity of others. The main sense given to this contrast in the context of quantitative research involves reliance upon a notion of procedural objectivity, which assumes that the only, or the most effective, means of minimizing error is through reducing data collection to following a set of explicit, standard procedures. However, while such standardization may sometimes be of value, there are limits to how far it can be achieved, and it carries threats to validity of its own. Moreover, it does not exhaust all aspects of methodological objectivity, some others of which would be espoused by some qualitative researchers (Hammersley 2010).

Not only are these various contrasts a good deal more complex, uncertain and contested than is often assumed, and are frequently matters of degree rather than dichotomies, but also the relationships among them are relatively weak: adopting a particular position on one does not *require* adoption of particular positions on the others (Symonds and Gorard 2010). Indeed, there have been respects in which more or less the same stance has been found on both sides of the divide at different times. This is illustrated, for example, by the shift among quantitative researchers during the first half of the twentieth century from an anti-realist position to a form of realism, and the way in which qualitative researchers tended to move in the opposite direction, from realism to anti-realist forms of constructionism, in the *second* half of that century (Hammersley 1992).

All this should make clear that there are *not* two quite distinct quantitative and qualitative ways of thinking. Of course, we do not deny the major divergences in methodological view and practice currently to be found within social science, or that whether researchers are engaged primarily in quantitative or qualitative work is implicated in these. But there is no justification for the claim that there are distinct and contrasting logics inherent in work on each side of the divide. Many fundamental methodological differences in orientation actually occur *among* qualitative researchers, as well as *among* quantitative researchers, as much as *between* quantitative and qualitative approaches. Indeed, there is now a complex mélange of methodological ideas differentially distributed across the diversified field of social science, these often being discrepant with one another, or at least having somewhat indeterminate mutual relations, as well as differing considerably in cogency. At the same time, we suggest that, in practice, there is a great deal more overlap in the character of what are conventionally included under the heading of quantitative and qualitative methods than is generally recognized, especially in practical terms.

This complexity and overlap have been obscured by the 'politics of method' (Steinmetz 2005) inherent in the 'paradigm wars' characteristic of recent decades (Gage 1989; Bryman 2008). In its extreme manifestations, this politics has taken the form of promoting some particular theoretical and/or methodological approach as of unique value and rejecting all else. However, looking across the history of social science since the beginning of the twentieth century, it is possible to distinguish a slightly wider range of more subtle attitudes that have been taken towards the qualitative–quantitative divide. We can identify four main ones. These assume that qualitative and quantitative approaches are:

1. Based on fundamentally discrepant sets of philosophical assumptions, with one being treated as legitimate while the other is dismissed as 'unscientific', 'positivist', etc.

2. Founded on divergent philosophical assumptions but with each approach viewed as legitimate in its own terms, to be selected as a matter of fundamental, and therefore necessarily non-rational, commitment by researchers. In effect, here the divide is seen as amounting to a difference in 'taste', analogous to an artist choosing one style over another.

3. Based on different methodological assumptions that are regarded as appropriate for addressing quite different general types of question, for example those concerned with understanding individual cases versus those seeking universal laws,

those focusing on social meanings versus those demanding causal analysis. From this point of view, one or other *whole approach* must be selected – according to the nature of the research question being investigated.

4. Finally, there have been some social scientists who have rejected the idea of any fundamental incompatibility between the two approaches, in favour of a more pragmatic concern with what method, or methods, are required in order to answer the particular research question being addressed. Here specific quantitative or qualitative methods are to be selected solely on this basis, and it is assumed that it will frequently be necessary to combine these types of method; with few philosophical or methodological problems envisaged in doing so. Thus, the terms 'quantitative' and 'qualitative' are treated simply as labels for two sets of data collection and analysis techniques that each share distinct characteristics, rather than being discrepant paradigms involving diverging methodological and/or philosophical assumptions.[5]

Clearly, some of these stances, notably the first, encourage paradigm war. Others involve less openly aggressive stances towards the other side: for instance the second is compatible with a tolerant détente, though this has by no means always been the attitude taken in practice. Much the same is true of the third stance: this does not present the two approaches as necessarily hostile to one another, even if it leaves room for disagreement about which sorts of question are the more important. Where the first two stances are inclined to treat the formulation of purpose, goal and research question as internal to each paradigm, this third one views them as external. The final stance, which underpins much recent argument for the 'mixing' of quantitative and qualitative techniques, also treats research questions as prior to, and as properly driving, the selection of methods. Even here, though, quantitative and qualitative methods are treated as quite different in character; despite a tendency to ignore the divergent methodological assumptions built into many of the methods, or for those associated with quantitative method to be adopted as the standard (Howe 2004).

Our position

In our view none of these stances is entirely satisfactory, though we are closest to the third and fourth. Indeed, our arguments in this book might be seen as simply another version of the fourth position outlined above, and

---

5 For early examples of this argument, see Trow 1957 and Sieber 1973.

to some extent that is true. We are certainly not opposed to the 'mixing' of quantitative and qualitative methods. However, we do not believe that this is a requirement in all or even most research projects. Nor do we think that it always solves the methodological problems faced. Indeed, to some extent we believe that it covers over problems that need addressing, as a result of a tendency to accept conventional interpretations of quantitative and qualitative methods, and to take for granted too readily the claims made about the effectiveness of those methods in causal analysis.

For us, the various contrasts that have at different times been taken to be central to the qualitative–quantitative divide, or to the opposition between positivist and anti-positivist approaches, need differential treatment. Some are indeed matters where an immediate and exclusive choice has to be made for one side; whereas others involve some genuine methodological problems that need to be addressed in ways that recognize the force of the arguments on both sides. For instance, the contrast that is sometimes drawn between idiographic and nomothetic forms of investigation raises a fundamental issue about what sorts of social science are possible and desirable, one that must be addressed by philosophical and methodological reflection on particular studies that attempt to produce these different sorts of knowledge (see Hammersley 2011b). Much the same is true of Znaniecki's arguments about the capacity of case study to produce general theories, the nature of causality (as deterministic or probabilistic), and the strengths and weaknesses of 'statistical method'. These topics are among the central themes of our book.

However, we take a very different attitude towards some of the other contrasts that have been presented under the heading of the qualitative–quantitative divide, and the associated contrast between 'positivism' and various forms of 'anti-positivism'. For example, the opposition between a focus on explicating meanings and causal analysis seems to us to be false, especially if the former is regarded as setting the goal for social science. There is no incompatibility between investigating meanings and causes, this only arises with particular interpretations of causality, notably those of a behaviouristic or determinist kind.

In the case of constructionism, there is an important distinction to be drawn between, on the one hand, those versions that suspend assumptions about the reality of the constructed phenomena, or about the truth of the discursive claims being examined, in order to focus exclusively on how these phenomena were socially constructed, and, on the other, those that treat constructionism as a sceptical philosophical position throwing into doubt or uncertainty *all* claims to knowledge or judgements about existence and truth. The first is a reasonable strategy, though it may imply a disciplinary difference in focus from conventional social science. By contrast, the more radical position breaches the essential assumptions of any kind of enquiry. If we cannot take it that the phenomena investigated, and this includes discursive practices, exist independently of any account we give of them, and/or if we are barred from assuming that reasonable judgements are possible about which account is more likely to be true, then enquiry is impossible. Whatever the philosophical value of scepticism of this kind, it is not a position that a social scientist can adopt: it is incompatible with empirical research. We take the same attitude towards the insistence that social enquiry is a form of philosophy, in the manner of Wittgenstein (Hutchinson et al. 2008) or a kind of literature (Denzin and Lincoln 2005). For us, all of these approaches simply lie outside the scope of social science (Hammersley 2008).

Our attitude is similar towards those conceptions of qualitative research that seek to redefine its goal as challenging dominant ideas, pursuing some political or practical goal, 'giving voice' to people, producing art works or exemplifying some ethical ideal. In effect, these are attempts to turn research into a quite different activity: away from its distinctive and exclusive operational goal of producing humanly relevant knowledge. While the other activities preferred by some qualitative researchers may well be of value in their own terms, and their demands may be urgent, they should not be confused with social science or pursued under its guise (Hammersley 1995, 2000).

So, we believe that different attitudes need to be taken towards the various methodological disputes that have been discussed under the heading of the qualitative–quantitative divide. And our focus here is solely on those issues that we regard as genuine methodological problems facing social scientific enquiry.

A parallel universe

The very brief historical sketch of the development of social science that we provided earlier, reflecting what has happened in the main areas in which we have worked, does not capture accurately what has happened in all fields. An interesting deviant case is US political science during the second half of the twentieth century. Here, qualitative case study, often historical in character, having previously played an influential role, was increasingly marginalized by the development of sophisticated quantitative work. However, in the past two or three decades there has been a growing methodological defence of case study (Bennett and Elman 2006). This has not involved rejection of quantitative research, but rather the identification of weaknesses within it, and case study has been portrayed as a powerful alternative for discovering causal relationships, on the grounds that it combines within-case and cross-case analysis. Among the most important products of this renaissance of case study has been Ragin's invention of Qualitative Comparative Analysis (QCA) and his subsequent development of this by drawing upon fuzzy logic.

We focus on QCA in several chapters in this book. An important feature of this approach is the fact that, despite its name, rather than lying clearly on the qualitative side of the divide, it has been explicitly presented as a bridge between the two (Ragin 2000: 28–30). It amounts to an attempt to produce a more systematic approach to comparative analysis than has been common on the part of qualitative researchers. But it can also be applied to large quantitative data sets, as is demonstrated in Chapters 6 and 7. Moreover, Ragin draws on the resources of mathematics, particularly set theory, not just as a means of conceptualizing what is involved in comparative analysis but also to develop techniques that render it more rigorous and effective. While the configurational strategies he recommends are very different from the dominant correlational approach within quantitative analysis, he does not dismiss the latter. Instead, he points out that it has important weaknesses that have not been given sufficient attention by most quantitative researchers, and that QCA, and configurational approaches more generally, offer a valuable complement.

Another striking difference between the accounts of qualitative methodology developed in political science and those that have become dominant in most other fields concerns the attitude towards causal analysis. QCA exemplifies the position taken by most case-study researchers in political science: it is explicitly committed to causal analysis, so that its goal is the same as that of most quantitative research today. While, as we saw earlier, in the 1930s and 1940s the influence of operationism and logical positivism discouraged appeal to the idea of cause, focusing instead on discovering correlations within data that provide a basis for prediction, in the second half of the twentieth century there was a move away from this radical position within quantitative research (Abbott 1998); and, in recent years, this has been reinforced by some analyses of causality that seem to claim it can be discovered through statistical analysis (Spirtes et al. 2001; Pearl 2009).

The trajectory of qualitative research in most fields outside of political science has been precisely the reverse of this: from an early explicit commitment to causal analysis, as we saw most notably on the part of Znaniecki (see also MacIver 1942), but also later in the form of Glaser and Strauss's grounded theorizing (discussed in Chapter 3), to a widespread tendency on the part of qualitative researchers today to reject causal analysis as unnecessary, undesirable, and/or impossible. This has often been formulated as dismissal of the project of discovering universal laws. For example, in a discussion of the similarities between ethnography and Foucauldian genealogy, Tamboukou and Ball (2003: 4) declare that both these approaches deny that the social world can be understood 'in terms of causal relationships or by the subsumption of social events under universal laws'. However, as Max Weber made clear long ago, identifying singular causes does not necessarily assume the prior establishment of empirical laws (Weber 1949; Turner and Factor 1984; Ringer 1997). Moreover, in practice, almost all qualitative research reports use verb forms that imply causal relations of some kind, such as 'influence', 'shape', 'leading to' or 'resulting in'. Indeed, they sometimes even employ terms that imply strong causality, such as 'determine'. Thus, Tamboukou and Ball go on to state that 'instead of asking in which kinds of discourse we are entitled to believe, genealogies pose the question of which kinds of practices, linked to which kinds of external conditions, *determine* the different knowledges in which we ourselves figure' (Tamboukou and Ball 2003: 4; emphasis added). Thus, there is often an inconsistency between what many qualitative researchers say about causality and what they actually do when it comes to making knowledge claims (including knowledge claims about what determines the knowledge we can have!).

While, in our view, there is little doubt that social science can and should engage in causal analysis, there are genuine problems about how to go about this, and difficult questions about the nature of social causality (Tooley 1987; McKim and Turner 1997). On this issue, as on several others, we regard many of the criticisms directed across the divide, from *both* sides, as convincing. In other words, we see both quantitative and qualitative researchers as frequently rather more optimistic about the capabilities of their own methods for identifying causes than they have reason to be; though we also believe that they are often rather more dismissive than is justified of what is available on the other side of the fence. While we would certainly not suggest that social science has made no methodological progress, there are nevertheless often considerable gaps between the claims that social scientists make for their work and the doubts and problems recognized within the methodological literature. In practice, researchers often pay little or no attention to threats to validity that have long been emphasized within that literature (see Hammersley 2003).

Case-focused versus aggregate-focused strategies

One of the ways in which the difference between quantitative and qualitative approaches to causal analysis has been conceptualized in political science and elsewhere involves a distinction between aggregate-focused and case-focused modes of analysis, though a more common formulation uses the phrases 'variable-based' and 'case-based' (Byrne and Ragin 2009). This distinction is related to the broader one between survey and case-study research, with most survey work adopting the first approach and much case-study research the second. However, there are significant exceptions, and these indicate that neither mode of analysis belongs exclusively on one side of the qualitative–quantitative divide.

The predominant analytic approach in quantitative survey research sets out to identify systematic patterns among values on a set of variables across cases in an aggregate. Some of the methods for doing this were developed in experimental research in agriculture, where the focus was on identifying trends within aggregates of cases that had been subjected to different 'treatments', in order to discover their effects: to find out whether there is a pattern of consistent variation between the cause and effect variables and, if there is, to assess how big a contribution the causal variable (the treatment) makes to determining scores on the effect variable (see Grigerenzer et al. 1989: ch3). Statistical techniques like correlation coefficients, significance tests, and regression analysis are employed in this task in order to assess the strength of particular patterns and/or to check whether they have been produced by random sampling or measurement error. In non-experimental research the aim has usually been to assess the relative contribution of different factors to some variation in one or more outcome variables – what Ragin (2006) has referred to as a concern with 'net effects' – while allowing for random error.[6]

---

6 For a comparison of conceptions of causality involved in aggregate-focused and case-focused research in political sciences, see Mahoney 2008. There is, of course, a wide range of statistical

By contrast, case-focused research is concerned with documenting causal and other relations *within* one or more cases. Here, the concern is usually with a larger number of variables than would normally be included in an aggregate-focused study. It is sometimes argued that these relations can be directly observed or 'traced', but in our view this is neither cogent nor essential. A more defensible formulation is that through within-case analysis indications of likely causal processes can be detected, thereby generating ideas about relevant candidate causal processes and allowing some testing of these. Moreover, this intra-case analysis may be complemented with comparative analysis: cases are to be selected and compared in such a way as to discover what features within cases seem to be associated, typically in combination, with the outcome that the researcher is interested in explaining (see Mahoney 2004). Often this is formulated in the language of necessary and sufficient conditions, though it need not be. Comparative analysis is also crucial in enabling causal hypotheses to be tested, complementing within-case analysis in this respect too.

In concrete terms, the contrast we are drawing here can be illustrated by comparing how social mobility has typically been investigated with how it can be investigated using a case-focused approach.[7] Many studies in this field have been concerned with investigating causal relations between such background factors as social class origin and parental level of education, on the one hand, and occupational destination, on the other. Specifically, the aim has been to discover the relative causal contributions that these background variables make to variation in occupational destination, on average across the aggregate studied (see Chapter 2). Case-focused work in this area is also concerned with discovering causal relations between background variables and occupational destinations, but it investigates a wider range of background variables. Moreover, there is a focus on how these various potential causal factors relate to one another *within* cases – within the lives of individual people, relevant social institutions, etc. – so as to generate differences in outcome.

---

techniques now employed in non-experimental quantitative research, of varying degrees of sophistication. For the purposes of our argument here in this Introduction we will restrict the discussion to the kind of correlational analysis that is most common in quantitative studies. We will not, for example, examine the case of multi-level modelling, which is one procedure for exploring interaction effects.

7   For the purposes of our argument here, we are ignoring variation in quantitative approaches to the study of social mobility, on which see Savage 1997: 305–6.

The resulting causal accounts are conceptualized in terms of typologies that capture characteristic combinations of factors that tend to lead to particular types of occupational trajectory.[8]

We are being intentionally parsimonious here in what we include under the heading of this distinction between aggregate-focused and case-focused modes of analysis. We have left out of account some differences that are commonly seen as underpinning the distinction between survey and case-study work. These include the number of cases analysed: while it is common for case-focused work to investigate a very small number of cases, there is nothing intrinsic to the approach (as we have defined it here) that requires this. Similarly, while much case-focused research explores changes over time, not all of it does. And, of course, some aggregate-focused work looks at temporal patterns, via panel studies or other means of longitudinal investigation. Further features we have left out of account concern whether the focus is on probabilistic or deterministic relations, and whether the variables are conceptualized in categorical or continuous terms. We will discuss many of these issues in subsequent chapters, but we are not treating them as essential to the aggregate-focused/case-focused distinction. This is because we want to leave space to explore the variation to be found within case-focused approaches.

It is also worth emphasizing that if we examine the range of methods used by social scientists, in terms of the aggregate-focused/case-focused distinction, we find that, while there has undoubtedly been a very strong tendency for survey research to adopt an aggregate-focused approach, there are some quantitative techniques that are case-focused in character, notably cluster analysis and perhaps also correspondence analysis (see Byrne and Ragin 2009). Perhaps even more surprisingly, within qualitative research we sometimes find aggregate-focused analysis employed, a point explored in Chapter 3: what has been called the qualitative survey is quite a common form in some fields, and relies upon an aggregate-focused mode of analysis; furthermore, it could also be argued that grounded theorizing is aggregate-focused rather than case-focused.

It is important to emphasize that both these modes of analysis are means of discovering and assessing the strength of *associations*, synchronic and/or diachronic, among variables or combinations of variables. Thus, both must be carried out alongside attempts to construct plausible models of the causal

---

8 For examples of case-focused, qualitative research on social mobility, see Bertaux and Thompson 1997.

processes operating on the phenomena being investigated, these models specifying the types of phenomena they are, the dispositions and relations they typically have, and so on. The two modes of empirical analysis we are distinguishing here provide means whereby causal hypotheses can be developed and tested, but *they are no substitute for theorizing, even if they represent an essential complement to it.*[9] In other words, it must be remembered that neither of these modes of analysis 'captures' causal relations in operation, they only provide evidence that can be used as a basis for inference about such relations, inference that must necessarily draw upon theoretical ideas.

In this book we will be examining various kinds of case-focused modes of analysis, each normally placed on one side of the divide or the other, and comparing them with standard forms of aggregate-focused analysis. We are interested in the similarities and differences as regards methodological assumptions among these approaches, and in assessing the findings they produce when applied to the same data. In doing this, we have chosen to concentrate in substantive terms on the area of educational inequalities and social mobility, to a large extent.[10] This is, of course, an important field in which a huge amount of social scientific work has been carried out, both quantitative and qualitative. In addition, dealing with a single substantive focus facilitates clear methodological discussion. However, our arguments apply much more widely.

Outline of the chapters

The first part of this book examines quantitative and qualitative approaches to social research, looking at the problems and challenges that each faces, and locating these within a general conception of social science as engaged in causal analysis. The second part is concerned with comparing correlational and configurational modes of analysis, and also with assessing various kinds of case-focused strategy. Many of the same issues are encountered, from different directions, in these chapters. Nevertheless, we have sought to make the

---

9   In this respect, what is referred to in the quantitative tradition as causal modelling, including structural equation modelling and 'path analysis' (as exemplified in Blau and Duncan 1967 and much subsequent work), is misnamed. See Pawson 1989.

10   An exception to this is our discussion of AI in Chapter 5, where the classic studies are located in the fields of drug use and financial crime.

chapters as independent of one another as possible, so that readers can use them separately. As a result, there will be some redundancy for any reader who reads the book from cover to cover, but we hope that there will be more than adequate compensation for this in terms of understanding the complex interrelations among issues and approaches.

Chapter 1 focuses on standard forms of quantitative research whose value is, in some influential quarters on both sides of the Atlantic, currently being re-emphasized against what is seen as the dominance of qualitative work. The chapter provides reminders about the serious difficulties faced by the predominant methods of quantitative analysis, especially in non-experimental research. The problems relate to: errors resulting from large-scale data production, measurement problems, sampling error, difficulties with counterfactual comparison, the limitations and misuse of significance tests, the danger of ecological invalidity, the disadvantages of a preoccupation with hypothesis-testing, and the problems generated by the complexity of causal processes. In discussing each of these issues there is an attempt to clarify the nature of the problem and what would be required to tackle it. The aim of the discussion is not to claim superiority for *qualitative* method, but rather to underline the limits to what social science of any kind can currently supply, as regards causal knowledge. Thus, the criticisms do not rely upon distinctive epistemological assumptions; indeed, many of these problems have been discussed by quantitative methodologists, even if their severity and combined effects have not always been given sufficient recognition.

The next chapter explores a particular mode of inference that is characteristic of research on social class inequalities in education and on social mobility, concerned with meritocracy. This inferential practice involves drawing conclusions about inequality of opportunity from inequalities in educational outcomes, or from inequalities in occupational destinations, at the level of national societies. The main problem here concerns the assumptions about causal mechanisms on which reliance is placed: that skills, knowledge, credentials, and/or occupational positions are distributed as goods or that they are allocated as rewards in relation to degrees of 'merit' defined in a generic way. Each of these models is examined, and it is argued that neither fits well the processes actually involved in educational selection and occupational recruitment. It is suggested that there is a need for more specific investigations of selection processes within the education system and in processes of occupational recruitment, employing qualitative and/or quantitative data. The conclusion reached is that research on outcome inequalities in educational achievement, and on social mobility, can tell us much less about whether meritocracy has been achieved, and if not why not, than is frequently claimed or assumed.

Chapter 3 explores some of the ways in which qualitative researchers have pursued causal analysis. It begins with an examination of what is currently the most popular approach of this kind, grounded theorizing (GT), comparing it with analytic induction (AI). There are significant differences, as well as similarities, between these approaches, with GT being closer to an aggregate-focused than to a case-focused approach in some respects. In the second half of the chapter there is an assessment of a study that claims to apply GT in focusing on how applications to UK universities are structured by social class, race and gender. Of particular importance for our purposes here is that this study takes the form of what has been referred to as a qualitative survey. And, as this label might suggest, to a large extent it adopts an aggregate-focused rather than a case-focused analytic strategy. By comparing how the researchers went about their task, both with the character of GT and with how quantitative researchers would have tackled it, some questions are raised about the effectiveness of this approach to causal analysis. While this study is by no means representative of all qualitative research – no study could be – the points raised here have wide relevance. It is concluded that what is required, in particular, is more careful attention to the meaning of the concepts employed, to how these relate to the data used, to the modes of inference being employed and to the threats to validity associated with them.

The next chapter focuses on one of the key tasks in qualitative research aimed at the explanation of educational inequalities: the detection of causal relationships that explain aggregate patterns, such as national variations in educational achievement as regards social class, gender or ethnicity. Two sorts of inference that carry significant dangers are outlined. One is what has been referred to as the 'ecological fallacy' or the 'fallacy of division'. This involves false inference from associations among variables found in a population to conclusions about relations among variables within cases. The other is the 'fallacy of composition': false inference from patterns identified within one or a few cases to conclusions about statistical patterns or causal processes occurring across a whole population. In both forms, the problem is the assumption, without further evidence, that relations among variables at one level are replicated at the other. The fallacy of composition is explored in detail, in relation to qualitative studies of one or a few schools in the UK that aimed to explain ethnic differences in educational achievement at the national level. Here, researchers have frequently assumed, without sufficient evidence, that what has been observed to happen in a particular case can explain national ethnic inequalities. It is demonstrated that the contribution of the processes observed in a particular school to the numerical tally for a whole population of schools, or of individuals, depends both on the degree of diversity within that population and on the way in which the particular case contributes to this. It is suggested therefore that, before researchers make general claims on the basis of individual case studies, it would be wise for them to map the wider population of cases in terms of relevant variables, and to locate the case(s) they have studied within this. For this purpose, quantitative research based on surveys, or administrative data, is a necessary complement.

The next chapter compares two case-focused approaches that are generally seen as being on the qualitative side of the divide: QCA and AI. As we saw earlier, Znaniecki (1934), who first developed AI, explicitly contrasted it with what he referred to as 'statistical method', dismissing this as relying upon a misconceived notion of science. A key element of his argument here was that analysis must produce determinate laws that apply to *all* cases of the relevant type, rather than probabilistic statements about tendencies. However, this was not just a disagreement about what form scientific knowledge should take. There was an insistence that, without this requirement, the key device that allows for the production of sound scientific knowledge – treatment of a single negative example as refuting the hypothesis – cannot be applied. This insistence that causal relations must be deterministic, not probabilistic, was shared with early forms of QCA, and in this chapter these two approaches are compared and contrasted. AI and crisp set QCA share a number of features in common: the search for causal theories that explain some specific type of outcome; commitment to the use of procedures derived from Mill's methods of agreement and difference; the use of categorical rather than continuous data; a concern to find, wherever this is possible, deterministic rather than probabilistic relations; and an insistence on the importance of studying deviant cases. At the same time, there are also some important differences between these two methods, mainly deriving from AI's insistence on identifying causal factors that are both necessary and jointly sufficient to produce the outcome. Further differences arise when AI is compared with Ragin's fuzzy set Qualitative Comparative Analysis (fsQCA). This chapter concludes by assessing the general implications for how social scientists should approach causal analysis.

Chapter 6 compares and contrasts correlation-based approaches to causal analysis, such as regression analysis, with a set theoretic, configurational approach – represented here by fsQCA. Here the comparison is in terms of how these can be applied in working with the same dataset, and what differences in results are produced. The chapter uses the relationship between educational achievement and measured ability – and the way this varies across social classes of origin and by gender – as a running example. The chapter begins by exploring a simple, invented dataset and then goes on to examine real data from the National Child Development Study (NCDS) to show that some important features of relationships among these variables are often missed, or treated as anomalies, within the framework of correlational analyses. These features become readily visible and non-anomalous when a set-theoretic analysis of the necessary and sufficient conditions for an outcome to be achieved is undertaken. The analysis of the NCDS data is unusual in incorporating three generations (respondents, parents, grandparents) in its exploration of the ways in which the *nature* of the relationship between ability and achievement varies across social classes and by gender. The chapter ends by relating the arguments to some general debates about causality and methods.

The final chapter follows on from the previous one, comparing QCA with another technique for creating typologies of cases: cluster analysis. Again, the data used for purposes of illustration relate to educational inequalities. Commonly used classificatory methods like cluster analysis employ conventional distance-based approaches to construct empirical typologies, but there are also versions drawing on the fuzzy set theoretic idea of partial membership, here within a cluster. This chapter compares and contrasts fuzzy cluster analysis with fsQCA. Both types of strategy adopt a case-focused approach, albeit in different ways. Using, first, simple invented data, and then real data from the National Child Development Study, the chapter explores similarities and differences in the typologies these methods create. It explains the source of these similarities and differences, and also compares the predictive power of the two approaches in accounting for how highest-qualifications-achieved varies by social class, gender and measured ability. The chapter ends by considering the generalizability of the results presented.

In the Conclusion we review our arguments in the book, separating out a number of issues that have arisen in our discussion that represent areas of strategic choice in carrying out causal analysis. These issues are largely independent of one another, rather than representing any simple dichotomy between quantitative and qualitative, or even between aggregate-focused and case-focused approaches. Moreover, decisions about them are largely strategic in character, rather than involving ontological or epistemological assumptions. There are, nevertheless, some more fundamental issues that are important, relating to the nature of causation in the social world and the primary purpose of causal analysis in social science, and we briefly consider these. We end by stressing the need to recognize the limits on what social science can currently achieve, to recognize the range of different options available in relation to types of data and forms of analysis, and to examine closely the strengths and weaknesses of these options, as regards threats to validity.

This book comprises chapters that report the results of work carried out by the authors independently, but which shares the common aim of questioning the qualitative–quantitative divide and exploring the nature of a case-focused approach to social science – with the result that, in many ways, the chapters complement one another.

References

Abbott, A. (1998) 'The causal devolution', *Sociological Methods and Research*, 27, 2, pp. 148–81.

— (2001) *Time Matters*, Chicago: University of Chicago Press.

Ashmore, M. (1989) *The Reflexive Thesis: wrighting sociology of scientific knowledge*, Chicago: University of Chicago Press.

Bennett, A. and Elman, C. (2006) 'Qualitative research: recent developments in case study methods', *Annual Review of Political Science*, 9, pp. 459–60.

Bertaux, D. and Thompson, P. (eds) (1997) *Pathways to Social Class: a qualitative approach to social mobility*, Oxford: Oxford University Press.

Blau, P. and Duncan, O. (1967) *The American Occupational Structure*, New York: Free Press.

Bridgman, P. (1927) *The Logic of Modern Physics*, New York: Macmillan.

— (1938) 'Operational analysis', *Philosophy of Science*, 5, pp. 114–31.

Bryman, A. (1988) *Quantity and Quality in Social Research*, London: Allen and Unwin.

— (2008) 'The end of the paradigm wars?', in Alasuutari, P., Bickman, L. and Brannen, J. (eds) *The Sage Handbook of Social Research Methods*, London: Sage.

Byrne, D. and Ragin, C. (eds) (2009) *The Sage Handbook of Case-Based Methods*, London: Sage.

Chalmers, I. (2003) 'Trying to do more good than harm in policy and practice: the role of rigorous, transparent, up-to-date evaluations', *Annals of the American Academy of Political and Social Science*, 589, pp. 22–40.

Cook, T. and Reichardt, C. (eds) (1979) *Qualitative and Quantitative Methods in Evaluation Research*, Beverly Hills CA: Sage.

Cresswell, J. W. and Plano Clark, V. L. (2007) *Designing and Conducting Mixed Methods Research*, Thousand Oaks CA: Sage.

Denzin, N. and Lincoln, Y. (eds) (2005) *Handbook of Qualitative Research*, Third edition, Thousand Oaks CA: Sage.

Foster, P., Gomm, R. and Hammersley, M. (1996) *Constructing Educational Inequality*, London: Falmer.

Gage, N. (1989) 'The paradigm wars and their aftermath: a "historical" sketch of research on teaching since 1989', *Educational Researcher*, 18, pp. 4–10. (Reprinted in Hammersley 2007.)

Grigerenzer, G., Swijtink, Z., Porter, T., Daston, L., Beatty, J. and Kruger, L. (1989) *The Empire of Chance: how probability changed science and everyday life*, Cambridge: Cambridge University Press.

Hammersley, M. (1989) *The Dilemma of Qualitative Method*, London: Routledge.

— (1992) 'Deconstructing the qualitative-quantitative divide', in Brannen, J. (ed.) *Mixing Methods: qualitative and quantitative research*, Aldershot: Avebury.

— (1995) *The Politics of Social Research*, London: Sage.

— (2000) *Taking Sides in Social Research*, London: Routledge.

— (2002) 'Ethnography and the disputes over validity', in Walford, G. (ed.) *Debates and Developments in Ethnographic Methodology*, New York: JAI Press.

— (2003) 'Recent radical criticism of interview studies: any implications for the sociology of education?', *British Journal of Sociology of Education*, 24, 1, pp. 119–26.

— (2005a) 'Should social science be critical?', *Philosophy of the Social Sciences*, 35, 2, pp. 175–95.

— (2005b) 'Is the evidence-based practice movement doing more good than harm? Reflections on Iain Chalmers' case for research-based policymaking and practice', *Evidence and Policy*, 1, 1, pp. 85–100.

— (ed.) (2007) *Educational Research and Evidence-based Practice*, London: Sage.

— (2008) *Questioning Qualitative Inquiry*, London: Sage.

— (2010) 'Is social measurement possible, or desirable?', in Tucker, E. and Walford, G. (eds) *The Handbook of Measurement: how social scientists generate, modify, and validate indicators and scales*, London: Sage.

— (2011a) 'Objectivity: a reconceptualisation', in Williams, M. and Vogt, P. (eds) *The Sage Handbook of Methodological Innovation*, London: Sage.

— (2011b) 'The nature of social science explanation', unpublished paper.

Howe, K. R. (2004) 'A critique of experimentalism', *Qualitative Inquiry*, 10, pp. 42–61.

Hutchinson, P., Read, R. and Sharrock, W. (2008) *There is No Such Thing as Social Science*, Aldershot: Ashgate.

Johnson, R. and Onwuegbuzie, A. (2004) 'Mixed methods research: a research paradigm whose time has come', *Educational Researcher*, 33, 7, pp. 14–26.

MacIver, R. (1942) *Social Causation*, Boston: Ginn and Co.

Mahoney, J. (2004) 'Comparative-historical methodology', *Annual Review of Sociology*, 30, pp. 81–101.

—. (2008) 'Toward a unified theory of causality', *Comparative Political Studies*, 41, 4/5, pp. 412–36.

McKim, V. R. and Turner, S. P. (eds) (1997) *Causality in Crisis? Statistical methods and the search for causal knowledge in the social sciences*, Notre Dame IND: University of Notre Dame Press.

Oakley, A. (2001) *Evidence-informed Policy and Practice: challenges for social science*, Manchester: Manchester Statistical Society. (Reprinted in Hammersley 2007.)

Pawson, R. (1989) *A Measure for Measures: a manifesto for empirical sociology*, London: Routledge.

Pearl, J. (2009) *Causality: models, reasoning, and inference*, Second edition, Cambridge: Cambridge University Press.

Pearson, K. (1892) *The Grammar of Science*, London: Walter Scott.

Ragin, C. (2000) *Fuzzy-Set Social Science*, Chicago: University of Chicago Press.

— (2006) 'The limitations of net effects thinking', in Rihoux, B. and Grimm, H. (eds) *Innovative Comparative Methods for Political Analysis*, New York: Springer.

Ringer, F. (1997) *Max Weber's Methodology*, Cambridge MS: Harvard University Press.

Russell, B. (1912) 'On the notion of cause', *Proceedings of the Aristotelian Society*, New Series, Vol. 13, pp. 1–26; reprinted in J. Slater (ed.) *The Collected Papers of Bertrand Russell v6: logical and philosophical papers 1909–1913*, London: Routledge, 1992, pp. 193–210.

Savage, M. (1997) 'Social mobility and the survey method: a critical analysis', in Bertaux and Thompson (eds).

Sieber, S. D. (1973) 'The integration of fieldwork and survey methods', *American Journal of Sociology*, 78, 6, pp. 1335–59.

Spirtes, P., Glymour, C. and Scheines, R. (2001) *Causation, Prediction and Search*, Second edition, Cambridge MS: MIT Press.

Steinmetz, G. (ed.) (2005) *The Politics of Method in the Human Sciences: positivism and its epistemological others*, Durham NC: Duke University Press.

Symonds, J. and Gorard, S. (2010) 'Death of mixed methods? Or the rebirth of research as a craft', *Evaluation and Research in Education*, 23, 2, pp. 121–36.

Tamboukou, M. and Ball, S. J. (eds) (2003) *Dangerous Encounters: genealogy and ethnography*, New York: Peter Lang.

Tashakkori, A. and Teddlie, C. (eds) (2003) *Handbook of Mixed Methods in Social and Behavioral Research*, Thousand Oaks CA: Sage.

Teddlie, C. and Tashakkori, A. (2009) *Foundations of Mixed Methods Research*, Thousand Oaks CA: Sage.

Thyer, B. (ed.) (1999) *The Philosophical Legacy of Behaviorism*, Dordrecht: Kluwer.

Tooley, M. (1987) *Causation: a realist approach*, Oxford: Oxford University Press.

Trow, M. (1957) 'Comment on participant observation and interviewing: a comparison', *Human Organization*, 16, pp. 33–5.

Turner, S. P. and Factor, R. A. (1984) *Max Weber and the Dispute over Reason and Value*, London: Routledge and Kegan Paul.

Weber, M. (1949) *The Methodology of the Social Sciences*, New York: Free Press.

Wetherell, M., Taylor, S. and Yates, S. (eds) (2001) *Discourse Theory and Practice: a reader*, London: Sage.

Woolgar, S. (1988) *Science: the very idea*, London: Routledge.

Znaniecki, F. (1934) *The Method of Sociology*, New York: Farrar and Rinehart.

Part I
Problems with Quantitative and Qualitative Research

What's Wrong with Quantitative Research?

Martyn Hammersley

1

As we saw in the Introduction, the division between quantitative and qualitative approaches has long been central to discussions of social science methodology, and over the second half of the twentieth century, especially in the UK, there was in many fields a shift away from the previous dominance of quantitative methods to a situation where most work was qualitative in character. Recently, however, there have been signs of a move back in the opposite direction, in the wake of pressure from governments and funders to increase training in quantitative method, and as a result of the rise of the evidence-based policymaking and practice movement, which initially took the randomized controlled trial in medicine as its methodological standard, and often continues to treat quantitative methods as essential for causal analysis (Hammersley 2002: Intro; Denzin and Giardina 2006; Biesta 2007).

With the benefit of hindsight, it is difficult to claim that these changes in the fortunes of quantitative and qualitative inquiry have amounted to much more than fluctuations in methodological fashion.[1] Moreover, the debates that have taken place have not always been very illuminating. A central feature of what came to be referred to as the 'paradigm wars' has been the tendency to use methodological and philosophical arguments as weapons, without paying careful attention to their validity or implications. Another significant element has been the capacity to forget or to downplay methodological principles when actually doing research, this sometimes being excused or even justified in the name of realism or pragmatism.[2] Elsewhere I have questioned whether qualitative research has lived up to the claims originally made for it (Hammersley 1992, 2008: ch1; see also Chapter 3), and here, in the light of the recent, and welcome, resurgence in the fortunes of quantitative inquiry, I want to make an assessment of *its* capabilities. In particular, my aim is to highlight some of the methodological problems it faces, lest these be forgotten in the new enthusiasm. Many of these problems are well-known to thoughtful practitioners of quantitative method, but in my view their nature and significance is often underplayed or overlooked.[3]

It is common to complain that much criticism of quantitative research is ill-informed, and/or that it focuses on poorly executed work rather than on high-quality examples. There is some truth in the latter claim, but we *do* need to be aware of differences between precept and practice. Another complaint is that many of the criticisms effectively undermine *any* kind of research, if

---

1 And some of the views underpinning the rise of qualitative method necessarily lead to this conclusion, since they deny the very possibility of progress in the cumulation of social scientific knowledge, and therefore presumably also in methodology. See Hammersley 1998.

2 What is feasible given the resources available always shapes research, there will inevitably be methodological problems that have to be managed rather than solved, and frequently trade-offs will have to be made between competing considerations, see Seale 1999; Seale et al. 2004. However, this does not mean that doing what is feasible will always enable us to answer effectively the question being investigated, and this must be recognized. Indeed, the constraints under which we are operating will sometimes mean that we have no hope of answering the question addressed, *and in these circumstances we should make this clear and not pretend that having 'done our best' is sufficient.*

3 I have drawn heavily on the work of several writers who have raised serious questions about various aspects of quantitative research practice from within, notably Pawson 1989; Lieberson 1985; Freedman 1987; Berk 1988, 2004 and Abbott 2001. Another key source is an early article by Turner (1948) on 'statistical logic in sociology'.

this is conceived as concerned with producing causal knowledge. This is also sometimes true; though we should not shrink from recognizing the severity of the difficulties faced. My aim here is to address general principles and practices, rather than particular studies, and to do so in a way that takes account of the arguments that underpin them. I am certainly not starting from the position that 'there can be no such thing as social science' (see Hutchinson et al. 2008), that the very focus of social research needs to be re-specified (Button 1991), that social inquiry must rely upon 'understanding' rather than seeking 'explanation' (von Wright 1971), that it involves writing fictions rather than seeking factual knowledge (Denzin 1997), or that it should be continually 'troubled' in the name of anti-authoritarianism or an aversion to any kind of fixity (Lather 2007). Instead, I share much the same conception of the goal of social research, and of its ontological and epistemological commitments, as many quantitative researchers. The difference, perhaps, is in my assessment of its capacity to achieve that goal.

I have already noted that 'quantitative research' is a label that covers a variety of research designs and methods of data collection and analysis, as well as a range of methodological ideas. This is a point that needs underlining, not least because my focus here will be on a few of the more influential types of quantitative work. It is important to remember that there are significant differences between experimental and non-experimental research; as well as more specific variations in practice that reflect the sort of data that are used, theoretical orientations, and also the disciplinary contexts in which researchers are operating. For example, there are differences between research employing randomized controlled trials to assess the effectiveness of some form of policy or practice and how social psychologists use experiments to develop and test their theories. Variation is also to be found within non-experimental research, for example between that using available statistics and that carrying out surveys, between cross-sectional and longitudinal designs, and between econometric and sociological research, and so on. In addition, there are important differences in strategies for identifying causal relationships (compare, for example, Abbott 2001 and Morgan and Winship 2007). In my discussion here I will focus on issues that are relevant to a great many quantitative studies; though, for the most part, my emphasis will be on non-experimental work. Furthermore, I am not primarily concerned with the use of numerical data in itself, or with basic techniques of descriptive statistics; my main interest is in assessing quantitative research strategies that are commonly used in seeking to identify causal relations.

The challenges I will discuss facing quantitative work of this kind relate to the following issues: large-scale data production; measurement; sampling; counterfactual comparison and the exercise of control; the use of significance tests; the issue of reactivity; a preoccupation with hypothesis-testing; and the nature of causality.

Problems of large-scale data production

It is important to start with the data production process, even though this is sometimes seen as a relatively mundane or pragmatic matter. A great deal of quantitative research draws data from a large number of cases, this being required for the sorts of multivariate statistical analysis employed. Sometimes, reliance is placed upon 'official', or what might be better referred to as 'available', statistics, for example about the incidence of suicide or crime, about the economic performance of some organization or national society, and so on. In other cases, the data are generated by researchers themselves, for example via observational or questionnaire surveys.

There are well-known problems with researchers using statistical data produced by organizations whose purpose is different from, or goes beyond, the production of research data. One is that there may be a substantial difference between the concepts that inform the data collection and those that are the focus for researchers' analyses. To use an early, classic example: defining the concept of suicide was an important theoretical task for Durkheim (1897), but he was forced to rely upon data about the incidence of suicide from various countries in which it had been operationally defined in ways that did not match his definition. A second problem is that there may be variation *among* the people generating the data in how they define relevant concepts in practice, so that the data produced disguise what may be significantly divergent conceptions of the phenomena concerned. At best, these may produce considerable noise. This, too, was a problem that Durkheim would have encountered. Closely related is a third point: that there are various factors operating upon those responsible for producing data that may endanger accurate recording or reporting, or produce systematic error. For example, there may be pressure on people producing government statistics to reduce the reported incidence of some type of social phenomenon at particular times, or to increase it. There may also be workplace factors that tend to generate substantial haphazard error in the reporting of data (Levitas and Guy 1996).

Where the data are being collected by researchers themselves, more control can often be exercised over the data production process, but this is rarely easy and can generate problems of its own. Once again, these stem from the large-scale nature of the data production process, as well as from usually unavoidable reliance on what Roth famously referred to as 'hired hands' (Roth 1965; Staggenborg 1988). If we take the case of observational surveys, problems arise partly from the fact that multiple observers are involved in producing the data. This has led some researchers to recognize the substantial task involved in training and monitoring observers if an acceptable level of consistency is to be established and maintained. However, no set of instructions can be exhaustive, and the more detailed the instructions the harder they may be to memorize and to apply; and this can itself generate inconsistency across observers, as well as inaccuracies, or drift in interpretation over time. Also relevant here is variation in the complexity of the category systems being used, in the number of variables about which data are being collected simultaneously, as well as in time sampling strategies.[4] Many of the same sorts of issue also arise with questionnaire surveys, and there are also long established points about reactivity and the danger of mismatches between the interpretive frames of researcher and researched, and the implications of these for inference from what people say to what they believe and do (see Cicourel 1964; Phillips 1971; Converse and Schuman 1974).

Thus, with both already available data and that collected by researchers for specific purposes, there may also be problems of inference involved. This is true even in the case of variables that may seem to be relatively unproblematic in theoretical and practical terms. For instance, in using gender as a variable, reliance is often placed upon official records, or even on differences in first name, in order to identify people as female or male. This will never be without error, even if most of the time it will amount to a low level of haphazard error.[5] However, the danger is greatly compounded in the case of more complex concepts. One example is social class. Aside from the range of different category systems or scales available, these often being associated with different theoretical rationales, there are also serious problems with

---

4   On the various issues associated with observational surveys, see Croll 1986. See also McCall 1984.

5   Other face-sheet data categories can be more problematic, see Phillips 1971: 101–2 and *passim*.

operationalization.[6] Even self-report of occupation, usually taken as the key indicator, is by no means entirely accurate, for a variety of reasons (ambiguity of occupational titles, prestige bias, etc.); but, often, reliance is placed upon even less reliable sources, such as organizational records or children's reports about parental occupation.

A further level of threats to validity is added when we recognize that the meaning of indicators is determined by the way in which they are linked to particular variables through the data structure employed in a particular study. As Abbott (2001: 47–51) notes, much quantitative research tends to assume that what are taken as indicators have univocal meaning, whereas in fact their status and causal effects may be more complex, so that they may actually carry contradictory implications. The example he uses is a measure of 'self-directedness' in a study of the reciprocal effects of job conditions and personality; he points out that, from the point of view of influential theories, self-directedness may lead both to increased and to reduced autonomy, via different routes. This problem of the potential multivocality of indicators not only generates problems of comparability across data (such as that while, from the point of view of the researcher, those studied were all responding to 'the same' stimulus or situation, in fact there may have been variability in how the stimulus or situation was interpreted), it also raises questions about individual cases, since individuals' responses may themselves be ambivalent.

These problems with data production are often acknowledged, at least to some degree, but they are easily forgotten at the stage of analysis: it is a constant temptation to assume that the numbers forming the data accurately represent what they were intended to represent, or what they are taken to imply. This is especially likely where those carrying out the analysis have not been directly involved in the data production process, as is quite common in quantitative research. Moreover, even if the problems are borne in mind, it is often not clear how the errors involved can be estimated or remedied effectively. There is a temptation to believe that these errors will all cancel one another out, yet this is unlikely. At the very least, they will generate interference that obscures significant differences, but they can also generate spurious differences or associations.

---

6 On the problems associated with producing occupational and social class scales measuring prestige or status, see Coxon et al. 1986.

The problem of measurement

Measurement is a central requirement in most forms of natural science, and it is also essential for much of the statistical analysis that is used by quantitative social scientists. The term 'measurement' can be interpreted in different ways. One common, rather broad, definition is that it is the rule-guided allocation of objects to mutually exclusive categories or to points on an ordinal, interval or ratio scale – in such a way as to capture difference or variation in a property possessed by that type of object. Other interpretations of the term restrict its meaning to the use of interval or even ratio scales, this sort of data being demanded by some of the statistical techniques used by social scientists, such as regression analysis.

A central problem in social science measurement, long recognized, is that there is often a gap between the meaning of concepts as these function within theories or explanations and the meaning that is implied by the procedures used to measure objects in terms of relevant variables. To use a classic example, it is arguable that what Marx meant by 'alienation' is rather different from what Blauner's (1964) operationalization of that concept captures; an example that illustrates that there can be problems on both sides. Much the same is true where research employs concepts with everyday meanings: in the process of measurement these are usually transformed into more specific and univocal concepts. This may or may not represent an advance, but it raises difficulties for the interpretation of findings. It may also be discovered that the original concept cannot be interpreted in a single, coherent and satisfactory way. One example here is the concept of homelessness.[7] All this constitutes a barrier to finding ways of linking data to the concepts embedded in knowledge claims in ways that, taken together, provide a basis for reasonably strong inference from the data to the truth or falsity of the knowledge claim concerned.

In part, this problem derives from the very attempt to develop standardized, objective measurement procedures. The term 'objective' here is usually taken to mean 'minimizing or eradicating the role of judgement'. However, it is rarely, if ever, possible to eliminate judgement altogether, even if that which remains amounts only to making a decision about to which of several closely specified categories a respondent's answer belongs. Moreover, the attempt

---

7 On this, see Williams 2001, who argues that a realist approach that recognizes social complexity and focuses on probabilities at the level of individual cases is required.

to minimize judgement via standardization or proceduralization can sometimes worsen rather than improve the chances of accuracy. This is not always recognized because the meaning of 'objective' is variable. Besides the sense already mentioned (namely, 'what is in accord with an explicit procedure, as against being a matter of unguided judgement') it carries at least three other potential meanings. It can refer to: what is 'of the world rather than of the mind'; 'what was reached by using an unbiased process of inference'; and, 'what is true, as against what is a misleading impression'. The problem is that the distinctions between 'objective' and 'subjective' on these four interpretations are not isomorphic, though the two terms are often used as if this were true. To underline the point: a statement could be about something that is 'of the mind', such as an attitude (and therefore in this sense be SUBJECTIVE); but may have been produced through an unbiased approach (and therefore in those terms be OBJECTIVE); however it need not have been generated by following any explicit procedure (therefore being SUBJECTIVE in that sense); but could at the same time be true (and in *this* sense OBJECTIVE).[8]

So, following procedures is not necessarily an unbiased process and may lead to false conclusions, while exercising unguided judgement need not be biased and can result in sound conclusions. Moreover, we need to recognize that procedures can vary in the level and kind of guidance they provide; *and also that maximum guidance is not necessarily beneficial.* This last point arises because, aside from informational overload, while guidelines can be useful – for example in reminding us of what needs to be taken into account – exclusive reliance on procedures may prevent us from employing our observational and interpretative skills, and relevant background knowledge, in drawing inferences about the nature of the particular phenomena we are dealing with. Yet these capabilities can be essential given the cultural and contextually variable character of human behaviour. For example, very often, in order to record observations or answers to questionnaire items, we will need to understand the language that the people concerned use to communicate with one another. But this is not just a matter of knowing the vocabulary and grammar of that language, we must also have pragmatic competence, in order to grasp *what the language is being used to do on any particular occasion.* Moreover, this competence is closely associated with understanding people's intentions, their likely reasons for doing what they are doing, the motives that might lead

---

8 For an example of the usage of 'objective' that conflates these meanings, see Kish 1970: 132–3.

them to react in the ways that they do to others' actions, and so on; and much of this knowledge is tacit (Polanyi 1959 and 1966). As a result of this, while standardization of data collection processes to facilitate measurement may sometimes increase the likely validity of the results, it can also reduce their validity: consistency may be attained at the cost of accuracy.

A related problem concerns one of the demands that measurement is usually taken to place upon research: that data be classified in terms of a clearly differentiated and exhaustive category system, or located on a properly calibrated scale. The way in which this has often been interpreted is that there must be some set of explicit criteria that identify what is essential for allocation to each category or to each point on a scale: in other words, necessary and sufficient conditions must be specified that allow the unique and certain allocation of every item to a particular category or scale position. Yet there are arguments to suggest that social science concepts may not be open to this sort of rigorous definition. Like commonsense concepts, they often seem to be defined via prototypes or exemplars that are used for determining what counts and does not count as an instance; and they may not just have fuzzy boundaries but also rely upon a family resemblance structure (Rosch and Lloyd 1978; Lakoff 1987; Rosch 1999; see also Taylor 2001 and 2003).[9] This perhaps reflects the fact that social research always depends upon social scientists' ordinary cultural capabilities, as already noted, and that these practices too will involve flexible, context-sensitive categorization. Equally important is that in order to explain people's behaviour, we need to represent the categories *they* use within our theories and explanations, yet those categories will be fuzzy in character and their meaning cannot therefore be captured by a specification of necessary and sufficient conditions.[10]

My argument here is not that the fuzzy and internally ambiguous nature of our categories is an insurmountable barrier to quantitative analysis, but rather that we must recognize the serious problems it causes for current classification and measurement strategies, and find ways of dealing with these adequately.[11] This is part of a more general problem, concerned with whether

---

9 This relates to a broader philosophical issue about the existence and nature of natural kinds. See Bird 2008.

10 For a more detailed discussion of these problems, see Hammersley 2009.

11 For an attempt to do this, see Ragin 2000 and 2008. See also Goertz 2006.

the object-properties to be measured in any piece of research have the character that is demanded by metric measurement (see Michell 2007; Prandy 2002). Michell claims that in psychology, despite the fact that a great deal of attention has been given to problems of measurement, it is often simply *assumed* that the properties to be measured are at least ordinal in character, and that the methods used to gauge them effectively generate at least an interval scale. In effect, what he is identifying here is what Cicourel, many years ago in the field of sociology, labelled 'measurement-by-fiat' (Cicourel 1964: 12); in other words, measurement that fails to ensure that the assumptions built into measurement procedures correspond to the structure of the phenomena being investigated.

A final problem relating to measurement is that very often in non-experimental research there is reliance upon proxy measures rather than direct measurement of key variables. For example, in UK research 'number of free school meals provided in a school' is often used as a proxy measure for the social class composition of the student body. It should be clear that such measures are crude – they do not provide the basis for delicate or precise discrimination – and they may also involve considerable error which it is difficult to discount.

As with the first set of problems, all of this raises questions about what the data produced by much quantitative research can reasonably be taken to represent. Moreover, there is a temptation, deriving from continuing influence of a now discredited operationism, to dismiss these problems by implying that it is the data that are being represented not phenomena lying beyond them. As I will emphasize later, it is essential to retain a clear distinction between the use of statistical inference within the data set and scientific inferences about what is going on in the world for which these may serve as evidence. Correspondence between the two cannot be assumed. But the very rationale of science relies upon its identifying causal processes operating in the world.

Problems with sampling

It is quite commonly stated that quantitative inquiry can produce generalizations while qualitative research cannot. At face value, this claim is clearly false. For one thing, qualitative research *can*, and almost always does, produce generalizations. The key question, of course, concerns the likely validity of these generalizations. Furthermore, as I have argued elsewhere, it should not be assumed that generalizations will always be false if they do not rely upon probability sampling and statistical analysis (Hammersley 1992: ch5). And there are sophisticated arguments about how generalization in qualitative research can be improved (see Schofield 1989). Here, though, I want to focus on the other side of the issue: namely, some well-known obstacles to the claims of quantitative research to produce sound generalizations from samples to populations.

First of all, it is necessary to draw a distinction between empirical generalizations about finite populations and the testing of theoretical propositions, which are intended to apply to all cases that would fall within the (necessarily open-ended) population marked out by the conditions specified by an explanatory theory. My concern in this section is only with the first sort of inference, in other words empirical generalization to a specified and limited population from which a sample has been drawn.

In non-experimental quantitative work the emphasis is usually very much on empirical generalization in this sense; though it is frequently conflated with theory-testing. Sampling is a reasonable and often unavoidable practice, and where it is carried out on a probabilistic basis, statistical theory can help us to decide how large our sample needs to be to minimize the danger of random sampling error, and to determine the likelihood that the sample characteristics deviate from the population characteristics. However, meeting the requirements of statistical sampling theory is more demanding than is sometimes recognized, and the result is that there are often genuine doubts about whether inference to the population is justified.

To start with, as is well-known there are frequently practical problems in finding a sampling frame that covers the whole population of interest, and there will almost always be some errors in the listing. A second problem concerns the sort of sampling strategy adopted. Even simple random sampling on the scale recommended by statistical theory does not *guarantee* that any particular sample will be representative. Furthermore, the likelihood of it being representative in the required respect varies according to the heterogeneity of the population as regards the variable or variables concerned. The greater the heterogeneity, the less likely it is that a simple random sample of a relatively small size will accurately represent the population in terms of those variables.

A further issue concerns the use of stratified random sampling strategies, which are very much more common than reliance upon simple random sampling.[12] There are various reasons why stratification is used, some methodological in character, others to do with administrative convenience (Cochrane 1963: 87–8). The fundamental idea is that we can use what reliable knowledge we have about relevant ways in which the population is heterogeneous to try to improve the likely representativeness of our sample. However, much depends here upon how reliable this knowledge of the population is and on our use of it. Indeed, where the information is misleading or misused it is possible for stratification to make a sample less rather than more representative.

Beyond this, there are the problems of gaining access to and getting agreement from all respondents in a sample; in other words, the issue of response rate. There will almost always be a less than a 100 per cent response, and in many surveys the rate is very much lower, sometimes below 50 per cent. The problem here is not just that this may render the number of cases in relevant cells too small to carry out the sorts of analysis required, but, equally importantly, that it tends to undercut any confidence we can have on the basis of statistical sampling theory that our sample is likely to be representative of the population. This is because, as is widely recognized, there are good reasons to believe that those who do not 'respond' will be distinctive in relevant respects. The fact that some of the responses will be incomplete or unintelligible, or unusable for other reasons, will also further reduce the effective sample size and in ways that could also introduce sampling bias. There are, of course, various strategies for minimizing non-response and for estimating and allowing for the sampling error resulting from this and other sources. However, these strategies are unlikely to be fully successful, and may sometimes introduce further error. Moreover, they are by no means used in all non-experimental research.

Counterfactual comparison

The task of much quantitative work is causal analysis. It is generally recognized that, in order to identify a causal relationship, it is not sufficient simply to show that the occurrence of some type of event, the presence of some

---

12   There are problems surrounding the formulae to be used in assessing the likelihood of error in stratified random as opposed to simple random sampling, see Selvin 1970: 95, note 2. However, I will leave this issue on one side.

feature or variation in some object-property, is frequently associated with the occurrence of, or variation in, the outcome to be explained. This is the standard warning that correlation is not causation. In order to identify causes, we must find some means of checking whether, in any particular case, the outcome effect *would have* occurred even if our hypothetical cause had not been operating (the counterfactual situation). This is why comparative method is essential to causal analysis. Ideally, in terms of the logic of much quantitative analysis, if we are to be able to come to a conclusion about what causes what, we need to be able to compare cases in which the hypothetical causal variable is operating at a high level with cases where it is not operating, or operates at a low level, and preferably where the cases share all other features in common.[13] This is never fully achievable in non-experimental research (and, in practical terms, not in experimental research either). Therefore the strategy employed is to examine the relationship between putative cause and effect in sets of cases where *some* potentially confounding variables are constant or their effect is low or absent.

Given the need for these sorts of comparison, the experiment is often taken to be an essential means of investigating causal relations: because, in principle at least, it enables us to exercise control over both the hypothetical cause and extraneous factors. One of the means often used to control extraneous variables in psychological and social science experiments is random allocation of subjects to treatment and control groups (or to experimental groups receiving different treatments). This reduces the likelihood that there will be aggregate differences between the groups in relevant background variables. Moreover, we can use a significance test to estimate the likelihood that such differences have generated any variation between the groups in relevant outcomes.

However, even experimental control will not always allow us to compare the cases we need to examine so as to reach reasonable conclusions about a hypothetical causal relationship. In particular, it will not always be possible to control all extraneous variables. For example, in randomized controlled trials in social science, blinding is often not feasible, so that people's knowledge of what treatment they are receiving may have a systematic effect on the outcome. There may also be variations in how the 'treatment' is administered; in fact, often the treatment will be a complex process of symbolic interaction that is fundamentally resistant to standardization. Furthermore,

---

13 This is what Mill referred to as 'the method of difference'.

where people are brought into communication with one another as members of experimental groups they may generate local social relations and cultures that shape experimental outcomes. There are also practical problems, such as differential dropout, which may affect our ability to draw conclusions about whether it was the treatment that had the effect, rather than some other factor.[14]

Needless to say, the problem of facilitating counterfactual comparison is even more challenging in the case of non-experimental quantitative (and qualitative) research. The main reason is that in order to control for extraneous variables we must first *identify* these. Yet, specifying all the factors that might shape a particular outcome is by no means straightforward, and necessarily relies upon theoretical assumptions. Furthermore, having identified these factors, we then need to find ways of gaining valid data about them. This is often impossible where reliance is being placed upon already available data. But even in the case of social surveys carried out by researchers for the purposes of particular studies, these can rarely provide accurate data about *all* the variables that could be acting on the outcome.

The weakness of non-experimental research in this respect is often recognized, but the seriousness of the problem is frequently underestimated. An experimental study that employs careful selection of potential subjects to maximize relevant homogeneity, random allocation to treatment and control groups and double-blinding procedures, can often make a relatively strong claim to have minimized the effect of any potentially confounding variables; especially if the results are confirmed through several replications. However, as soon as we move to quasi-experimental designs, and then on to the non-experimental designs of much survey research, the control exercised over variables becomes very much weaker, and the confidence we can reasonably have in the validity of the findings is considerably less.

The point here is not that reasonable conclusions about likely causal relations can never be drawn from such research, it is rather that they always involve judgements that rely upon substantive or theoretical as well as methodological assumptions. No statistical analysis can tell us, on its own, whether the hypothesized cause generated the outcome. Moreover, for the reasons indicated, the statistical evidence for coming to such a decision is quite weak

---

14 For two interesting evaluations of RCTs from a philosophy of science perspective, see Worrall 2007 and Cartwright 2007.

in the case of much non-experimental research. This means that the likely validity of the conclusions is often rather uncertain.

Reliance on significance testing

Significance testing has been the subject of recurrent criticism within the quantitative methodological literature (see Morrison and Henkel 1970a; Oakes 1986; Harlow et al. 1997; Ziliak and McCloskey 2008), but it continues to be widely employed. The central criticism has been that this set of techniques is frequently misused, in particular that it is often applied where the assumptions on which it relies do not hold, or the results are interpreted in ways that these assumptions cannot sustain.

There are two uses of significance testing that are widely recognized to be legitimate. First, in the context of survey research, it can be used to assess the likelihood that random sampling has produced a sample that is unrepresentative of the population sampled. Second, in experimental research significance tests can be used to assess the likelihood that random allocation has generated experimental groups that are sufficiently different in relevant background characteristics to have produced the size of difference in outcome actually discovered between the groups.

There is a third sort of application that is also legitimate, in my view.[15] This is where we are concerned to discover whether or not a systematic causal process has been in operation on some occasion, rather than the variation documented having been generated by a concatenation of many factors whose overall effect approximates to being random. The first step here is a kind of thought experiment: to compare the actual distribution of some outcome across cases studied *with what we might have expected to find had the distribution process been random*. For example, if we were interested in whether the allocation of students to sets in a secondary school might have involved ethnic bias, we could document the allocation of students with the same level of ability but from different ethnic groups to the various sets, and

---

15   In this I am departing from the views of some critics of the use of significance tests: see, for example, Morrison and Henkel 1970b. It is important to underline that the use of significance tests in this third way is quite different in character from its use in the context of probability sampling: there is no implication that what is involved is assessment of the likely accuracy of a generalization from the cases studied to some larger population by means of the significance test.

then compare this with the distribution in terms of ethnicity that would be expected if no other factor than ability were operating.[16] If we find a difference we could then use a significance test to assess the likelihood of this having arisen 'by chance'. In effect, this part of the thought experiment involves imagining that the allocation of students across sets had been carried out a large number of times, producing a distribution of allocations whose mean involves no proportional ethnic differences, whereas some of the allocations will involve over-assignment of members of one ethnic group to the top sets while others will show under-assignment of members of that group to these sets. Given that this distribution of allocations will approximate to a normal curve, we can use standard deviations as a scale to assess the likelihood that random allocation would have produced the ethnic differences in allocation discovered in the case being studied.[17] Of course, even if this significance test shows that the distribution was very unlikely to have been produced by haphazard factors, this would not tell us that ethnic discrimination had occurred (since other systematic factors could have generated the outcome, for example the ethnic groups in the school may have different social class profiles). What it *would* indicate is that a systematic causal relation, over and above ability, was probably involved in generating the differences in outcome found in the particular allocation studied; and that this might repay further investigation.[18]

It is important to repeat that this thought experiment can only tell us what the likelihood is that this particular allocation, on this particular occasion, was generated by one or more systematic rather than haphazard factors. It does not, *in itself,* tell us whether, say, the teachers involved have a disposition to allocate members of ethnic groups in this way or whether they have done so (or will do so) on other occasions. To establish these claims would require further evidence. Similarly, if we were to treat this allocation as a sample from the yearly allocations that are made in the school so as to generalize about what typically happens in that school, we could not legitimately use a significance test to assess the likelihood that this allocation is representative or

---

16   On some further complexities involved in such an investigation that I have left on one side here, see Gomm 1993.

17   In practice, significance tests may use other sorts of distribution, see Gold 1970: 176 on the chi-squared test.

18   Of course, it could also indicate systematic measurement error in relation to ethnicity, ability and/or set allocation.

typical. This is because the data come from studying only one allocation, and even if we studied allocations carried out in successive years these would not have been *randomly* selected from the larger population (of allocations).

The same points apply if we are interested in whether what happened in this school is typical of what happens in other schools. Here again the use of significance tests is not appropriate. As already noted, in non-experimental research the analytic task is to identify and examine cases where the hypothetical cause varies and where relevant extraneous variables have been controlled. If, across these cases, we find that variation in the outcome is closely in line with variation of the cause, and in the predicted direction, then (assuming no serious level of measurement or sampling error) we might reasonably conclude that our hypothesis is true (until further notice). However, generally speaking in social science what we find is not an all-or-nothing, or even a very large, average difference in outcome between those cases where the hypothetical causal factor is operating and those where it is not. Instead, the differences discovered are usually relatively small. Given this, there is always the suspicion that the finding could be a spurious, haphazard product of uncontrolled variables, errors in measurement or sampling, etc., rather than signifying a causal process of the kind suspected. Significance testing is often used to assess the likelihood of this. However, this is not justified.

Above all, what significance testing cannot tell us is whether any difference in outcome found in some set of cases would be found in *all* cases where the factor hypothesized as the cause is present. In other words, it cannot test a theoretical hypothesis.[19] As indicated earlier, what is involved in theory-testing is not generalization from a randomly selected sample to a finite population (what I referred to earlier as empirical generalization), but rather inference to what is true about a set of cases, infinite in extent, defined by the scope conditions of the theory being tested (theoretical inference). Significance tests can tell us nothing about the likely validity of this sort of theoretical inference. Yet this is the purpose for which they are frequently used in the social science literature, explicitly or implicitly.[20]

---

19 In fact, the outcome of a test of statistical significance only tells us the chances of the result we have found arising via random processes, not the probability of the null hypothesis being false: see Cohen 1997.

20 Whether significance tests can legitimately be used in this way is a matter of dispute. Gold 1970: 76–7 provides what is perhaps the clearest explication of what is involved. However, it is significant that he assumes a finite population, and it seems to me that the logic of the thought

The point is worth elaborating. In quite a lot of non-experimental quantitative research there seems to be a confusion between two rather different issues: whether we can reasonably conclude that an association among variables found in a sample would also be discovered in the population from which the sample was drawn; and whether this association indicates a systematic rather than a haphazard relationship among those variables *that would also be found in other populations*. Furthermore, despite frequent statements to the effect that correlation is not causation, there is often slippage into a third issue: whether the association indicates that a causal process of the kind hypothesized actually operates. It is quite reasonable to use a significance test to tackle the first issue, assuming that the sample has been drawn randomly from the population (though note the problems mentioned in an earlier section). There are also cases where we can use significance testing in judging how likely it is that a difference in outcome of the size discovered in some particular context on some particular occasion was generated by haphazard (rather than systematic) factors. However, where the task is to test a theoretical hypothesis about the effect that some causal factor always has or tends to have, within the relevant scope conditions, significance testing cannot legitimately be applied. This would only be appropriate if the population of cases defined by the scope conditions of the theory were finite, and if we could ensure that the cases examined were randomly selected from that population. However, neither condition is met because theories relate to all cases which meet their scope conditions that have occurred in the past, exist in the present, will happen in the future; and indeed even those that *could* happen.[21]

---

experiment he deploys does not apply where the population is infinite, as is the case with any domain marked out by the scope conditions of a theory. Furthermore, the problem with much usage of significance tests in this way is that no attempt is made to specify scope conditions, what is involved is simply a search for relationships that might be 'significant' in some body of data.

21 My argument here is a contentious one. It is more or less in line with the position taken in Selvin's (1970) classic discussion of the subject. For a different view, criticizing that position, see Kish (1970). Note, however, that the limit of the latter's claim, even if accepted, is that significance tests can tell us whether or not a difference in outcome is likely to have been produced by haphazard error. His arguments do not justify the widespread practice of using significance tests as evidence for specific causal claims.

Ecological validity and reactivity

As indicated in the previous section, very often in carrying out social research we are aiming to discover causal relationships or tendencies that operate in the world *generally*; we are not concerned simply with whether the outcome we are interested in was produced by the hypothesized cause *in the particular cases studied*. Experiments are specifically designed to discover general causal relationships through the direct control of variables. However, such control can itself create threats to the validity of inferences about what has happened, is happening, will or would happen in similar situations outside of the experimental situation. This is often referred to as the problem of ecological validity.

The key source of invalidity in this respect is reactivity: the extent to which people's behaviour is affected by the fact that they know that they are participating in an experiment, by the distinctive features of the experimental situation, and/or by the particular characteristics of the experimenter. It is on these grounds that experiments are sometimes dismissed as 'artificial'. While the artificial/natural contrast is misleading (given that experiments are themselves part of the social world, and so-called natural situations are frequently influenced by the researcher), nevertheless reactivity in experiments can be a major problem. Both the way in which the experiment is set up so as to control key variables, for example the use of blinding, and the usually highly structured means by which data are collected, may have the effect of rendering doubtful any inference from what people do in the experimental situation to what they would do in non-experimental situations to which the theory is intended to apply.[22] In part, what is being pointed to here is the contextually variable character of human behaviour: people may obey commands to carry out what seems like cruel behaviour in an experiment in a way that they would not do in other contexts; or they may *not* obey such commands in an experimental situation but would do so in other contexts, where they believed in the rationale for the demands concerned, feared the consequences of refusal, etc.[23]

---

22 This is an issue that was addressed by Egon Brunswik, who proposed the notion of representational design, see Hammond and Stewart 2001, especially pp. 4–5. On the wider range of criticisms made of experimental psychological research, see Rosnow 1981.

23 The reference here is, of course, to the infamous experiments by Milgram (2005). For discussion of what a partial replication of his study reveals today, see *American Psychologist*, 64, 1, 2009.

The problem of reactivity also occurs in non-experimental quantitative research. As already noted, the presence of an observer in a 'natural' situation may change it in significant ways, and the use of standardized (or non-standardized) elicitation techniques in interviews or questionnaires can increase reactivity because this makes the situation in which data are being collected different in character from those to which the findings will be applied. Furthermore, research participants in non-experimental research often know that they are being studied (or that data are being collected about them) and this may lead to various sorts of systematic error; this deriving, for example, from their desire to present themselves or others in the best possible light.

These sources of error take on slightly different forms depending upon whether the aim is to identify attitudes, personality attributes, etc. that are exemplified in responses to questionnaire items, and that are assumed to govern behaviour in other contexts as well, or to obtain reports from respondents about what they or others have done or would do in various types of situation. Survey researchers have long been aware of problems of ecological invalidity, and there are means that can be used to reduce them, but these strategies are not always employed, and their success is by no means guaranteed.

A preoccupation with hypothesis-testing?

In much quantitative research, the emphasis is on hypothesis-testing, and it often seems to be assumed that *any* hypothesis of interest can be tested and is worth testing (see Lieberson 1985: 6–12).[24] In part, this preoccupation reflects a failure to recognize the need for conceptual and theoretical development in many areas of research. Thus, most non-experimental quantitative research takes the conceptual categories it starts with as relatively fixed and seeks to discover relations among the variables those categories identify. What this ignores is that if the categories and variables do not approximate closely to the nature of the relevant causal relations then there will be, at the very least, a great deal of noise in the results; and those results will not give

---

24 There are of course exceptions to the emphasis on hypothesis-testing, for example the use of factor and cluster analysis for exploratory purposes (Neill 2008), the techniques for exploratory data analysis developed by Tukey and others (Tukey 1977; Erickson and Nosanchuk 1979). See also Marsh 1988; Marsh and Elliott 2008; and Baldamus 1976.

us a reliable understanding of the causal relations involved.[25] Many years ago Turner (1948) pointed to the problem here: that, unless what we are studying is a sample or population that corresponds to the domain of the causal system we are investigating, as represented by the scope conditions of a theory, we cannot conclude that frequency differences within the aggregate being investigated indicate causal tendencies on the part of units within that aggregate.

Of course, quantitative researchers recognize that many concepts initially adopted as part of research problems are vague or ambiguous in meaning. But usually their solution to this problem is the use of stipulative definitions, ones that are simultaneously 'operational' in character, specified in terms of indicators or measurement procedures. However, this effectively prevents the kinds of re-conceptualization that may be necessary if causal relations are to be discovered. This is the insight that lies at the core of approaches employed by qualitative researchers like grounded theorizing and, especially, analytic induction (see Hammersley 1989). What it points to is the need to explicate the causal mechanisms which are assumed to operate across the variables being investigated (Pawson 1989). This has implications for research design, for example that the population to be studied must be defined theoretically, in relation to suspected causal mechanisms; *and may need to be redefined during the course of the research*. In other words, the nature of the causal mechanism, and the scope conditions built into the theory about it, must usually be *discovered*. We cannot presume to know these, or the variables they imply, at the start of a study; unless they have already been well established by previous research that has itself adopted a more exploratory or developmental orientation.

Finally, we should perhaps note that there is often *post hoc* hypothesis-generating in quantitative research: ideas are brought in *after* data collection and analysis in order to explain unexpected findings. Yet they are rarely subjected to further investigation, and are sometimes even presented as if they were conclusions that had been confirmed by the evidence presented.

Causal process

The final problem I will discuss relates to the *nature* of causality. There are some quantitative researchers, and many qualitative researchers, who deny

---

25 See Rozeboom's (1997) argument for an abductive rather than hypothetico-deductive approach in psychology.

that causality operates in the social world, and/or that causal explanation of human behaviour is possible. But much depends here on what is meant by the term 'causality' (McKim and Turner 1997). If we interpret it in a broad sense to mean that the occurrence of one sort of event, or the presence of some type of feature in cases, or variation in some object-property dimension, tends to generate a particular type of outcome or change in it (in ways that may or may not have been intended by the human actors involved), then it is clear that causal relations are endemic in the social world. Qualitative researchers sometimes explicitly accept this but still criticize quantitative research for failing to recognize the complexity of those relations. I will argue that this charge is true in some key respects; though we should not assume that capturing the full complexity of the social world is desirable for analytic purposes (Hammersley 2008: ch2), even less that qualitative research is more effective in discovering causal relations (see Chapter 3).

If we start with experimental research, the concept of causality usually involved assumes that there are necessary and jointly sufficient conditions that must be met for the production of some outcome, or for there to be a strong correlation between a set of causal and a set of outcome variables. The concept of causality assumed here is a very stringent one.[26] Generally speaking, non-experimental quantitative research relies on weaker interpretations of causality. It is usually concerned with assessing *the degree to which a particular factor contributes to producing some type of outcome.*[27] A problem with this, however, is that there is generally a failure to identify the conditions under which this causal factor operates, in other words to discover the scope conditions of the theory involved, so as to be able to investigate cases where these do and do not hold (Walker and Cohen 1985; Lucas 2003). As a result the cases making up the aggregate studied will often include both those where the conditions are met and those where they are not (Turner 1948). This means that estimates of the contribution made by any factor are likely to include error or noise from this source, on top of any from measurement and sampling error. Closely associated with this problem is that these estimates

---

26 Interestingly, this conception of causality is shared by analytic induction (see Chapter 5). Whether experimental research is necessarily committed to this concept of cause may be open to question. It is possible that instead it could be concerned simply with finding out whether a particular intervention can have the effect predicted.

27 What Ragin (2006) refers to as 'net effect'.

are dependent upon how many and which other factors are included in the multivariate analysis.[28]

A more basic question, though, concerns the extent to which it is realistic to think of causal factors as each operating independently of others in bringing about an outcome. It seems likely that they will often operate in some combination. As a result, important causal contributions may be missed by the sorts of statistical analysis applied in much non-experimental research (Abbott 2001: 56–9; Ragin 1987 and 2008). This will be true unless there is systematic exploration of various configurations of factors through studying interaction effects. Moreover, given the problems involved in obtaining data on a large number of factors, and the huge number of cases that would need to be studied to ensure sufficient numbers in each cell, this is usually very difficult to achieve. Configurative analysis is an important alternative here.[29]

There is at least one further aspect of complexity that neither experimental nor most forms of non-experimental quantitative research are able to deal with easily. While it is widely recognized (though occasionally disputed) that causal relations involve temporal ordering – that the cause must occur before the effect – time can play a more substantial role in the way in which outcomes are generated.[30] This is illustrated by the fact that we will find instances of particular categories of outcome being generated by different causal routes; in other words, by different sequences in the incidence and timing of factors. Similarly, trajectories that produce diverse outcomes may start from more or less the same situation and involve more or less the same sorts of factors operating, but in different sequences or timings. Partly involved here is the idea that causes can perform different sorts of role: for instance, they may operate as underlying background variables, sleeper factors that may be present in many situations but only have a causal effect when certain conditions apply, trigger factors that set off mechanisms, and

---

28 For these reasons, and others, some commentators have pointed to the importance of focusing on the development and testing of particular theories, identifying particular candidate causal relationships, rather than estimating the contribution of all the factors that seem likely to play a role in bringing about an outcome: see Pawson 1989 and Lieberson 1985.

29 Ragin's qualitative comparative analysis, based on Boolean algebra, is specifically designed to identify configurations of causal factors: see Ragin 2000 and 2008; Rihoux and Ragin 2008. For an application of this technique to an issue and data set that has previously been subjected to conventional kinds of quantitative analysis, see Cooper 2005 and Cooper and Glaesser 2008. See also Chapters 6 and 7.

30 See Abell 1971: 2–4 and *passim*, and Abbott 2001.

so on. Arguments about the importance of these aspects of social causation have been extended in recent years by the growing influence of complexity theory, where the emphasis is on how outcomes at higher organizational levels can emerge from the interaction of factors at lower ones (see Byrne 1998). The overall argument is that outcomes may be strongly path-dependent, that we need to understand how outcomes were reached in particular cases because the sequence and pacing of causal factors may be different across cases, and differences in these may have affected the nature of the outcome (see Abbott 2001).

Finally, there are questions about the *nature* of the causal relations that can be assumed to operate in the social world. Several, by no means incompatible, possibilities arise here. One is the sort of causal relation assumed by psychological behaviourism. Here we have a situation that may seem to approximate to physical causation in character: once response habits have been established, there will be a relatively determinate or at least predictable relationship between a stimulus and the response of the organism. However, we should note that this relation is dependent upon the development of specific habits, and that these may decline, drift or be transformed over time. Furthermore, there are, of course, more complex, and more plausible, models of the human agent, in which cognition and other factors mediate the production of behaviour, with the result that the relationships involved are even further away from the model of physical causal relations.[31] This is a point that is given great emphasis by interpretive social scientists, who often imply that the relationship between background factors and outcomes is entirely contingent (which, if true, would presumably render social science, and perhaps commonsense understanding of human behaviour too, impossible). Moreover, if we recognize that some of the agents whom social scientists study are collective in character, rather than being individual people, then the complexity of the processes by which behaviour in any situation is generated probably increases still further; since the 'internal relations' of such agents are perhaps even less determinate.

The methods of analysis currently employed in most quantitative research do not allow us to investigate the sorts of complexity in causal relations outlined here. Yet, arguably, this is essential if we are to answer many of the kinds of questions such research typically addresses.

---

31   One of these relies on the notion of evolutionary explanation, see van Parijs 1981.

Conclusion

The short answer to the question posed in my title is that there is nothing wrong with quantitative research *per se*, but that there are many theoretical and practical problems involved in much current practice. In my view the same is true of qualitative research, so my arguments here do not amount to further shots in the 'paradigm wars' (Gage 1989). The aim is more constructive: to highlight the weaknesses in influential quantitative research strategies currently employed by many social scientists. This is necessary because these weaknesses are frequently forgotten by both researchers and their audiences, and because they urgently need to be addressed. Moreover, this kind of forgetfulness is especially dangerous when quantitative methods are held up as the gold standard.

Each set of problems I have discussed is potentially quite severe in character, although the severity will vary across particular studies, depending upon the aim involved, the sort of data employed, and so on. Taken together, these problems imply that, currently, we should exercise extreme caution in accepting the findings of much quantitative research, just as we should with the findings of most qualitative studies. Given this, we need to find an appropriate balance between portraying the significant contribution to public knowledge that social science can provide while emphasizing the limits currently operating on this contribution. Equally important, we need to give more attention to understanding the problems and finding better remedies.

There is a widespread human tendency to treat numbers in a taken-for-granted way as accurately representing what they purport to represent. This probably operates in all of us, even when we know better. It certainly infects much discussion in the media, and the thinking of many politicians, policy-makers, managers and others. In the face of this tendency, it is an important public obligation on the part of the social scientist to provide continual reminders of the error that may frequently be involved in numerical data, of the importance of other kinds of evidence, and of the need to exercise careful thought in using evidence of any kind to try to understand what happens in the world.

Another fundamental danger, this time more prevalent among quantitative researchers themselves, is the tendency to assume that causes and consequences can be discovered by primary or exclusive reliance upon statistical techniques, for example via so-called causal modelling, factor or cluster analysis, etc. What is neglected here is the essential role in causal analysis of substantive knowledge and of thought about the nature of the phenomena being investigated, the data being used, and so on. Mathematical techniques of various kinds can aid us in stimulating ideas and in checking them out; but they cannot, on their own, identify what are fruitful causal hypotheses or valid scientific conclusions. The tendency to neglect or overlook this fact perhaps stems from the idea that applying mathematical procedures is objective whereas thinking about the social world and how it operates cannot but be subjective, that word frequently being taken to mean 'speculative' or even 'biased'. The remnants of an influential kind of empiricism have not yet been entirely exorcized within social science, and are perhaps preserved via the way in which statistical computing packages are often employed.

An influential illustration of this point is Davis's critique of some sociologists' decisions not to use significance tests, in which he insists that we must have a 'formal criterion' by which to reach conclusions (Davis 1970: 91). What is involved here is a sharp distinction between fact and opinion, where the former must be determined by some 'objective procedure'. However, no procedure can eliminate the need for exercising judgement, nor can the use of any procedure guarantee validity. Indeed, as I argued earlier in this chapter, procedures can lead us astray as well as helping us. Moreover, what must be involved in scientific inference is a judgement of the likelihood that an explanation is true by comparison with alternatives, rather than a decision to 'accept' or 'reject' a null hypothesis mandated by whether or not a test result reaches a level of 'significance' set by convention (see Morrison and Henkel 1970b: 194–5).

Many of the ideas and techniques employed by quantitative researchers are essential if we are to answer the important descriptive and explanatory questions we ask about the social world. At the same time, there is a considerable danger of overlooking or downplaying the problems that quantitative work often faces, and of making excessive claims about what it can currently offer. Indeed, in my judgement such forgetting and over-claiming is common, and has very undesirable effects. So, the purpose of this chapter has been to sound a cautionary note, and to indicate that we need to find ways of addressing more effectively the serious problems often involved.

References

Abbott, A. (2001) *Time Matters*, Chicago: University of Chicago Press.

Abell, P. (1971) *Model Building in Sociology*, London: Weidenfeld and Nicolson.

Baldamus, W. (1976) *The Structure of Sociological Inference*, London: Martin Robertson.

Berk, R. A. (1988) 'Causal inference for sociological data', in Smelser, N. J. (ed.) *Handbook of Sociology*, Newbury Park CA: Sage.

— (2004) *Regression Analysis: a constructive critique*, Thousand Oaks CA: Sage.

Biesta, G. J. J. (2007) 'Why "what works" won't work: evidence-based practice and the democratic deficit of educational research', *Educational Theory*, 57, 1, pp. 1–22.

Bird, A. (2008) 'Natural kinds', *Stanford Encyclopedia of Philosophy*. Available at (accessed 14.07.09): <http://plato.stanford.edu/entries/natural-kinds/>.

Blauner, R. (1964) *Alienation and Freedom: the factory worker and his industry*, Chicago: University of Chicago Press.

Button, G. (ed.) (1991) *Ethnomethodology and the Social Sciences*, Cambridge: Cambridge University Press.

Byrne, D. (1998) *Complexity Theory and the Social Sciences*, London: Routledge.

Cartwright, N. (2007) 'Are RCTs the gold standard?', Centre for Philosophy of Natural and Social Science, Contingency and Dissent in Science, Technical Report 01/07, London School of Economics. Available at (accessed 5.02.09): <http://www.lse.ac.uk/collections/CPNSS/projects/ ContingencyDissentInScience/DP/Cartwright.pdf>.

Cicourel, A. V. (1964) *Method and Measurement in Sociology*, New York: Free Press.

Cochrane, W. G. (1963) *Sampling Techniques*, Second edition, New York: Wiley.

Cohen, J. (1997) 'The earth is round (p<.05)', in Harlow et al. (eds).

Converse, J. and Schuman, H. (1974) *Conversations at Random: survey research as interviewers see it*, New York: Wiley.

Cooper, B. (2005) 'Applying Ragin's crisp and fuzzy set QCA to large datasets: social class and educational achievement in the National Child Development Study', *Sociological Research Online*, 10, 2. Available at (accessed 27.05.09): <http://www.socresonline.org.uk/10/2/cooper.html>.

Cooper, B. and Glaesser, J. (2008) 'How has educational expansion changed the necessary and sufficient conditions for achieving professional, managerial and technical class positions in Britain? A configurational analysis', *Sociological Research Online*, 13, 3. Available at (accessed 27.05.09): <http://www.socresonline.org.uk/13/3/2.html>.

Coxon, A. P. M., Davies, P. M. and Jones, C. L. (1986) *Images of Social Stratification: occupational structures and class*, London: Sage.

Croll, P. (1986) *Systematic Classroom Observation*, Lewes: Falmer.

Davis, J. A. (1970) 'Some pitfalls of data analysis without a formal criterion', in Morrison and Henkel (eds).

Denzin, N. K. (1997) *Interpretive Ethnography: ethnographic practices for the 21st century*, Thousand Oaks CA: Sage.

Denzin, N. K. and Giardina, M. D. (eds) (2006) *Qualitative Inquiry and the Conservative Challenge*, Walnut Creek CA: Left Coast Press.

Durkheim, E. (1897) *Suicide: a study in sociology*, New York: Free Press, 1951.

Erickson, B. and Nosanchuk, T. (1979) *Understanding Data*, Milton Keynes: Open University Press.

Freedman, D. A. (1987) 'As others see us: a case study in path analysis' (with discussion), *Journal of Educational Statistics*, 12, pp. 101–223.

Gage, N. (1989) 'The paradigm wars and their aftermath: a "historical" sketch of research on teaching since 1989', *Educational Researcher*, 18, pp. 4–10.

Goertz, G. (2006) *Social Science Concepts: a users guide*, Princeton NJ: Princeton University Press.

Gold, D. (1970) 'Statistical tests and substantive significance', in Morrison and Henkel 1970a (eds).

Gomm, R. (1993) 'Figuring out ethnic equality', *British Educational Research Journal*, 19, 2, pp. 149–65.

Hammersley, M. (1989) *The Dilemma of Qualitative Method*, London: Routledge.

— (1992) *What's Wrong with Ethnography? Methodological explorations*, London: Routledge.

— (1998) 'Telling tales about educational research: a response to John K. Smith', *Educational Researcher*, 27, 7, pp. 18–21.

— (2002) *Educational Research, Policymaking and Practice*, London: Paul Chapman/Sage.

— (2008) *Questioning Qualitative Inquiry*, London: Sage.

— (2009) 'Is social measurement possible, or desirable?', in Tucker, E. and Walford, G. (eds) *The Handbook of Measurement: how social scientists generate, modify, and validate indicators and scales*, London: Sage, forthcoming.

Hammond, K. R. and Stewart, T. R. (2001) 'Introduction', in Hammond, K. R. and Stewart, T. R. (eds) *The Essential Brunswik*, Oxford: Oxford University Press.

Harlow, L. A., Mulaik, S. A. and Steiger, J. H. (eds) (1997) *What if there were no Significance Tests?* Mahwah NJ: Lawrence Erlbaum.

Hutchinson, P., Read, R. and Sharrock, W. (eds) (2008) *There is No Such Thing as a Social Science: in defence of Peter Winch*, Aldershot: Ashgate.

Kish, L. (1970) 'Some statistical problems in research design', in Morrison and Henkel (eds).

Lakoff, G. (1987) *Women, Fire, and Dangerous Things*, Chicago: University of Chicago Press.

Lather, P. (2007) *Getting Lost: feminist efforts towards a double(d) science*, Albany NY: State University of New York Press.

Levitas, R. and Guy, W. (eds) (1996) *Interpreting Official Statistics*, London: Routledge.

Lieberson, S. (1985) *Making it Count: the improvement of social research and theory*, Berkeley: University of California Press.

Lucas, J. W. (2003) 'Theory-testing, generalization, and the problem of external validity', *Sociological Theory*, 21, 3, pp. 236–53.

Marsh, C. (1988) *Exploring Data*, Cambridge: Polity.

Marsh, C. and Elliott, J. (2008) *Exploring Data*, Cambridge: Polity.

McCall, G. (1984) 'Systematic field observation', *Annual Review of Sociology*, 10, pp. 263–82.

McKimm, V. R. and Turner, S. P. (eds) (1997) *Causality in Crisis? Statistical methods and the search for causal knowledge in the social sciences*, Notre Dame IND: University of Notre Dame Press.

Michell, J. (2007) 'Measurement', in Turner, S. P. and Risjord, M. W. (eds) *Philosophy of Anthropology and Sociology*, Amsterdam: Elsevier.

Milgram, S. (2005) *Obedience to Authority: an experimental view*, London: Pinter and Martin.

Morgan, S. L. and Winship, C. (2007) *Counterfactuals and Causal Inference*, Cambridge: Cambridge University Press.

Morrison, D. E. and Henkel, R. E. (eds) (1970a) *The Significance Test Controversy*, London: Butterworths.

— (1970b) 'Significance tests reconsidered', in Morrison and Henkel (eds).

Oakes, M. (1986) *Statistical Inference: a commentary for the social and behavioural sciences*, Chichester: Wiley.

Pawson, R. (1989) *A Measure for Measures: a manifesto for empirical sociology*, London: Routledge.

Phillips, D. L. (1971) *Knowledge from What? Theories and methods in social research*, Chicago ILL: Rand McNally.

Polanyi, M. (1959) *Personal Knowledge*, Chicago ILL: University of Chicago Press.

— (1966) *The Tacit Dimension*, Garden City NY: Doubleday.

Prandy, K. (2002) 'Measuring quantities: the qualitative foundation of quantity', *Building Research Capacity*, Issue 2, pp. 3–4. Available at (accessed 13.01.08): <http://www.tlrp.org/rcbn/capacity/Journal/issue2.pdf>.

Ragin, C. (1987) *The Comparative Method: moving beyond qualitative and quantitative strategies*, Berkeley CA: University of California Press.

— (2000) *Fuzzy-Set Social Science*, Chicago: University of Chicago Press.

— (2006) 'The limitations of net effects thinking', in Rihoux, B. and Grimm, H. (eds) *Innovative Comparative Methods for Policy Analysis*, New York: Springer.

— (2008) *Redesigning Social Inquiry: fuzzy sets and beyond*, Chicago: University of Chicago Press.

Rihoux, B. and Ragin, C. (eds) (2008) *Configurational Comparative Methods*, Thousand Oaks CA: Sage.

Rosch, E. (1999) 'Reclaiming concepts', in Nunez, R. and Freeman, W. J. (eds) *Reclaiming Cognition: the primacy of action, intention and emotion*, Exeter UK: Imprint Academic. Published simultaneously in *The Journal of Consciousness Studies*, 6, 11–12, pp. 61–77. Available at (accessed 19.02.08): <http://psychology.berkeley.edu/faculty/profiles/erosch1999.pdf>.

Rosch, E. and Lloyd, B. (eds) (1978) *Cognition and Categorization*, Hillsdale NJ: Lawrence Erlbaum.

Rosnow, R. L. (1981) *Paradigms in Transition: the methodology of social inquiry*, New York: Oxford University Press.

Roth, J. (1965) 'Hired hand research', *American Sociologist*, 1, 1, pp. 190–6.

Rozeboom, W. W. (1997) 'Good science is abductive, not hypothetico-deductive', in Harlow et al. (eds).

Schofield, J. W. (1989) 'Increasing the generalizability of qualitative research', in Eisner, E. and Peshkin, A. (eds) *Qualitative Inquiry in Education: the continuing dialogue*, New York: Teachers College Press.

Seale, C. (1999) *The Quality of Qualitative Research*, London: Sage.

Seale, C., Gobo, G., Gubrium, J. F. and Silverman, D. (eds) (2004) *Qualitative Research Practice*, London: Sage.

Selvin, H. C. (1970) 'A critique of tests of significance in survey research', in Morrison and Henkel (eds)

Staggenborg, S. (1988) ' "Hired hand research" revisited', *American Sociologist*, 19, 3, pp. 260–9.

Taylor, J. R. (2001) 'Linguistics: prototype theory', in Smelser, N. J. and Baltes, P. B. (eds) *International Encyclopedia of the Social and Behavioral Sciences*, Amsterdam: Elsevier.

— (2003) *Linguistic Categorization*, Oxford: Oxford University Press.

Tukey, J. W. (1977) *Exploratory Data Analysis*, Reading MS: Addison-Wesley.

Turner, R. H. (1948) 'Statistical logic in sociology', *Sociology and Social Research*, 32, pp. 697–704.

Van Parijs, P. (1981) *Evolutionary Explanation in the Social Sciences*, London: Tavistock.

Von Wright, G. H. (1971) *Explanation and Understanding*, London: Routledge.

Walker, H. A. and Cohen, B. P. (1985) 'Scope statements: imperatives for evaluating theory', *American Sociological Review*, 50, pp. 288–301.

Williams, M. (2001) 'Complexity, probability and causation: implications for homelessness research'. Available at (accessed 11.03.08): <http://www.whb.co.uk/socialissues/mw.htm>.

Worrall, J. (2007) 'Why there's no cause to randomize', *British Journal for the Philosophy of Science*, 58, 3, pp. 451–88.

Ziliak, S. T. and McCloskey, D. M. (2008) *The Cult of Statistical Significance: how the standard error costs us jobs, justice, and lives*, Ann Arbor, Mich.: University of Michigan Press.

Quantitative Research on Meritocracy: The Problem of Inference from Outcomes to Opportunities

Martyn Hammersley

Having discussed a range of problems facing quantitative research in the previous chapter, here I want to focus in more detail on a particular problem that arises in a specific field. For me this exemplifies the way in which the conclusions of quantitative research often have a speculative character, despite sustained concern with providing detailed numerical evidence. The key point here is that what is involved in causal analysis is never simply a matter of assessing the strength of correlation between variables within a dataset, or even statistical inference from a sample to a population. Such analysis always involves theoretical inference to processes going on in the world, those that the data are taken to represent, and reliance upon assumptions about those processes cannot be avoided. Moreover, to the extent that they are open to reasonable doubt, these assumptions need to be made explicit, and their likely validity assessed. Obvious as all this may seem, it is easy to lose sight of these requirements. This is what I will argue has happened in much quantitative research on social mobility.

During the twentieth century, and continuing into the present one, social mobility has been a major area of sociological research, and one where quantitative method is dominant.[1] Indeed, it is perhaps the pre-eminent field of quantitative sociological investigation. In Britain, one of the main issues addressed has concerned the degree to which meritocracy has been achieved, or the extent to which there was a shift in this direction over the course of the twentieth century, and this will serve as a convenient focus here.[2] Moreover, the role of the education system has been seen as central, being regarded both as crucial to the achievement of meritocracy but also, frequently, to the reproduction of inequities.[3]

Much research in this field has been concerned with determining how closely processes of educational selection and occupational recruitment approximate to what we might call the meritocratic paradigm. This is a set of assumptions about how people involved in the occupational and educational systems – both those who operate selection processes and those subjected to them – would act if meritocracy were in place. For example, the paradigm assumes that those engaged in educational assessment or occupational recruitment make judgements exclusively on the basis of the relative merit of the candidates. Similarly, it is expected that those subject to selection processes will be primarily concerned with maximizing their educational and occupational achievements. Any deviation from this paradigm is treated as inequitable, or at least as an inequality that is relevant to judgements about whether or not meritocracy has been achieved (Hammersley 2009). And it is deviation from the paradigm that is seen as requiring explanation, not conformity to it.

In this chapter I want to examine a central methodological feature of this body of research: a mode of inference that moves from the discovery of

1 For views on its current state and future prospects, see Morgan et al. 2006.

2 See, for example, Heath and Ridge 1983; Heath et al. 1992; Saunders 1994, 1995, 1996, 1997, 2002; Marshall and Swift 1993 and 1996; Goldthorpe 1996a, 1996b and 2003; Lampard 1996; Hellevik 1997; Marshall et al. 1997; Savage and Egerton 1997; Breen and Goldthorpe 1999, 2001 and 2002; Bond and Saunders 1999; Ringen 2005; Cooper 2005, Cooper and Glaesser 2008; Bynner and Joshi 2002; Swift 2003; Gorard 2008.

3 For an assessment of work claiming to document the reproduction of inequities within the education system, see Foster et al. 1996.

inequalities of *outcome* to conclusions about the existence of inequalities of *opportunity*.[4] Commitment to this mode of inference was stated many years ago by Halsey, who wrote that, for the egalitarian: 'unless there is proof to the contrary, inequality of outcome in the social distribution of knowledge is a measure of *de facto* inequality of access' (Halsey 1981: 111).[5] We can interpret this statement as implying that, without strong evidence the other way, any inequality in outcome should be interpreted as indicating a corresponding inequality of opportunity, in the form of a set of barriers that lowers the performance of the relevant category of actor compared to others. And this is an assumption that underpins the dominant approach in studying social mobility, and is not uncommon in studies of educational inequalities as well. For example, Goldthorpe writes:

> the pattern of relative mobility chances [. . .] associated with the British class structure over the decades in question embodies inequalities that are of a quite striking kind [. . .]. Where inequalities in class chances of this magnitude are displayed – of the order [. . .] of over 30:1 – then, we believe, the presumption must be that to a substantial extent they do reflect inequalities of opportunity that are rooted in the class structure, and are not simply the outcome of the differential 'take-up' of opportunities by individuals with differing genetic, moral, or other endowments that are unrelated to their class position. At all events, this is the interpretation that must stand until latter-day Social Darwinists or Smilesians are able to offer some alternative account of an empirically credible kind. (Goldthorpe 1988: 328)[6]

---

4 Most of this work is concerned with social class inequalities, and this will be my focus here, but the argument applies to work on other kinds of inequality too.

5 Halsey's qualification 'for the egalitarian' points to the way in which research in this field has been framed by a set of value assumptions, and the ambiguous status of this framework. Elsewhere, I have argued that this framework must be treated as no more than a basis for identifying questions that are worth investigating and determining what would be relevant answers to them: Hammersley 2009.

6 As Swift has pointed out, use of the concept of 'chances' in this context risks confusion between the statistical sense of that term, which is the one that is built into the method employed by most research on social mobility, and the commonsense notion of 'having a chance' to do something (Swift 2004: 4). Elsewhere, Marshall and Swift (1999) have argued that many of those involved in recent social mobility research, including Goldthorpe, have been aware of the problems involved in inferring inequalities in opportunity from inequalities in outcome. However, my view is that they have by no means taken full account of the severity of these problems.

Thus, in much research on how far Britain deviates from being a meritocracy, and why, there is investigation of the extent to which there are social class differences in occupational destination and/or in educational achievement, and these are treated (with or without controlling for other variables, such as 'ability') as evidence for the existence of inequalities in opportunity. In other words, outcome inequalities are taken to indicate deviation from the meritocratic ideal in how people are selected within the education system or recruited to occupational positions, and/or it is assumed that there are factors serving to lower the aspirations or modify the preferences of working-class children and thereby their acquisition of relevant abilities, credentials and/or occupational positions.

Explanatory models relating to these processes, of various kinds, have been sketched, ranging from those that treat criteria of selection and recruitment as biased against working-class candidates to those that use rational choice or causal explanations to show how the aspirations and preferences of working-class children and adults could have been distorted away from what is required by the meritocratic paradigm.[7] So, rather than a meritocratic evaluative standard being applied directly to the behaviour of people involved in the occupational and educational systems, there is an attempt to infer how close their behaviour is to the meritocratic ideal solely from the outcomes produced by those systems, bolstered by explanatory models that point to potential processes that would account for the pattern of outcomes found.

This mode of inference necessarily assumes that there is a direct causal link between those processes that determine the distribution and take-up of educational and occupational opportunities and system outcomes, so that the latter can be treated as a sound measure of relevant attitudes and behaviour. But the question is: what is the nature of the causal mechanisms assumed here, and how convincing is the claim that they are actually operating and that they thereby enable inequalities in outcome to be read as indicators of inequalities in opportunity? In practice, the fundamental mechanisms assumed seem to derive from the conceptions of justice that frame research on social mobility and educational inequality.[8] There are two of these – what

---

7 There are serious questions to be raised about these latter explanations, in that they assume meritocratic motivation on the part of the working class to be the only rational option. See Murphy 1981 and 1990.

8 For excellent discussions of the value principles underpinning research on social mobility, see Marshall et al. 1997; Swift 2000 and 2004.

I will call the distribution of benefits model and the allocation of rewards model – and each will be examined in turn.

The distribution of benefits

Halsey's statement, quoted above, refers to 'the social distribution of knowledge', effectively alluding to the notion of distributive justice. Of course, the word 'distribution' can have different meanings. One sense, central to statistics and by no means irrelevant here, refers to an array of figures showing how many instances are to be found within each of a set of categories, or at each point on a scale, representing some variable. In the case of social mobility research for example, the interest is usually in how people born into each social class are 'distributed' across categories relating to occupational destination.[9] However, this statistical meaning of the term does not imply any causal mechanism and is therefore insufficient on its own as a basis for inference. Instead, it must be assumed that there is an *active process of distribution by some agent or set of agents*. Only this could allow inference back from unequal outcomes to the existence of inequality in the processes that produced them.

The canonical case would be where a single agent has goods to give away, and does this across a small and well-defined population.[10] For example, a child has some sweets and decides to share these with her friends. Looking at the outcome distribution we can ask whether the distributive process was fair, in terms of some interpretation of fairness, such as equal provision: if the friends receive unequal numbers of sweets then we can assume, other things being equal, that they were *given* different numbers of sweets.

However, the case of equality of opportunity for educational achievement and occupational positions departs considerably from this model, and in significant ways. First of all, there is no single agent distributing either educational credentials or occupational positions; even less, the knowledge, skills and virtues required to obtain these. Rather, what we have is a *statistical* distribution of outcomes that has been generated by diverse local processes in a very large number of situations, at many points in time.

---

9 In practice, the focus is often on the social class position of parents at some point in the respondent's childhood, and his (rarely her) occupational position at a point later in life. There are well-known problems here about how far 'origin' and 'destination' are actually captured.

10 Note that it could equally involve the distribution of detriments, such as pay cuts or redundancies.

So a crucial issue is how much coordination, or at least alignment, there is among these processes. For instance, in the case of educational credentials, we cannot sensibly talk about their 'distribution', in terms of a causal mechanism operating, unless we assume that it could be within the power of some coordinated or aligned set of distributors to transmit the knowledge and skills that the credentials represent equally across students irrespective of their social class backgrounds. It is also essential that the distributive agent begins the process of distribution from children's birth onwards, and is a monopoly supplier of these goods. Furthermore, this system of distribution must be capable of playing an overwhelming role in children's lives over the course of their development through to the point where they enter work; since other substantial influences operating on them could generate inequalities.

Any complexity in selection or recruitment processes, in the form of operational divergences among 'distributors', factors that are not under their control, delay in the point of intervention, or countervailing processes, would subvert the validity of inferences from inequality of outcome to inequality in the distributional process, *unless we can assume that these forms of complexity themselves represent deviation from the meritocratic ideal on the part of the system concerned*. Given that, in fact, there is probably a rather low level of alignment across any large national society, in terms of criteria and forms of evaluation, as regards either processes of educational selection or occupational recruitment, this additional assumption, italicized above, seems to be the lynchpin of the argument from unequal outcomes back to inequality of opportunity in terms of the distributive model.

However, there are two questions that might be raised about this lynchpin. The first amounts to a challenge on the basis of other value principles than those embodied in the meritocratic paradigm. For example, in terms of the liberal values of negative freedom and institutional or communal autonomy, questions can be raised about the desirability of the nature and scale of the intervention that would be required significantly to reduce local variation in the 'distribution' of knowledge, skills and occupational positions. The policy measures needed to attempt some sort of approximation to random variation in credential-earning capabilities as regards social class would be draconian, including major interventions into family life and/or the removal of babies to places where their treatment could be directly controlled (Fishkin 1983; Munoz-Dardé 1999), plus the standardization of both educational processes and of occupational recruitment procedures (Cavanagh 2002). While there are arguments in favour of such interventions, there are even more obvious ones against. So there is an issue here about what value judgements should and should not be included within the meritocratic value framework that guides research on social mobility, and above all about the need for clarity about this.

The second question is to do with feasibility. Even if we put aside these liberal objections, it seems very unlikely that it would ever actually be possible for the state to exercise the wide scope and sustained intensity of control that is required to bring about an approximation to the distributional model. Doubts arise here not just because of the range of processes, locales and people involved but also from the fact that any effects produced are likely to come about through complex causal interactions that depend upon the differential responses of people to 'the same' conditions. Here, the doubt concerns the factual assumptions on which the meritocratic framework can reasonably rely.

To elaborate, even putting aside the possibility that genetic variation relevant to educational and occupational achievement in Britain may be associated with social class, and also the effects of parental variation in life condition and lifestyle on embryos in the womb, it seems likely that there may be differences in how babies and young children are treated in the first two or three years of life, and later, that could have consequences for the development of various sorts of learning and ability. We can also expect there to be a variety of processes shaping appetites and aspirations, what is and is not found appealing by children, young people and adults in different social classes, etc. These processes will include modelling on significant others, such as kin and peers; availability of various kinds of knowledge and skills and of support in acquiring them; competition with others and available opportunities for engaging in activities of varying kinds, achieving status in diverse ways, etc.; variation in level of motivational support for knowledge and skills relevant to educational or occupational achievement; compositional effects of neighbourhoods and schools working via the above, though no doubt also shaped by the role of the media in projecting models about kinds of people, what are virtues and vices, what is and is not worthwhile, how people should spend their time, etc. It seems unlikely that levelling out all these processes or their effects as regards social class would ever be possible, and that any attempt on the part of the education system, or the state, to do so would meet considerable resistance. As regards both value assumptions and factual assumptions, what I have called the lynchpin argument is, at the very least, in need of explicit justification.

There is a further, even more serious, problem with the distribution model as an inference ticket from inequalities in educational outcome back to inequalities in opportunity. This is that what is conceptualized as being distributed is not the sort of thing that *can* be 'distributed'. In what sense can knowledge and skills be simply allocated by teachers? The process of learning is much more complex and interactive than this notion implies, despite the now popular discourse of curricular content being 'delivered'. What is assumed in the distributional model is an extreme version of the transmission mode of teaching, in which students are vessels to be filled by teachers (or perhaps a better analogy would be that it is their schoolbags that are to be filled with the necessary knowledge and skills, that they can then 'use' as resources later). This would be hard to defend as practically possible, even if it were educationally desirable.

Similar issues arise as regards social mobility. Even if we could think of the attachment of particular levels of income to particular occupational positions as a process of distribution, and there are doubts about this for reasons already explained, we certainly cannot sensibly conceive of the allocation of people to jobs as equivalent to the distribution of goods. Indeed, generally speaking, it is people who are appointed to jobs rather than jobs that are distributed among people. In other words, occupational recruitment is primarily a matter of matching the capabilities and virtues possessed by the candidates that are available to those required by the particular position currently open. Of course, other processes may also be involved, or even dominate, such as nepotism; but there is no reason to assume that these are central in most occupational recruitment processes in Britain.[11] Even aside from this, there is a significant distinction to be drawn between the distribution of 'livings', in other words rewards tied to jobs, and the process of recruiting people to jobs, where the appointee is expected to carry out the tasks involved, and where much may hang on how effectively this is done, including continued employment.

In summary, then, the assumption that what is involved in educational selection and occupational recruitment is the distribution of goods or benefits is a highly questionable basis for inference from outcome inequalities to inequalities in opportunity. Neither the education system nor the occupational system operates in the way assumed by this model, and any assumption

---

11 However, see Jackson 2007 for evidence about criteria used in occupational recruitment.

that its failure to do so amounts to deviation from meritocracy needs to be made explicit and is open to challenge. In particular, neither educational credentials, knowledge and skills, on the one hand, nor jobs, on the other, are the sorts of thing that can be distributed (or, arguably, *should* be distributed) in the way that, say, shares in a windfall profit might be.

The allocation of rewards

A rather different principle of justice could conceivably supply an alternative underpinning for inference from outcome inequalities to inequalities in opportunity. Moreover, this one is perhaps even more closely linked to the notion of meritocracy than is distributive justice. This is the idea of desert-based justice: the dispensing of differential rewards *in return for differential performance*. Here, we might reason as follows: if rewards were dispensed on the basis of merit this would lead to no social class inequalities in outcome, so that if such inequalities are found then we can conclude that rewards have not been dispensed fairly in relation to the distribution of merit across the social classes. This is to assume, of course, that there are no systematic differences among members of social classes in terms of the relevant kind of merit, or that any such differences have been controlled for in the analysis.

How far does this model provide us with a sound basis for drawing inferences from outcome inequalities to the existence of inequalities of opportunity? The answer, it seems to me, is that it does not. We can certainly ask of any particular process of educational selection or occupational recruitment whether it operated in such a way as to reward those who possessed or displayed the set of capabilities and virtues assumed to be relevant, and whether any deviation from this pattern was correlated with the social class origins of candidates. However, it is much more problematic to compare a statistical distribution of occupational destinations with a statistical distribution of ability and motivation possessed at an early age, and to conclude that any mismatch between the two amounts to deviation from meritocratic educational selection and/or occupational recruitment in terms of desert-based justice.

If we could assume that there were single generic kinds of ability and motivation whose possession ought to constitute a necessary and sufficient condition for high levels of educational and occupational achievement, then inference from inequalities in outcome to inequalities of opportunity might well be viable. But this assumption is very implausible. After all, ability is always the capacity to engage successfully *in some particular activity* or in *a specific range of activities*. The notion of an ability *to do anything at all* makes no sense. Nor, I suggest, does the more specific idea of a single form of ability that enables one to, say, obtain *any* university degree, or carry out *any* high-level occupational task.

To develop this point, it is fairly clear that the tasks involved in educational or occupational achievement do not belong to a homogeneous set such that more or less the same ability is involved. What we find instead is a diversity of tasks and kinds of success, requiring a variety of kinds of knowledge, skill, and virtue. In the case of education, the tasks involved would include learning mathematics, English literature, geography, etc. sufficient, for example, to get an upper second or a first at a particular university. As regards occupational work, the tasks might be, for instance, developing the knowledge and skills required to prepare and present a case in court, to diagnose and treat illnesses, to run a business effectively, to make 'an original contribution to knowledge' in a specific field, and so on. It is patently obvious that becoming able to do one of these things does not enable one to do the others, that some people are likely to be capable of one but not of the others, and perhaps even that acquiring one sort of knowledge, skill, or virtue actually makes it harder to acquire some of the others.

Now, of course, it is almost certainly true that there are some elementary capabilities that operate as a foundation for all or many of these sorts of achievement: particular levels of literacy and numeracy, for example. However, the point is that while these may be a necessary condition they are not sufficient for any such achievement – other more specific forms of ability are required, and we cannot assume that these are simply more refined, differentiated versions of a foundational general ability. It follows that, at each point of selection and recruitment, what is being assessed is the display of *some particular set of capabilities and virtues,* and moreover the display of these *at a particular point in time.* What is *not* being assessed, even indirectly, is the possession at birth or soon after of generic kinds of ability.

Much the same is true of motivation. While it might seem to make sense to identify a form of motivation that is focused on maximizing educational credentials and/or gaining *any* high-level occupational position, we might ask whether this is what motivates most people, and how effective it is likely to be in facilitating high-level educational and/or occupational achievement.[12] Are not people usually motivated by the desire to achieve rather more specific goals? Most important of all, must we assume that any more specific motivation amounts to deviation from meritocracy? This is what inference from outcomes to opportunities on the basis of the notion of reward allocation effectively presupposes.

In short, processes of educational selection and occupational recruitment are usually carried out on the basis of specific criteria relevant to the context, not in terms of what is required to achieve some overall level of qualification, or to gain access to service class occupations. These processes are also often carried out in contexts where there is a limited number of places, and where the candidates concerned are evaluated against the others available at the time for selection (see Gomm 1993). So, once again, we are not faced with a single agency engaging in selection for a single or standard purpose, across the whole relevant population, at one point in time, but rather with a complex and heterogeneous set of processes, occurring in many different places and times, whose effects will themselves inevitably be complex and situationally variable. A further key point is that the sorts of ability and virtue singled out as relevant in selection and recruitment processes necessarily vary considerably across different phases and parts of the education system, and even more across different occupations.

For all these reasons, it makes little sense to ask whether the statistical distribution of educational credentials towards the end of young people's educational careers, or the statistical distribution of eventual occupational destinations, amounts to fair reward in relation to the initial distribution of generic ability and motivation that people had, or were capable of, at the start of their lives – as young children. Or perhaps I should say that this would only make sense if it were reasonable to expect that educational selection and occupational recruitment decisions *ought to be made* in terms of generic ability and motivation in the early years, *and that any deviation from this itself amounts to deviation from meritocracy*. Once again, a lynchpin assumption is called for; and, once again, it seems very hard to justify.

If we were looking at whether or not recruitment to some position in an organization was fair, we would be concerned with whether those who had

---

12 Attempts to identify some generic form of 'achievement orientation' and to use these to explain achievement levels, and even countries' relative levels of economic growth, such as the work of McClelland 1961 have been subjected to cogent criticism, see for instance Schatz 1965; Mazur and Rosa 1977; Lewis 1991.

the personal capabilities and characteristics necessary for the job in the same amounts had an equal chance of being appointed, irrespective of social class origin, gender, ethnicity, etc. However, it is a very questionable procedure to ask whether Britain, or any other national society, is meritocratic – in the sense that recruitment across a very wide range of posts demanding different knowledge, skills, personal characteristics etc., and over a lengthy period of time, was in line with differences in ability and effort, or perhaps more accurately in the potential for acquiring these, when the applicants were children. What we could reasonably ask, instead, is whether or not processes of selection and recruitment at key points in educational and occupational trajectories within a society are fair, in the sense that the best qualified people tend to be selected. But this necessarily moves away from inferences relying primarily on outcome inequalities. And we would also need to look at the effects of different sorts of home background on the development of relevant kinds of ability or motivation. Moreover, if selection and recruitment were fair in this sense, it would not guarantee an outcome pattern in which no social class inequalities appeared.

Conclusion

I began this chapter by noting that most quantitative research on social mobility, and much investigation of social class inequalities in educational achievement, is underpinned by a set of assumptions about the behaviour of those engaged in educational and occupational selection and those subject to these processes of selection: what I called the meritocratic paradigm. I noted how this body of research typically relies on inferring inequality of opportunity from the existence of outcome inequalities. I argued that this mode of inference must rely on one or other of two models of how meritocracy would operate. The first derives from the principle of distributive justice, where what is assumed is distribution by a single agent of some set of goods or benefits to members of a well-defined population, in a way that corresponds to a criterion of fairness. I pointed to two respects in which educational selection and occupational recruitment do not, and almost certainly cannot, fit this model: that there is not and probably never could be a single coherent agent capable of distributing the goods involved (whether educational credentials, knowledge and skills or occupational positions and the benefits attached to them); and that these 'goods' are not of a kind that can be, or are, 'distributed' by agents – they are acquired in more complex ways. The mechanism implied by the other value perspective that usually frames studies in this field, allocation of rewards for past performance, draws on the principle of just deserts. This too fails to provide the inference ticket required. Here, the unavoidably heterogeneous character of relevant abilities and motivations, and criteria, involved in both educational selection and occupational recruitment make any assessment of equity on the basis of outcomes hopelessly unreliable.

While systematic social class inequalities in educational and occupational outcomes should certainly prompt investigation of the processes that might have produced them, this is the *starting point* for an investigation, not the end point. It tells us neither whether inequalities in opportunity exist, as defined by some interpretation of the meritocratic paradigm, nor provides us with a reliable explanation for any that may be present. Instead, it seems clear that, if we are to generate knowledge relevant to judgements about whether educational selection and/or occupational recruitment is fair in Britain or elsewhere, we need to rely primarily upon studies of particular processes of selection and recruitment at key points in educational and occupational trajectories; investigations of outcome inequalities can only play a background role in this respect.[13]

References

Bond, R. and Saunders, P. (1999) 'Routes to success: influences on the occupational attainment of young British males', *British Journal of Sociology*, 50, 2, pp. 217–49.

Breen, R. and Goldthorpe, J. H. (1999) 'Class inequality and meritocracy: a critique of Saunders and an alternative analysis', *British Journal of Sociology*, 50, 2, pp. 217–50.

— (2001) 'Class, mobility and merit: the experience of two British birth cohorts', *European Sociological Review*, 17, 2, pp. 81–101.

— (2002) 'Merit, mobility and method: another reply to Saunders', *British Journal of Sociology*, 53, 4, pp. 575–82.

Bynner, J. and Joshi, H. (2002) 'Equality and opportunity in education: evidence from the 1958 and 1970 birth cohort studies', *Oxford Review of Education*, 28, 4, pp. 405–25.

Cavanagh, M. (2002) *Against Equality of Opportunity*, Oxford: Oxford University Press.

---

13 It is perhaps necessary to make clear that this is not an argument for qualitative rather than quantitative research. The sorts of study I am recommending may well need to employ quantitative techniques. See, for example, Jackson's (2007) analysis of job adverts.

Cooper, B. (2005) 'Applying Ragin's crisp and fuzzy set QCA to large datasets: social class and educational achievement in the National Child Development Study', *Sociological Research Online*, 10, 2. Available at (accessed 2.12.08): <http://www.socresonline.org.uk/10/2/cooper.html>.

Cooper, B. and Glaesser, J. (2008) 'How has educational expansion changed the necessary and sufficient conditions for achieving professional, managerial and technical class positions in Britain? A configurational analysis', *Sociological Research Online*, 13, 3, pp. 1–22. Available at (accessed 2.12.08): <http://www.socresonline.org.uk/13/3/2.html>.

Fishkin, J. (1983) *Justice, Equality of Opportunity, and the Family*, New Haven CT: Yale University Press.

Foster, P., Gomm, R. and Hammersley, M. (1996) *Constructing Educational Inequality*, London: Falmer Press.

Goldthorpe, J. H. (1988) *Social Mobility and Class Structure in Modern Britain*, Second edition, Oxford: Oxford University Press.

— (1996a) 'Problems of "meritocracy"', in Erikson, R. and Jonsson, J. O. (eds) *Can Education be Equalized? The Swedish case in comparative perspective*, Boulder Co: Westview Press.

— (1996b) 'Class analysis and the reorientation of class theory: the case of persisting differentials in educational attainment', *British Journal of Sociology*, 47, 3, pp. 481–505.

— (2003) 'The myth of education-based meritocracy: why the theory isn't working', *New Economy*, 10, 4, pp. 234–9.

Gomm, R. (1993) 'Figuring out ethnic equality', *British Educational Research Journal*, 19, 2, pp. 149–65.

Gorard, S. (2008) 'A re-consideration of rates of "social mobility" in Britain: or why research impact is not always a good thing', *British Journal of Sociology of Education*, 29, 3, pp. 317–24.

Halsey, A. H. (1981) *Change in British Society*, Oxford: Oxford University Press.

Hammersley, M. (2009) 'Can social science tell us whether Britain is a meritocracy? A Weberian critique', paper given at a symposium on Methodological Issues in Research on Social Class, Education and Social Mobility, British Educational Research Association annual conference, Manchester, September 2009.

Heath, A. and Ridge, J. M. (1983) 'Schools, examinations, and occupational attainment', in Purvis, J. and Hales, M. (eds) *Achievement and Inequality in Education*, London: Routledge and Kegan Paul.

Heath, A., Mills, C. and Roberts, J. (1992) 'Towards meritocracy? Recent evidence on an old problem', in Crouch, C. and Heath, A. (eds) *Social Research and Social Reform: essays in honour of A. H. Halsey*, Oxford: Oxford University Press.

Hellevik, O. (1997) 'Class inequality and egalitarian reform', *Acta Sociologica*, 40, pp. 377–97.

Jackson, M. (2007) 'How far merit selection? Social stratification and the labour market', *British Journal of Sociology*, 58, 3, pp. 367–90.

Lampard, R. (1996) 'Might Britain be a meritocracy? A comment on Saunders', *Sociology*, 30, 2, pp. 387–93.

Lewis, J. (1991) 'Reevaluating the effect of N-ach on economic growth', *World Development*, 19, 9, pp. 1269–74.

Marshall, G. and Swift, A. (1993) 'Social class and social justice', *British Journal of Sociology*, 44, 2, pp. 187–211.

— (1996) 'Merit and mobility: a reply to Peter Saunders', *Sociology*, 30, 2, pp. 375–86.

— (1999) 'On the meaning and measurement of inequality', *Acta Sociologica*, 42, pp. 241–50.

Marshall, G., Swift, A. and Roberts, S. (1997) *Against the Odds? Social class and social justice in industrial societies*, Oxford: Oxford University Press.

Mazur, A. and Rosa, E. (1977) 'An empirical test of McClelland's "achieving society" theory', *Social Forces*, 55, 3, pp. 769–74.

McClelland, D. (1961) *The Achieving Society*, New York: Free Press.

Morgan, S. L., Grusky, D. B. and Fields, G. S. (eds) (2006) *Mobility and Inequality: frontiers of research in sociology and economics*, Stanford CA: Stanford University Press.

Munoz-Dardé, V. (1999) 'Is the family to be abolished then?', *Proceedings of the Aristotelian Society*, New Series, 99, pp. 37–56.

Murphy, J. (1981) 'Class inequality in education: two justifications, one evaluation, but no hard evidence', *British Journal of Sociology*, 32, pp. 182–201.

— (1990) 'A most respectable prejudice: inequality in educational research and policy', *British Journal of Sociology*, 41, 1, pp. 29–54.

Ringen, S. (2005) 'The truth about class inequality'. Available at (accessed 05.02.09): <http://users.ox.ac.uk/~gree0074/en/en-publications.htm>.

Saunders, P. (1994) 'Is Britain a meritocracy', in Blackburn, R. M. (ed.) *Social Inequality in a Changing World*, Cambridge: Sociological Research Group, Faculty of Social and Political Sciences.

— (1995) 'Might Britain be a meritocracy?', *Sociology*, 29, 1, pp. 23–41.

— (1996) *Unequal but Fair? A study of class barriers in Britain*, London: Institute of Economic Affairs.

— (1997) 'Social mobility in Britain: an empirical evaluation of two competing theories', *Sociology*, 31, 1, pp. 261–88.

— (2002) 'Reflections on the meritocracy debate in Britain: a response to Richard Bereen and John Goldthorpe', *British Journal of Sociology*, 53, 4, pp. 559–74.

Savage, M. and Egerton, M. (1997) 'Social mobility, individual ability and the inheritance of class inequality', *Sociology*, 31, 4, pp. 645–72.

Schatz, S. (1965) 'Achievement and economic growth: a critique', *Quarterly Journal of Economics*, 79, 2, pp. 234–41.

Swift, A. (2000) 'Class analysis from a normative perspective', *British Journal of Sociology*, 51, 4, pp. 663–79.

— (2003) 'Seizing the opportunity: the influences of preferences and aspirations on social immobility', *New Economy*, 10, 4, pp. 208–13.

— (2004) 'Would perfect mobility be perfect?', *European Sociological Review*, 20, 1, pp. 1–11.

Qualitative Causal Analysis: Grounded Theorizing and the Qualitative Survey

3

Martyn Hammersley

As we saw in the Introduction, at the level of methodological discourse, it is now common for qualitative researchers – in many fields – to deny any commitment to causal analysis; on the grounds that causality does not operate in the social world and/or that pursuing causal knowledge is ethically or politically undesirable.[1] Yet, in practice, virtually all qualitative researchers routinely make causal claims, for example about what factors have 'influenced', 'shaped', 'formed', 'brought about' etc. some outcome; indeed, it would be hard for them to avoid doing this (Hammersley 2008a). Furthermore, not only have some older qualitative approaches focused directly on causal analysis, notably analytic induction (AI), but in addition one of the currently most

---

1 In the Introduction we also noted an important exception: in recent case-study research in political science there has been an explicit commitment to causal analysis, and strong engagement with quantitative methodology (Bennett and Elman 2006). Qualitative Comparative Analysis has been one product of this. Interdisciplinary accounts of case-study method have also often presented it as an alternative means of causal analysis to quantitative research, notably Yin (2009).

influential ones, grounded theorizing (GT), was explicitly introduced as a form of causal analysis and is still treated in this way (see Dey 2007: 178–9), despite various attempts to excise earlier 'positivist' aspects of it (see Charmaz 2000, 2006: 9–10; Bryant and Charmaz 2007: 36–41).[2]

In this chapter, I will begin by exploring what is involved in GT as a means of identifying causal relations, comparing it with AI since they have significant similarities and differences. In the second half of the chapter I will look at a particular study that claims to apply GT but which departs from it in overall research design, albeit in illuminating ways: it is closer to what might be described as a qualitative survey (Jansen 2010). Through this discussion, I hope to illustrate some of the variation in approach, as well as the problems, to be found within Qualitative Causal Analysis.

An outline of grounded theorizing

Glaser and Strauss formulated GT in the 1960s as a set of 'strategies for qualitative research'.[3] The approach drew on Strauss's experience of doing case-study work in the tradition of Chicago sociology (Becker et al. 1961; Strauss et al. 1965), and on Glaser's familiarity with the primarily quantitative tradition of 1950s Columbia sociology, and with Merton's pursuit of middle-range theory (Lazarsfeld and Rosenberg 1955; Merton 1957; Glaser 1964). Glaser and Strauss's book *The Discovery of Grounded Theory* (henceforth DGT) arose out of a research project on which they worked together concerned with issues around dying in hospitals (see Glaser and Strauss 1965).

In DGT Glaser and Strauss challenged a then influential model of inquiry in quantitative research concerned with testing hypotheses drawn from the sociological literature (Glaser and Strauss 1967: ch1). Against this 'verificationism', they insisted on the importance of generating and developing theoretical ideas in an inductive way through systematic data collection and analysis.[4] However, their argument also represented a challenge to much qualitative

---

2 There has also been an attempt to redirect Qualitative Comparative Analysis away from the investigation of causes, see Rantala and Hellström 2001.

3 It should be remembered, however, that they included a chapter in their book concerned with 'theoretical elaboration of quantitative data'. Glaser and Strauss subsequently came to disagree sharply about the nature of GT (Dey 1999: ch1), and some of the issues are relevant to my discussion here.

4 It is worth pointing out that what is meant by 'verification' here is different from the verificationism characteristic of logical positivist philosophy, on which see Misak 1995.

research at the time, in both anthropology and sociology – where this adopted a primarily descriptive orientation, and therefore did not engage *systematically* in the development of theory. From Glaser and Strauss's point of view, while such work generated theoretical ideas through empirical investigation it did this in an informal, and therefore in a less than fully effective, way.

So, what Glaser and Strauss sought to provide in DGT, and in subsequent methodological texts, was a systematic strategy for developing theories through the collection and analysis of qualitative data. Moreover, they argued that, because it had been produced in a rigorously inductive fashion, grounded theory was much more likely to be valid than that produced by armchair theorists, and that for many purposes further testing is not required (Glaser and Strauss 1967: 4 and 233).

Key features of the approach they recommended include the following:

1. An insistence on the importance of starting with close examination of social processes in particular settings, looking for the patterns that can be discovered in data generated in this way. In order to achieve this, they suggest that researchers should not read the research literature prior to going into the field – so as to avoid imposing prior theoretical notions that might obscure what actually occurs (Glaser and Strauss 1967: 37; Covan 2007: 68).
2. Rather than data collection being completed before analysis formally begins, bouts of data analysis must be interspersed with periods of data collection, each informing the other.
3. Closely related to this is the strategy of theoretical sampling: after an initial exploratory period, the cases – locations and/or people – to be studied should be specifically selected in a manner designed to facilitate further development of the emerging theory. This involves comparing both cases that seem to be similar in terms of the theory, *and* cases that would be at opposite ends of dimensions identified as important by the theory.
4. In examining data relevant to particular theoretical categories, there must be constant comparison of different segments of data classified in the same way, and of these with current conceptualizations of the relevant categories. It is argued that this will facilitate clarification and development of the categories, in particular identifying new properties, dimensions and relations; and that it will eventually lead to the emergence of an integrated theoretical account.

A comparison with analytic induction

In the course of discussing the distinctive features of GT, Glaser and Strauss contrast it with analytic induction (AI), an approach that had been developed much earlier in the century, also in the context of Chicago sociology.[5] The pioneer here was Znaniecki (1934). He argued that statistical method was defective from a scientific point of view because science is necessarily concerned with discovering universal laws that apply to *all* relevant cases rather than with producing probabilistic generalizations that apply only to some of them. He claimed that such laws could be derived from close analysis of one or a small number of cases, and that an important aspect of this process was to discover to what theoretical, in other words to what causally homogeneous, outcome category the case being investigated belongs. He argued that in doing this the researcher would be identifying the semi-closed system of causal factors that distinctively produces this type of outcome. AI was further developed and applied by Lindesmith (1937/1947) in his study of opiate addiction. He examined quite a large number of cases, seeking to identify the *combination* of features that seemed always to be present when addiction occurred. In addition, he investigated other cases where only some of the component causal factors he had identified were present, in order to check the sufficiency of the full set of conditions. Subsequently, Cressey applied the same approach to a study of embezzlement, coming to redefine what it was he was trying to explain as 'financial trust violation', in order to produce a causally homogeneous category by eliminating those cases of embezzlement where the offender specifically took on a position of financial trust in order to exploit it.[6]

There are important similarities between GT and AI. These include:

- They are both designed primarily for use with qualitative data drawn from case-study investigations.
- Both are 'inductive' in orientation: they recommend beginning with an investigation of one or a small number of cases of the type of phenomenon that is of interest.
- Both reject the goal of achieving representative sampling of cases. For advocates of AI, as already noted, this is because the aim is deterministic laws not probabilistic generalizations. As regards GT, representative sampling is downplayed in favour of selecting cases that will facilitate development of the emerging theory.

---

5 For an exploration of the historical relationship between GT and AI, see Hammersley 2010.

6 Other applications include Becker's (1953, 1955) work on marihuana use, and Katz's (1982) investigation of lawyers.

- In both approaches decisions about whether to analyse further cases should be based on judgements about whether or not these are likely to provide valuable information: the analysis stops when this no longer seems likely, at the point of what Glaser and Strauss call 'theoretical saturation'. So, in neither approach is there any requirement for full coverage of a previously identified sample or population.

There are also important *differences* between AI and GT, and these highlight issues that are of central concern for any qualitative causal analysis:

1. The starting point for AI is an interest in why some particular type of quite specific outcome occurs, such as opiate addiction or financial trust violation. This provides a relatively narrow focus for enquiry, cases being selected for study that display this outcome; though, as already noted, it is also recognized that the nature of what is to be explained may subsequently need to be reformulated. By contrast, the initial focus for GT is much vaguer and broader. It is concerned, for example, with what is going on in a particular type of setting or scene – the 'basic social process' occurring there – or issues surrounding a key dimension of it, for instance that of who is and is not aware that a patient is dying.
2. A related difference concerns the nature of the theory that is pursued. AI focuses on a single causal hypothesis, albeit usually involving a combination of factors, as to why some particular type of outcome (opiate addiction, financial trust violation) occurs. By contrast, the sort of theory that GT aims at is an integrated system of ideas which is designed to explain, or to provide a conceptual language for understanding, *the whole range of behaviour associated with some social process or aspect of a setting.*
3. While AI tends to employ categorical variables (addicted/not addicted, symptoms recognized/not recognized, opiates used/not used), GT often deals with variables that are conceptualized in terms of degree (awareness as high or low; social status as high or low).
4. The concept of theoretical sampling in GT requires that new cases for investigation be selected according to which are most likely to facilitate the developing analysis, through maximizing similarities on some occasions and maximizing differences on others. By contrast, in AI new cases analysed are, for the most part, simply further cases where the outcome to be explained is present (or, more rarely, where it is absent despite the presence of some candidate causal factors).
5. This partly reflects the fact that GT is primarily concerned with the *development* of theoretical ideas, whereas AI is explicitly concerned with both developing and *testing* causal hypotheses. For Glaser and Strauss, comparative analysis of cases is directed towards the former rather than the latter. Indeed, there is an often noted ambiguity in *DGT*, and for that matter in their later methodological writings, about whether or not the theories produced via GT need to be formally tested

(see Hammersley 1989: 198–204; Dey 1999: 18, 20–1, 34–5). In some places the authors suggest that this is unnecessary because the process of theory development itself involves testing; in others they deny this, indicating that grounded theories can subsequently be tested by other means, though they often seem to imply that this is not necessary. The underlying idea here may be that the need for testing only arises where theoretical ideas have been produced by speculation, that where theories are generated through empirical investigation their validity is more or less assured.

6. While AI involves quite a demanding notion of the threshold that must be reached if a hypothesis is to be accepted – namely that it must fit *all* the cases where instances of the explanandum type occur – adherents of GT seem to be satisfied with tendencies, in a similar way to most quantitative analysis. In other words, a single exception is not treated as refuting the emerging theory, but rather (at most) as indicating the need for further elaboration of the theory. Once categories have 'emerged', they are unlikely to be abandoned later as failing to fit the data, the only grounds for dropping categories seem to be that they are not central to the emerging theory. This contrasts with AI's emphasis on the need for either the explanans or the explanandum to be reformulated in the face of a single discrepant item of data.

7. This raises the question of what 'grounded' means in the context of 'grounded theorizing' and 'grounded theory'. It seems to imply a thorough familiarity with the phenomena being investigated, and systematic comparison of cases in order to identify the variable properties that are associated with particular types of phenomenon.[7] As Dey (1999: 33–9) shows, in accounts of GT there is heavy reliance upon the discovery metaphor, and indeed it seems to be assumed that causal relations can be observed directly. Thus, at one point Glaser and Strauss (1967: 40) claim that 'in field work [. . .] general relations are often discovered in vivo; that is, the field worker literally sees them occur'. By contrast, at least in the form developed by Lindesmith, and subsequently used by Cressey, AI specifically assumes that causal relations cannot be found in studying a single case but only through analysis of multiple cases in terms of the presence and absence of relevant features.[8] In other words, comparative analysis, not just within-case analysis, is required for identifying causal relations.

8. Both Znaniecki and Lindesmith insist that the scientific concepts emerging from AI involve a significant break from commonsense categories. While the latter necessarily provide a starting point for social research, it is argued that they

---

7 However, Glaser and Strauss's studies do not provide in-depth accounts of particular locations, and narrative accounts of particular sequences of events, in the manner of many ethnographic studies (Dey 1999: 30).

8 This contrast is less clear in the case of Znaniecki.

will often need to be reformulated if causally homogeneous categories are to be discovered. This is why, in the face of failure of a hypothesis to match the evidence, it is explicitly recognized that the explanandum may require reformulation. By contrast, Glaser and Strauss do not seem to draw a distinction between scientific and commonsense categories, even though they insist that GT develops new categories that are 'analytic' in character. The lack of such a distinction is reflected in the fact that they also require that the categories it produces be 'sensitizing': they must 'yield a "meaningful" picture, abetted by apt illustrations that enable one to grasp the reference in terms of one's own experience', helping 'the reader to see and hear vividly the people in the area under study' (Glaser and Strauss 1967: 38–9).[9] This suggests that Glaser and Strauss see the categories forming part of grounded theories as amounting to no more than refinements of the commonsense categories used by the people being studied. If scientific concepts were more than this, then they could not serve a sensitizing function, they would be alien and therefore opaque to people's ordinary ways of thinking about the world, for instance in the way that the concepts of twentieth-century Physics are.

9. Closely associated with this is the fact that Glaser and Strauss assume what Dey refers to as 'interpretive stability': 'though mediated by the researcher's own sensitivities, categories are "indicated" by the data in an essentially straightforward way. They do not have to compete for attention with other, rival ways of categorizing the data' (Dey 1999: 28).[10] Thus: 'Glaser and Strauss seem to imply that categories can emerge from the data almost without requiring any act of interpretation on the part of the researcher. The categories may be constructs, but these are constructs that directly reflect reality as experienced rather preconceived'. And it seems to be assumed that reality imposes itself in this way upon actors and researchers alike, thereby implying that the experience of actors and researchers in the field is 'pre-theoretical', in other words is simply given (Dey 1999: 29). Furthermore, Glaser and Strauss suggest that this experience arises from pragmatic engagement in the world, this view contrasting sharply with Znaniecki's rejection of pragmatic categories as unscientific. This

---

9 Blumer's (1940 and 1969) original usage of 'sensitizing concepts' seems to refer to analytic fruitfulness, indicating 'directions in which to look', though such concepts may also have been intended to capture the everyday understandings of actors. Dey (1999: 30–3) argues that there is a tension between the two requirements that Glaser and Strauss place upon concepts: that they be analytic and sensitizing.

10 As Dey points out, this also tends to neglect the 'diffusion, difficulties, and diversity of interpretations among those being studied. [. . .] There is little sense of the deceits and self-deceptions, or conflicts and contradictions, that might make meaningful behavior so hard to interpret – even for the actors themselves' (Dey 1999: 28).

leads Glaser and Strauss to comment that 'informed laymen and social scientists manage to profit quite well from the merely plausible work of discovery published by sociologists who carefully analyze their qualitative data, and so the need for highly rigorous research is forestalled' (1967: 235). By contrast, Znaniecki sees scientific theory as of pragmatic value, in providing for control of social phenomena, *precisely because* it is the result of highly rigorous research that involves testing hypotheses and thereby overcomes the limitations of commonsense knowledge.

From the point of view of causal analysis, GT has some clear strengths. It involves detailed examination of cases in a concern with 'process tracing' (Brady and Collier 2004; George and Bennett 2005): with identifying sequential patterns among multiple features within cases that may indicate the operation of causal mechanisms. In addition, comparative analysis of cases is central to the approach, and cases are selected strategically so as to develop the emerging causal theory. Moreover, at different times, this selection of cases involves both maximizing and minimizing the differences between cases on particular dimensions, and this seems likely to be a fruitful strategy in identifying causal relations (Collier et al. 2004: 92–4 and *passim*).

However, there are also potential weaknesses. GT does not involve a single-minded focus on explaining a specific type of outcome. Instead, the goal seems to be to produce representations of specific parts of the social world, these being treated as typifying more abstract social forms. Furthermore, there is a failure to recognize that the development and testing of theories are mutually dependent. As a result of these two weaknesses, little systematic testing of causal interpretations seems to be involved in GT, so that the validity of the conclusions is questionable. What is overlooked is how easy it is to be mistaken about causal relationships, and the consequent importance of checking appearances, for example taking account of confounding variables. This is an aspect of the naïve realism that Dey (1999: ch2) detects in GT.

GT has been applied, in one manner or another, in a very large number of studies. Most of these have taken the form of case-study investigations relying on participant observation and/or on interview data. However, there are exceptions. In the remainder of this chapter I want to examine an unusual example, one that comes closer to the survey rather than to the case-study model.

Causal analysis in practice: a qualitative survey of educational inequalities

While, as I have noted, the GT model is frequently appealed to by qualitative researchers today – and while, in practice, such research is almost always concerned with identifying causal relations – much of it does not correspond *closely* to the recommendations laid down by Glaser and Strauss, in their original book and in subsequent accounts (see Benoliel 1996). The example I will examine here is no exception. However, it is of particular interest because it moves away from the case-study mould, towards a research design that shares some features in common with the quantitative survey: it studies a relatively large number of cases, these mostly being selected at a single point in time, with the main focus being on cross-case, rather than within-case, analysis. Furthermore, the primary strategy seems to be to use associations among variables in the data to draw inferences about what causes a particular type of outcome. In the terms used in our Introduction, this study is, to a large degree, aggregate-focused rather than case-focused. However, it is representative in this respect of a significant body of qualitative work today, not least in the study of educational inequalities (see, for instance, Ball et al. 1995; Gewirtz et al. 1995; Ball 2003).

In their book *Degrees of Choice*, Reay et al. (2005) are concerned with documenting and explaining differences in how people in the UK decide to which universities they will apply. The investigation is described in the blurb as 'a rich empirical study of 500 applicants to higher education'. The data consisted of questionnaire and interview data from applicants, and also from interviews with some parents and teachers, plus a small amount of observation of relevant events in the schools and colleges where the applicants were students.

The researchers conclude that there are significant social class differences in application decisions; and they claim that these derive, in large part, from differential social class and ethnic distribution of social and cultural capital, and from the very different 'habituses' associated with the social classes and with specific class fractions. They give particular attention to emotional factors, these being concerned with people's sense of where they belong, and where they would and would not 'fit in'; suggesting that this is a neglected aspect of decision making in currently influential rational choice accounts. Along with Bourdieu (1984), they argue that what is involved here is a choice of lifestyle (Reay et al. 2005: 29), with the middle class having been socialized into an appreciation of what elite universities have to offer, while the working class have not been. These factors shape decision-making processes, producing a strong tendency for working-class applicants to apply to non-elite universities, while middle-class applicants tend to apply to elite ones. The authors suggest that these differences in decision-making processes make an important contribution to the reproduction of social class inequalities in the education system, and in wider UK society. They emphasize that in examining the role of higher education in this process, it is no longer just a matter of who goes and does not go to university but rather of *to which type of university* they go.

While there are a few places in the book where the authors examine individual cases in some level of detail, for the most part their analysis seems to have consisted of examining frequencies across cases; in other words, associations among scores on variables, notably between social class background and differences in the processes (specifically search procedures employed and criteria of selection) by which applicants chose to which universities they would apply.

I will examine two methodological aspects of this study, in each case comparing it with both GT and with the *quantitative* survey: first, the issue of how cases were selected; second, how the data were analysed.

Sampling strategy

Reay et al. draw on questionnaire data from 502 students, and interview data from 120 students, in 6 schools and colleges in the London area. These institutions varied sharply in academic status, and in the social class composition of their student bodies: from a comprehensive school and an FE college running higher education access courses to two elite, single sex, private schools. As far as one can tell, the questionnaire was distributed to all students in years 12 and 13 in the 6 institutions. It is reported that 502 students filled in the questionnaire, but it is unclear what response rate this represents, though we can perhaps assume it was relatively high.

As regards selection of applicants to interview, the authors report that: 'At first we interviewed those who had volunteered through the questionnaire, but then attempted to broaden the sample to address imbalances, notably in relation to gender, and also to include a range of interesting cases, for example first generation students and Oxbridge entrants in state schools' (Reay et al. 2005: 11). The result was interviews with 120 students, 54 per cent of whom were female, 34 per cent working class, and 54 per cent from ethnic minority backgrounds. Data from applicants themselves were supplemented by interviews with 40 parents and 15 other key informants, for example sixth-form tutors; and by participant observation at a range of events in all 6 institutions, including parents' evenings, careers lessons, Oxbridge interview practice, and tutor group sessions on university application.

The authors report that they 'employed grounded coding techniques (Strauss 1987) in [the] analysis of the interview data'. However, it is clear that their sampling strategy deviated from the kind of theoretical sampling characteristic of GT. As we saw, the latter usually begins with investigation of a relatively small number of cases, *further cases being selected as part of succeeding waves of iterative analysis, in a manner that builds on prior analysis and is designed to develop the emerging theory.* By contrast, Reay et al. began with a large sample of students who answered a questionnaire, and then drew volunteers for interview from this. While they sought subsequently to 'broaden' the interview sample, this seems to have been partly in terms of improving representativeness by addressing 'imbalances', notably in terms of gender. While their inclusion of cases that were of particular interest for the study, such as people who were the first in their families to go to university, might seem close to GT, it does not constitute theoretical sampling because it does not seem to have arisen from systematic analysis of the data. Much the same judgement applies to what the authors describe as their 'deliberate focus on non-traditional – working class, ethnic minority, and mature women as well as white, middle class female and male applicants [. . .]' (Reay et al. 2005: viii). So, in terms of sampling strategy, the design of this study is some way from what Glaser and Strauss recommend: what seems to be involved is the construction of a relatively large and fixed sample prior to carrying out the data analysis, in a manner analogous to the quantitative survey.

However, if we compare Reay et al.'s study with the standard approach recommended for quantitative surveys, a number of differences emerge here too. First, there is no clear indication of to what population the authors are intending their findings to apply; though from their conclusions it seems likely that the intended population was something like 'applicants to higher education in the UK, at the end of the 20th century'.

The second issue concerns the strategies used to try to achieve representativeness. While the authors specifically selected institutions in a way that was designed to cover much of the range of variation in UK applicants as regards social class and ethnicity, as well as the various types of institution attended, this was *not* done in the way that would normally be recommended in survey research. In particular, the clusters – in this case the institutions – were not randomly selected from the relevant population, and the fact that they are all located in the same city itself raises questions about the representativeness of the questionnaire sample, as regards the UK or even England. The authors themselves note that 'the research has its limitations in terms of its particular location', since 'in many ways, London, with its heavy concentration of HEIs, is unique and stands out from the rest of the UK' (p. 11). They also acknowledge that the social class distribution of their sample differed significantly from that of the UK population (p. 13). This means that there are serious questions about what general conclusions can be drawn on the basis of the data used in this study about applicants in the UK generally: we simply do not know in what ways their sample is, and in what ways it is not, likely to be representative; though it probably has a higher chance of being representative of the population of London applicants.[11]

Equally important, as already noted, it is not clear what the response rate was for the questionnaire, and the authors indicate that they were only able to obtain usable information about occupation from 80 per cent of applicants so as to classify them in terms of social class. For these reasons too, the working sample that they employed might be unrepresentative, raising further questions about how generalizable conclusions drawn from the questionnaire can be about the UK population of applicants, or for that matter even about London applicants. Of course, by no means all quantitative surveys match the methodological ideal, and low response rates and other types of missing data are a common problem. However, the provision of information about such imperfections, and the use of strategies to reduce or allow for them, are normally required.

---

11 Of course, concentrating data collection in one location may carry advantages, not just in logistical terms but also for example in allowing for systematic comparison of cases that share some features of location in common. In addition, selecting institutions from the full range, in terms of social class and ethnic background of students, provides a basis for systematic comparative analysis. However, Reay et al. do not seem to exploit these possibilities to any great extent.

When it comes to the sample of applicants interviewed, from which much of the data used in the analysis are drawn, even more serious departures from the survey model are to be found. Not only was there no process of random sampling here, but placing reliance primarily on volunteers is almost certain to have introduced sampling bias. Equally important, the authors report that:

> In our qualitative sample we deliberately sought a different class profile to that of the quantitative sample. First, we included a far higher percentage of working class students (33%) than are to be found in the quantitative sample. Second, over 30 per cent of the qualitative sample were part of what we have termed the established middle classes. [. . .] The rest of the qualitative sample was predominantly middle class traditional graduates (28%) with a sprinkling of the routine, non-manual A-level (intermediate) grouping (8%). (Reay et al. 2005: 14)

The reasoning behind these decisions was presumably that the primary aim of the study was to explain why working-class applicants were much less likely to apply to elite universities than those from the established middle classes, so that this reflects a strategic judgement. Nevertheless, it does compromise even further any basis for claiming that the findings of the study apply to the whole population of UK applicants. We have a mode of sampling here that lies somewhere between the theoretical sampling of GT and the strategies for achieving representative samples that are characteristic of quantitative surveys. While there may be some distinctive benefits associated with this, the authors do not say what these could be, and the risks associated with it in terms of producing non-generalizable findings are obvious.

However, it should be noted that this relates to a fundamental issue as regards much survey research: whether the task is to provide an accurate representation of the characteristics of a finite population or to identify causal relations. To the extent that the aim of Reay et al.'s study was to identify the distribution of various features relevant to the application process across the UK applicant population, the concerns I have raised above are justified and serious. However, as with much survey research, the authors were also concerned to try to determine what factors caused an outcome – in this case the lower rate of working-class application to elite universities. And the means they employ for doing this seems to be comparative analysis, more or less along the lines of Mill's methods of agreement and difference: comparing those cases that display the outcome (working-class applicants not applying to elite universities) with other cases (working-class applicants who do, middle-class applicants who do and those who do not). The aim here is to try to identify potential contributory causes and to test hypotheses about them. Here, arguably, the aim is not to produce an account of what happens in the UK but rather to detect general causal relationships typically producing the outcome concerned. And we should note that there may be alternative causal paths by which that outcome is produced, and each of these causal relationships is likely to operate outside the population of UK applicants as well as within it. It must be said, however, that in their book Reay et al. engage in little or no explicit comparative analysis of a systematic kind: they limit themselves to reporting various correlations among key variables, treating these as picking out causal relationships.

The form of analysis

The authors report that the questionnaire data were used to generate 'contextual information and basic descriptive statistics of [the] sample, as well as [to] help in selecting students for interview'. They report that: the 'in-depth interviews elicited educational career histories from the students and a narrative account of their choice of higher education institutions. Specific questions were asked about information used, support received, constraints etc' (Reay et al. 2005: 12). As already noted, the authors report that they 'employed grounded coding techniques (Strauss, 1987)', and they provide some elaboration about what this involved: the transcripts were 'open coded initially but as the analysis proceeded, coding concentrated on the major emergent issues and allowed us to saturate our main hypothesis concerning the relationship between habituses and choice'. They continue:

> Bourdieu's three main concepts of habitus, field and cultural capital were all deployed in order to analyse sociologically the processes underpinning students' choice making practices. Work on developing the characteristics and dimensions of our primary codes was extended by using axial coding and constant comparison procedures. All the qualitative data was entered into Nudist, a qualitative data analysis package, which allowed us, using counts and searches, to verify or disconfirm the relevance of issues emerging through our manual coding. Nudist also allowed us to undertake a number of other frequency counts in relation to the interview data and was used throughout to search, sort and manage the data base. (p. 12)

Once again, this discussion raises a number of questions about the relationship of this study to GT. First, the nature of what is being studied here, and the kind of explanation or theory aimed at, show some differences from as well as some conformity to the GT model. In terms of its focus, *Degrees of Choice* seems rather closer to AI, in that the primary concern is to explain a quite specific outcome: why do proportionately fewer working-class people apply to elite universities? However, the theory that is developed to account for this is closer to the sort of theory aimed at by GT: it is concerned with modelling the application process.

We might also ask about the extent to which the analysis was directed at generating an emergent theory. We have already seen that the sampling strategy appeared to be concerned with representativeness rather than with theoretical sampling, and was framed in terms of variables that seem to have been identified as important from the start. Moreover, most of the data seems to have been already collected before the analysis began.

This is closely related to the question of the relationship between the 'open coding' that the authors employed and their use of Bourdieu's theoretical framework. They talk, for example, of viewing the application process 'through the lens' provided by this framework (Reay et al. 2005: ix).[12] They report that:

> drawing on Bourdieu's work on distinction and judgement, we take the concept of habitus, and the development of the concept to include institutional and familial habituses, and use them to understand and explain the choices students make of higher education. Our aim is to link school (institutional habitus) and family (class habitus) with individual choice-making and the workings of cultural capital in a sociologically informed dynamic. (Reay et al. 2005: viii)

In the body of the book, as with many qualitative research reports, the authors use concepts from the literature, and especially from Bourdieu, as a kind of scaffolding to provide for interpretation of the data. In effect, throughout, Bourdieu's theoretical apparatus is used as a means of reformulating the data in theoretical terms, pointing to what the authors take to be the underlying significance of what their informants say.

---

12 It may be worth commenting that what Bourdieu offers is not a theoretical language in the sense of a well-organized and tightly related set of concepts, by comparison for example with Marx's theory of capitalism, but something rather looser. Furthermore, there are serious questions to be raised about whether the assumptions built into Bourdieu's theoretical apparatus have been tested, see Jenkins 1992.

At face value, there is a contradiction between this use of Bourdieu's work and 'grounded coding'. Glaser and Strauss in 1967, and subsequently, seem to argue against the adoption of theoretical ideas from the literature in this way. Moreover, this was the central point in Glaser's critique of Strauss and Corbin's text, where he accused them of encouraging the imposition of a particular theoretical framework on data, rather than generating concepts *from* the data (Glaser 1992). And what Reay et al. adopt here is much more substantively specific even than the 'conditional-consequential matrix' proposed in *Basics of Qualitative Research* (Strauss and Corbin 1998: ch12).

The issue is more complex than this, however. Even in 1967, Glaser and Strauss comment at one point: 'a discovered grounded theory, then, will tend to combine mostly concepts and hypotheses that have emerged from the data *with some existing ones that are clearly useful*' (Glaser and Strauss 1967: 46, emphasis added). This leaves the door open for some use of prior concepts. Furthermore, Strauss (1970) wrote an article specifically concerned with developing a new theory from existing theory, even if what he proposes is very different from what Reay et al. do.[13] More fundamentally, as Dey (1999: ch1) points out, throughout much of the methodological literature on grounded theory, there is an at least apparent tension between the insistence that previously developed concepts must be avoided and an emphasis on the importance of 'theoretical sensitivity' (see, especially, Glaser 1978). In other words, it is not necessarily assumed that the concepts simply come out of the data or are impressed on the analyst by the world. He or she must have the necessary resources to make sense of what is going on.

What is at issue here is, perhaps, to do with how readily the analyst seeks to apply existing concepts, and in particular whether alternative conceptualizations are considered. Turning back to the work of Reay et al., it is hard not to conclude that Bourdieu's conceptual scheme guided the research more or less from the start. Moreover, throughout their discussion this scheme provides the main framework of analysis, and there are no very obvious signs of new concepts emerging from the data analysis.

It is also striking how, in their discussion of the analytic approach they adopted, Reay et al. mix an appeal to GT with language that would normally be regarded as at odds with this. In the extract quoted above, they talk of 'using counts and searches, to verify or disconfirm the relevance of issues emerging

---

13 This article is partially reprinted as an appendix to Strauss 1987, a text to which Reay et al. refer.

through our manual coding' (p. 12). As we saw, Glaser and Strauss specifically deny that GT is concerned with verification or disconfirmation. Furthermore, they do not explicitly recommend the use of 'frequency counts' (p. 12).

Here again, though, Reay et al.'s deviation from the GT model relates to a significant issue. As we noted earlier, Glaser and Strauss are ambiguous about whether or not GT involves *testing* the theory that is being generated and developed. Furthermore, while they do not explicitly recommend frequency counts, GT *does* seem to be concerned with identifying associations among variables and properties, and in these terms actual frequency counts could surely be appropriate. In other words, in a broad sense GT is correlational in character: the aim is to discover patterns across cases, and what 'patterns' means here seems, to a large extent, to be co-variation among variables; for example, that the higher the social status of the patient who is dying, the more likely it is that medical personnel will develop what Glaser and Strauss refer to as 'loss rationales'.

There is a clear parallel in *modus operandi* here with quantitative surveys, and so once again it is also worth comparing Reay et al.'s analysis with the form of analysis characteristic of that type of work. In terms of this comparison, their work is subject to some major criticisms; though many of these could also be applied to other examples of the qualitative survey genre; and, as with the comparison with GT, these criticisms involve assumptions that raise important issues.

A first point is that, from a survey research point of view, conceptualization and operationalization of the key variables in *Degrees of Choice* are weak in important respects. As regards social class, there are reasonable questions that might be asked about the scheme used, the Registrar General's classification of occupations, by contrast for example with that employed in recent social mobility studies (Goldthorpe 1988). While the authors refer to Goldthorpe's more recent classification system, this does not appear to have had much impact on their work in operational terms. It is also unclear how problems of conflict between father's and mother's occupation were handled. Beyond this, there is some ambiguity about which classification is being used at different points in the analysis, since the authors report: 'In addition to the traditional class categorization outlined above [the Registrar General's classification] we also constructed our own composite categorisation based on both parents' occupation, where present, and the parents' education' (Reay et al. 2005: 13). They report that they used this in discussing parental involvement in higher education choice, but it is unclear whether it was also used elsewhere. We are also left in the dark about how occupational and educational characteristics were combined in constructing this alternative scheme.

There are issues about the operationalization of the class categories as well as about their conceptualization. It seems that in the majority of cases reliance was placed upon questionnaire responses from students in order to identify parental social class, and this could have involved significant error. As we noted in Chapter 1, this is a notorious problem in the measurement of social class. While the authors report that they were able to assign over 80 per cent of questionnaire respondents to social classes (Reay et al. 2005: 12), it is impossible to judge sensibly how accurately this was done.

It may be that this was not a serious source of error since, while the Registrar General's scheme identifies six different classes, for the most part Reay et al.'s analysis relies on middle-class/working-class comparisons. Even so, there are places where questions arise. For example, at one point the authors note that, of their working-class sample of 41:

> Two were from self-employed backgrounds. Lesley's father managed a small jewelry shop where her mother worked as a shop assistant. [Lesley's] current partner is also self employed and runs his own sign writing business. Darren's father is a small property developer, although Darren works as a security guard. Both, however, self-identified as working class. Both [. . .] were the first in their families to aim for university, were on low incomes and living in public sector households. Accordingly, we have included them in our working class sample, while attempting to address the ambiguity of their situation. Thus some of our sample are already mobile, located in intermediate middle class positions or, in Bourdieu's terms, petit-bourgeois. (p. 84)

Even more importantly, reliance on middle-class/working-class comparisons offers little delicacy of analysis, a problem that the authors themselves note:

> The old binary between working and middle class has never explained enough about the myriad ways in which social class is acted out in people's lives. Even Jackson and Marsden [1962] wrote about different groupings within their working class category. Thirty-eight per cent of the working class sample were described as 'sunken middle class'. Similarly, current research indicates that it is important to disaggregate crude class categorizations and develop more subtle analyses which recognize rather than gloss over increasing horizontal and vertical segmentation within class groupings (Savage et al. 1992; Savage 2000; Power et al. 2003). (Reay et al. 2005: 5)

Despite this recognition of the problems involved, for most of their book Reay et al. rely on this 'crude' 'old binary'. Moreover, while they discuss segments within the middle and working classes at some points, these are not presented very clearly in conceptual terms, nor are we told how people were assigned to them, and so cannot judge how accurate this process is likely to have been.

Similar problems apply to Reay et al.'s treatment of other variables. Even the status hierarchy of universities is not specified clearly, nor is the issue explored of discrepancies between how the researchers conceptualized this hierarchy and applicants' perceptions of universities.[14] Equally important, the different types of choice process presented as characteristic of the social classes are not as clearly described as in earlier research of a similar kind on selection of secondary school (Ball et al. 1995; Gewirtz et al. 1995), and this makes understanding what causes them, and identifying their effects, more difficult.

In addition to these problems of conceptualization and operationalization, another feature highlighted by comparison with quantitative surveys is that we are not provided with full information about the frequencies that are central to the analysis. In many places, the information is simply absent. For example, we are not told what numbers of working-class and middle-class students in the sample chose each type of university, only what proportions at each school or college did so. Nor are national figures provided regarding the distribution of working-class and middle-class applicants across the hierarchy of universities. With other claims we are provided with verbal quantifications but not supplied actual figures, even though these were presumably available to the authors. For instance, we are not told what the frequencies were between the classes as regards various forms of cultural capital or the different types of selection process identified, only that these were very different for working-class and middle-class applicants.[15]

Another criticism from the direction of survey methodology would be that there is little or no testing of the causal hypotheses put forward, and no

---

14 This is explored to some extent elsewhere, see Ball et al. 2002.

15 There is also a tendency to conflate frequency across cases with intensity within each case. For example, the authors write that: 'The private school students express high levels of preference for Oxbridge and virtually no interest in the post-1992 universities. The FE students did not even consider Oxbridge. It is "not for the likes of them"' (p. 44). Also illustrated here is a mixing of presentation of what is to be explained and of what is held to explain it.

attempt to *specify* the relative contributions of the various factors mentioned: material circumstances, social and cultural capital and emotional habitus. Nor is there any explicit exploration of how the frequencies might change if other variables were controlled, even those that the study focused on, such as gender and ethnicity. This is despite the fact that the authors claim to have disentangled these factors (pp. 59–60). There are also variables that are not taken into account that may have played a crucial role in the decision-making process. The most obvious one is differences in academic ability among applicants, or in their perceptions of their own ability. Yet, given that applicants may well select institutions partly on the basis of judgements about their own ability in relation to the academic demands of courses at different universities, this would seem to have causal relevance. On most interpretations it would also be relevant to any evaluation of inequalities in educational outcome as just or unjust. Moreover, while the authors pay attention to mediating variables – notably school/college, indeed they claim to have documented a 'school effect' (pp. 36–8) – there is little indication of how this was done or what evidence the study provides about the contribution of mediating factors.[16]

Continuing with the comparison, we should give attention to features of Reay et al.'s study that are often (though not always) absent from quantitative surveys. In particular, they engaged in some within-case analysis to complement their cross-case comparisons. Of necessity, however, given the sheer number of cases they were dealing with, this could not but be rather superficial. Moreover, in this area their work shared a weakness that is also characteristic of much survey research: almost exclusive reliance upon questionnaire or interview data: in documenting the processes through which decisions were made about to which universities to apply, they are almost entirely dependent upon informants' retrospective accounts.[17] There is a sharp contrast here with case studies, such as those of Lacey 1970 and Ball 1981, that rely upon a range of different sorts of data and thereby ground their analyses of social processes much more effectively.

---

16 See also Reay et al. 2001. While I am not suggesting that the quantitative survey is the ideal against which all other research should be judged, I do believe that most of the problems raised by the comparison here are serious ones; indeed many of them seem to be breaches of what would be required whatever approach to causal analysis were adopted.

17 For a study of the same process that uses a more longitudinal approach see Brooks 2004. Some of the issues as regards primary reliance upon interview data are discussed in Hammersley and Gomm 2008.

For the most part, this type of data is all that the authors have available, for example as regards the criteria used to select universities, or the role of parents in this process. Only in relation to a few issues, notably differences among the schools and colleges, are these data supported by some observational material. The authors are clearly aware of the dangers of inference from interview data: for example, in one place they note the risk of rationalization (p. 58), and elsewhere discuss the problem of conflicts between accounts from different informants (see pp. 66, 68–70). However, these problems with inference from interview accounts are not systematically addressed, and in relation to most of their central claims the authors do not have the evidence required to check the reliability of the interview data. This seriously weakens their within-case analyses, as is true of a great deal of other interview-based qualitative research. While we need not adopt the extreme scepticism displayed by radical critics of interviews (Hammersley and Gomm 2008), there is room for doubt about the validity of Reay et al.'s conclusions on these grounds too.

Conclusion

In this chapter I began by examining grounded theorizing, one of the most influential current approaches to qualitative analysis; and one that, in its original form, is explicitly concerned with causal analysis. I compared it with analytic induction, an earlier approach with which it shares much in common, but whose differences from it are also significant. In the second part of the chapter I examined a particular study: Reay et al.'s investigation of social class differences in how people go about deciding to which UK universities they will apply. Like many who claim to be using GT, these researchers depart in some important ways from Glaser and Strauss's recommendations. In particular, where GT seems normally to involve a case-study design, Reay et al.'s work is closer to the survey model. It might be described as a qualitative survey in that, in terms of the dimension we introduced in the Introduction, it is more aggregate-focused than case-focused: in particular, while it uses both cross-case and within-case analysis, it concentrates more on the former than the latter; and adopts a correlational rather than a configurational approach. However, in this respect it is not unrepresentative of a considerable body of qualitative work. Furthermore, this orientation connects with GT, since this too tends to rely upon associations to identify causal relations, perhaps reflecting the influence of Glaser's Lazarsfeldian training at Columbia. Thus there is a sharp contrast with analytic induction, even though Reay et al. share the latter's concern with finding an explanation for a quite specific type of outcome. From the point of view of both GT and quantitative analysis their study displays important weaknesses, and these highlight key issues that need to be addressed as regards Qualitative Causal Analysis.

The aim of this chapter has been to map the main strategies by which qualitative researchers across most social science disciplines pursue the task of causal analysis, and to assess the likely effectiveness of these strategies. What is illustrated by Reay et al.'s study, through comparison with GT and quantitative research, is the heterogeneous character of qualitative causal analysis: the way in which a range of rather different strategies may be combined. This could be interpreted in a positive way as a form of bricolage: the use of whatever means and materials are at hand for present purposes (Denzin and Lincoln 2005: 4; see Hammersley 2008b: 137–40). However, in my view there is a need for more clarity about why particular methods are being used, the differences among them and their likely effectiveness.

References

Ball, S. (1981) *Beachside Comprehensive*, Cambridge: Cambridge University Press.

— (2003) *Class Strategies and the Educational Market: the middle classes and social advantage*, London: Routledge-Falmer.

Ball, S., Bowe, R. and Gewirtz, S. (1995) 'Circuits of schooling: a sociological exploration of parental choice of school in social class contexts', *Sociological Review*, 43, 1, pp. 52–78.

Ball, S., Davies, J., David, M. and Reay, D. (2002) ' "Classification" and "Judgment": social class and the "cognitive structures" of choice in higher education', *British Journal of Sociology of Education*, 23, 1, pp. 51–72.

Becker, H. S. (1953) 'Becoming a marihuana user', *American Journal of Sociology*, 59, 3, pp. 235–42.

— (1955) 'Marihuana use and social control', *Social Problems*, 3, 1, pp. 35–44.

Becker H. S., Geer, B., Hughes, E. and Strauss, A. (1961) *Boys in White: student culture in medical school*, Chicago: University of Chicago Press.

Bennett, A. and Elman, C. (2006) 'Qualitative research: recent developments in case study methods', *Annual Review of Political Science*, 9, pp. 459–60.

Benoliel, J. (1996) 'Grounded theory and nursing knowledge', *Qualitative Health Research*, 6, 3, pp. 406–28.

Blumer, H. (1940) 'The problem of the concept in social psychology', *American Journal of Sociology*, 45, pp. 707–19.

— (1969) *Symbolic Interactionism: perspective and method*, Englewood Cliffs NJ: Prentice-Hall.

Bourdieu, P. (1984) *Distinction*, London: Routledge and Kegan Paul.

Brady, H. E. and Collier, D. (eds) (2004) *Rethinking Social Inquiry: diverse tools, shared standards*, Lanham MD: Rowman and Littlefield.

Brooks, R. (2004) ' "My mum would be as pleased as punch if I actually went, but my dad seems a bit more particular about it": paternal involvement in young people's higher education choices', *British Educational Research Journal*, 30, 4, pp. 495–514.

Bryant, A. and Charmaz, K. (eds) (2007) *The Sage Handbook of Grounded Theory*, London: Sage.

Charmaz, K. (2000) 'Grounded theory: objectivist and constructivist methods', in Denzin, N. and Lincoln, Y. (eds) *Handbook of Qualitative Research*, Second edition, Thousand Oaks CA: Sage, pp. 509–35.

—Char (2006) *Constructing Grounded Theory*, London: Sage.

Cohen, A. K. (1955) *Delinquent Boys: the culture of the gang*, New York: Free Press.

Collier, D., Mahoney, J., Seawright, J. (2004) 'Claiming Too Much: warnings about selection bias'. In Brady and Collier (eds), pp. 85–102.

Covan, E. (2007) 'The discovery of grounded theory in practice: the legacy of multiple mentors', in Bryant and Charmaz (eds).

Denzin, N. and Lincoln, Y. (eds) (2005) *Handbook of Qualitative Research*, Third edition, Thousand Oaks CA: Sage.

Dey, I. (1999) *Grounding Grounded Theory*, San Diego CA: Academic Press.

— (2007) 'Grounding categories', in Bryant and Charmaz (eds)

George, A. and Bennett (2005) *Case Studies and Theory Development in the Social Sciences*, Cambridge MS: MIT Press.

Gewirtz, S., Ball, S. and Bowe, R. (1995) *Markets, Choice and Equity in Education*, Buckingham: Open University Press.

Glaser, B. (1964) *Organizational Scientists*, Indianapolis: Bobbs-Merrill.

— (1978) *Theoretical Sensitivity*, Mill Valley CA: Sociology Press.

— (1992) *Emergence v Forcing: basics of grounded theory analysis*, Mill Valley CA: Sociology Press.

Glaser, B. and Strauss, A. (1965) *Awareness of Dying*, Chicago: Aldine.

— (1967) *The Discovery of Grounded Theory*, Chicago: Aldine.

Goldthorpe, J. H. (1988) *Social Mobility and Class Structure in Modern Britain*, Second edition, Oxford: Oxford University Press.

Hammersley, M. (1989) *The Dilemma of Qualitative Method*, London: Routledge.

— (1992) *What's Wrong with Ethnography?*, London: Routledge.

— (2008a) 'Causality as conundrum: The case of qualitative inquiry', *Methodological Innovations Online*, 2, 3. Available at (accessed 7.12.10): <http://erdt.plymouth.ac.uk/mionline/public_html/viewarticle.php?id=63&layout=html>.

— (2008b) *Questioning Qualitative Inquiry*, London: Sage.

— (2010) 'A historical and comparative note on the relationship between analytic induction and grounded theorising', *Forum Qualitative Sozialforschung/Forum: Qualitative Social Research*, 11, 2, Art. 4. Available at (accessed 6.12.10): <http://nbn-resolving.de/urn:nbn:de:0114-fqs100243>.

Hammersley, M. and Gomm, R. (2008) 'Assessing the radical critique of interviews', in Hammersley 2008b (ed.).

Jackson, B. and Marsden, D. (1962) *Education and the Working Class*, London: Routledge.

Jansen, H. (2010) 'The logic of qualitative survey research and its position in the field of social research methods', *Forum Qualitative Sozialforschung/Forum: Qualitative Social Research*, 11, 2, Art. 11. Available at <http://nbn-resolving.de/urn:nbn:de:0114-fqs1002110>.

Jenkins, R. (1992) *Pierre Bourdieu*, London: Routledge.

Katz, J. (1984) *Poor People's Lawyers in Transition*, New Brunswick NJ: Rutgers University Press.

Lacey, C. (1970) *Hightown Grammar*, Manchester: Manchester University Press.

Lazarsfeld, P. and Rosenberg, M. (eds) (1955) *The Language of Social Research*, Glencoe ILL: Free Press.

Lindesmith, A. (1937) *The Nature of Opiate Addiction*, Chicago: University of Chicago Libraries.

— (1968) *Addiction and Opiates*, Chicago: Aldine.

Merton, R. (1957) *Social Theory and Social Structure*, Glencoe ILL: Free Press.

Misak, C. (1995) *Verificationism*, London: Routledge.

Power, S., Edwards, T., Whitty, G. and Wignall, V. (2003) *Education and the Middle Class*, Buckingham: Open University Press.

Rantala, K. and Hellström, E. (2001) 'Qualitative comparative analysis and a hermeneutic approach to interview data', *International Journal of Social Research Methodology*, 4, 2, pp. 87–100.

Reay, D., David, M. and Ball, S. (2001) 'Making a difference? Institutional habituses and higher education choice', *Sociological Research Online*, 5, 4. Available at (accessed 2.3.11): <http://www.socresonline.org.uk/5/4/reay.html>.

— (2005) *Degrees of Choice: social class, race and gender in higher education*, Stoke on Trent: Trentham Books.

Savage, M. (2000) *Class Analysis and Social Transformation*, Buckingham: Open University Press.

Savage, M., Barlow, J., Dickens, P. and Fielding, T. (1992) *Property, Bureaucracy and Culture: middle class formation in contemporary Britain,* London: Routledge.

Strauss, A. (1970) 'Discovering new theory from previous theory', in Shibutani, T. (ed.) *Human Nature and Collective Behavior*, Englewood Cliffs NJ: Prentice-Hall.

— (1987) *Qualitative Analysis for Social Scientists*, Cambridge: Cambridge University Press.

Strauss, A. and Corbin, J. (1990) *Basics of Qualitative Research*, Thousand Oaks CA: Sage.

Strauss, A., Schatzman, L., Bucher, R., Ehrlich, D. and Sabshin, M. (1965) *Psychiatric Ideologies and Institutions*, New York: Free Press.

Tooley, J. and Darby, D. (1998). *Educational research – a critique.* London: Office for Standards in Education.

Yin, R. K. (2009) *Case Study Research: design and methods*, Fourth edition, Thousand Oaks CA: Sage.

Znaniecki, F. (1934) *The Method of Sociology*, New York: Farrer and Rinehart.

4

Qualitative Causal Analysis and the Fallacies of Composition and Division: The Example of Ethnic Inequalities in Educational Achievement

Roger Gomm

Chapter Outline

This chapter is about what can be inferred with confidence about aggregates from their constituent cases, and what can be confidently inferred about cases from aggregates. Both kinds of inference are at risk of fallacious reasoning, if it is assumed that aggregates are composed of units which are very similar in ways relevant to the research and if it turns out that this is not so. And this is rarely so with social and cultural phenomena.

The *division fallacy* lies in inferring without sound evidence, that a component will show the same relationships between variables as have been found in some aggregate of which it is a part. In the social sciences it is best known in the form of the 'ecological fallacy'. For example, if in a neighbourhood there is both a high level of unemployment and a high level of property crime, it would be premature, without further investigation, to infer that unemployed people were the main perpetrators of the property crime (Robinson 1950; Freedman 1999).

The obverse of the division fallacy is the *fallacy of composition*.[1] This is committed when it is assumed without further evidence that an aggregate has the same relations between variables (causal or otherwise) as have been found in one (or a few) of the cases which comprise it. Drawing this sort of conclusion is particularly common in qualitative case-study research.

Both fallacies entail, first, an assumption of causal homogeneity: that there is only one kind of route to the outcome at aggregate level. Second, there is an assumption of social and cultural homogeneity: that what is true for some people at some times and in some place must be true for others, elsewhere at other times. Third, there is a failure to understand the relations between aggregates and the instances which compose them: particularly a failure to recognize that measures such as means or percentages are emergent properties arising from aggregation itself. A simple example to illustrate all this is that of electoral swings. A 'national swing' (say, from one of the losing parties to the victorious one) is often quoted. This is calculated by averaging the relevant differences between the current and some previous election, across all constituencies. Pundits then enthusiastically commit the fallacy of division by 'explaining' why there was a 'national swing' of some per cent, invoking causes alleged to influence all or most constituencies to a similar degree. But,

---

1 Also known as the 'fallacy of exception', the 'converse accident fallacy', 'over', or 'hasty generalization' '(the fallacy of) proof by example' and, if juxtaposed with the ecological fallacy, the 'individual fallacy'. It is also a variety of selection bias insofar as this means making generalizations to wider populations on the basis of unrepresentative samples. However, that term is sometimes restricted to bias arising from inferences based on samples which are unrepresentative specifically in having values more extreme than in the population from which the sample is drawn (Collier et al. 2004). This may in turn give rise to problems associated with regression to the mean or Kelly's paradox (Wainer and Brown 2004), as occurred with the well-publicized first Clackmannan experiment on the effectiveness of teaching reading via synthetic phonics (Johnston and Watson 2004) – see Torgerson et al. 2006: 20.

in reality, such 'national swings' are composed of constituencies 'swinging' in different directions to different degrees: for example, in 2005 the swing between Labour and Conservative in England varied between 17.3 per cent in favour of the Tories from Labour and 5.6 per cent against them towards Labour. This is to say nothing of the various movements involving other parties which are relevant when the results are expressed as percentages of the total vote, and different swings among different sections of the electorate differentially within different constituencies (House of Commons 2008). Similarly, it is not uncommon for radio or TV reportage to select a constituency which has shown locally something like the national swing and to interview voters there, allegedly to illuminate what has happened at national level; thereby committing the fallacy of composition. With this illustration in mind, we can say that drawing inferences from aggregates to cases, and from cases to aggregates is only likely to avoid error under the very special circumstances that the aggregate is composed of units very similar to each other (as relevant to the inference drawn), each of which makes a contribution of similar weight to the aggregate.[2] Whether the components of an aggregate – the cases – are very similar to each other and in what ways, is not something which can be established by case-study research.[3]

Ethnic gaps in educational performance

We shall illustrate this further from the field of ethnic 'gaps' in educational achievement, where both kinds of inference have been common.[4] Indeed they often appear together, researchers citing nationally aggregated

---

2 This is often created in the natural science experiments where similar, if not identical cases are created and subjected to different treatments. In social research, usually, the best that can be hoped for in experimental research or in analysing data from naturally occurring situations, is to create groups of cases with similar profiles, rather than groups of cases each similar to the others on a large number of criteria.

3 By case-study research here we mean the intensive study of one or a few cases. This is by contrast with 'case-focused' research, such as occurs with Qualitative Comparative Method or QCM (see Chapters 6 and 7) which typically involves the comparison of many cases on several dimensions.

4 The measurement of such gaps, and particularly of the way they change through time is controversial. See Gorard 1999, 2000; Hammersley 2001 and footnote 13.

figures on the relative educational performance of ethnic groups, with the assumption that these will be reproduced at local levels, thus risking the division fallacy and also treating case-study research as if it can immediately explain the nationally aggregated figures, thereby risking the composition fallacy (e.g. see; Commission for Racial Equality 1992; Eggleston et al. 1986; Gillborn 1990; Gillborn and Gipps 1996: 48–62; Troyna 1991, 1992; Troyna and Siraj-Blatchford 1993; Wright 1986, 1992; Gillborn and Youdell 2000; Rollock 2007). While these studies are in the tradition of qualitative research, what they set out to explain is the numerically expressed difference in educational achievement between ethnic groups. Thus numbers usually feature very strongly. However, these are rarely analysed further than eyeballing the data and computing means and percentages. The studies rarely feature measures of within-group dispersions, or correlations or statistical significance testing, and often include what Ian Schagan (2008) has called 'voodoo statistics': that is elementary flaws of numerical reasoning (see also Gomm 1993).

Most of the case studies of ethnic inequalities in educational achievement present themselves, and have usually been interpreted, as documenting processes going on in many schools, not just in the school or the small number of schools studied. More specifically, a common claim is that differential treatment by teachers of pupils from different ethnic groups has produced the differences in educational achievement among these groups as recorded at the national level (Foster et al. 1996). For instance, this idea underpinned Gillborn and Gipps' review of research in this field, where information is provided about national differences in performance among ethnic groups up to the mid-1990s, and links these data to qualitative studies that have claimed to document differential treatment of ethnic groups in particular schools (Gillborn and Gipps 1996: 48–62).

In effect, what is claimed in that review, and in many of the studies on which it draws, is that the alleged findings from case studies about causal processes can be generalized to the population of schools in England and Wales, thereby indicating widespread (witting or unwitting) unfair discrimination on the part of teachers; *and that* it is this discrimination which explains the lower performance *on average, nationally,* of some minority ethnic groups compared with the ethnic majority. We will note that describing pupils of different groups being treated differently, is not in itself a demonstration that such differential treatment is a cause of differences in achievement (Foster 1990, 1993; Foster et al. 1996, 2000: 107–38;

Gomm 2008: 333–5).[5] Moreover, the criticism made of educational practice is rarely simply that one group has been treated differently from another. Often the complaint is that where pupils should have been treated the same, they have been treated differently and, where they should have been treated differently, they have been treated the same. In these terms, the observation of treatment as inequitable is subject to a high degree of interpretation.[6] However, our exclusive concern here is with the problem of deriving causal explanations for aggregate phenomena from what is discovered in some cases. For the sake of argument we will assume that these studies have indeed accurately identified patterns of differential treatment within the schools studied.

Socio-economic status and ethnicity

In order to judge the confidence with which we should make generalizations from cases to aggregates we need to know how these studies relate to the relevant heterogeneity existing in the larger population of schools. One important dimension of variation is socio-economic differences among pupils, and

---

5 One or both of two mechanisms are suggested. One is essentially psychological, that low expectations by teachers are transmitted to pupils whose own expectations for themselves as learners are thereby lowered, and hence so is the level of their performance. Despite this being held as an item of faith by many researchers there is to date, little compelling empirical evidence that this psychological process is a major cause of differences in performance (Rogers 1982; Jussim and Harber 2005). The other mechanism, which we will exemplify later, is that prejudicial decisions by teachers limit the opportunities available to particular kinds of pupil: particularly decisions about allocation to teaching groups or entry to assessment. Again the evidence of the effects of setting and streaming on performance is unclear (Hallam and Toutounji 1996; Sukhnandan and Lee 1998; Ireson and Hallam 1999; Ireson et al. 2005). For both mechanisms direction of effect is problematic. Do teachers' attitudes/decisions create differences in educational achievement, or follow from those differences? Are they based on accurate predictions or are they self-fulfilling prophesies?

6 For example while some authors argue that the educational performance of African Caribbean boys is damaged by teachers' over-reaction to their torts (Wright 1986; Gillborn 1995; Tikly et al. 2006), others have argued that it is damaged by teachers' greater reluctance to control the misbehaviour of African Caribbean boys or to keep them 'on-task' compared with their responses to other kinds of pupil (Green 1983). Both, of course, are possible for different pupils of the same ethnicity and in different schools, or indeed different classrooms in the same school or different years for the same pupils.

it seems fairly clear from the literature that much of the difference in attainment between ethnic groups at the aggregate level disappears when social class and other measures of socio-economic difference are factored into the analysis. The scope for a simple mediation of this kind is mapped in Table 4.1, in terms of varying patterns of social class composition of the pupil body in schools, some of which schools might feature in case-study research.[7]

We might reasonably expect that social class would affect the treatment that pupils receive in school because of differential teacher expectations of pupils from different social classes, and or because factors beyond the schools such as family background, or material deprivation or poor health will affect the interaction of pupils and teachers, as well social class differences affecting levels of achievement independently of differences of treatment by teachers. To the extent that this is true, in order to check whether the differential treatment of pupils who belong to different ethnic groups within the case-study school is generalizable, we need studies that cover all or most of the cells in this diagram (Table 4.1). To generalize on the basis of one study, or of several studies all located in the same cell (or in one or two of the cells), risks error through conflation of the effects of social class and ethnicity.

Put another way, Table 4.1 stands as an example of one dimension of the kind of theoretical sampling framework which should be used in case-study research. While it is often practically impossible for the case-study researcher to select instances from each cell, the construction of such a frame at least allows for those cases actually studied, to be located in terms of theoretically interesting dimensions of diversity within the population constituted by all extant and theoretically possible cases (Glaser and Strauss 1967; Gomm et al. 2000). A similar approach is adopted in Charles Ragin's 'Qualitative Comparative Analysis (QCA)' (Ragin 1987; Ragin and Becker 1992; and see Chapters 6 and 7 in this book).[8]

---

7 For brevity we have used the term 'social class' or 'socio-economic status'. However some of the survey and census research in this area instead or in addition use measures of deprivation (or not): most often eligibility for free school meals, and nowadays for English pupils the locality deprivation indicator IDACI/CWI2009 http://www.communities.gov.uk/publications/communities/childwellbeing2009

8 Gender would be another important dimension of variation here, given that the sex-ratios of ethnic minority pupils vary from school to school more than those of 'white pupils' and that there are considerable gender differences in achievement within ethnic groups.

Table 4.1 Variation across multi-ethnic schools in proportions of middle-class pupils

		National ethnic majority group in case study school	
		Schools containing the same or a higher proportion middle class national ethnic majority pupils than the national average for the national ethnic majority group	Schools containing a lower proportion of the national middle class national ethnic majority pupils than the national average for the national ethnic majority group
A national minority ethnic group in the case study school	Schools containing the same or a higher proportion of middle class pupils of this national minority ethnic group than the national average for this national	Type 1.1	Type 1.2
	Schools containing a lower proportion of middle class pupils of this national minority ethnic group than the national average for this national minority ethnic group	Type 1.3	Type 1.4

Studies involving either logistic or linear regression and based on surveys such as the Youth Cohort Study (Drew and Gray 1991; Drew et al. 1992; Drew 1995; Rothan 2006; Connolly 2006), or the Longitudinal Study of Young People in England (LSYPE or 'Next Steps') (Strand 1999, 2007a,b, 2010, forthcoming a and b; Strand and Lindsay 2009) and studies using data from groups of schools (e.g. Smith and Tomlinson 1989) or from the school census data[9] (e.g. Wilson et al. 2006) show how closely associated is pupils' socio-economic status with their educational performance and hence how the distribution of socio-economic status through different ethnic groups relates to their different average or percentile achievement. While these studies do not entirely agree with each other, there is considerable consensus that Indian and Chinese pupils (as groups) achieve more at most stages of schooling than do white pupils of the same socio-economic

---

9 Successively, from the Pupil National Database (PND), the Pupil Level Annual School Census (PLASC) and the (Annual) School Census. http://www.dcsf.gov.uk/research/data/uploadfiles/DCSF-RR002.pdf

standing, and that Black Caribbean boys (and usually mixed heritage Black Caribbean/white boys) and travellers achieve less. All studies indicate that controlling for socio-economic status considerably reduces the gap between other ethnic/gender groups and white pupils, but there is less agreement on the extent to which this is so.[10] A problem with the sample survey studies is usually that the unit of sampling is the individual pupil so that we get no picture of how pupils of different kinds *in the same school* are treated compared with each other. If differential treatment of pupils by teachers is an important mechanism generating differences in educational perform-ance then this is something which is difficult, if not impossible, to observe in survey research where sampled pupils do not attend the same schools. To some extent this is overcome in the studies based on LSYPE *(op cit.,)* with an average of around 27 pupils from each of 629 schools. However, the samples are stratified for ethnicity at the level of the survey as a whole and not within schools, and 27 is a very small number when subdivided by ethnicity and gender, then by social class, prior achievement and a number of other factors. Ethnographic case studies could remedy this problem but only insofar as it is known how a particular school (or indeed a particular year group) fits within the overall picture. Knowing the socio-economic profile of different ethnic groups within a school, or year group, provides one co-ordinate for locating a case study within the overall picture. Other important co-ordinates are suggested below.

Levels of performance

Another dimension of variation relevant to the case-aggregate relationship is the relative level of performance of different ethnic groups within the schools studied, and how their performance relates to local or national averages. Table 4.2 outlines the variations that can occur in this respect.

Thus a school of type 2.1 would be one in which pupils from a particular minority ethnic group performed at a higher level than the national average for this ethnic group and at a higher level than the national ethnic majority in the school, who themselves scored at or above the national mean for this group. By contrast a school of type 2.8 would be one where members of a

---

10 At the time of writing the more up-to-date studies are Bradley and Taylor 2004; Connolly 2006; DfCSF 2005; Rothan 2006; Strand 2007 a and b, 2010, forthcoming a and b; Wilson et al. 2006.

Table 4.2 Variation across schools in terms of average levels of educational achievement

National minority ethnic group in the case-study school	National majority ethnic group in the case-study school	
	On average, members of the majority group achieve *at or above* the national mean (all pupils)	On average, members of the majority group achieve *below* the national mean (all pupils)
On average, this minority ethnic group achieves *at or above* the national average for this ethnic category		
On average, members achieve *at or above* the average performance of national majority group members in the school	Type 2. 1	Type 2.2
On average, members achieve *below* the average performance of national majority group members in the school	Type 2.3	Type 2. 4
On average, this minority ethnic group achieves *below* the national average for this ethnic category		
On average, members achieve *at or above* the average performance of national majority group members in the school	Type 2.5	Type 2.6
On average, members achieve *below* the average performance of national majority group members in the school	Type 2.7	Type 2.8

national minority ethnic group achieved less than the national average for that minority and less than their majority group peers in the same school, who themselves achieved below the national mean for the ethnic majority. What we are suggesting is that, without further evidence, it would be unsafe to assume that an association between school processes and different levels of academic achievement across ethnic groups in any one of these types of school could be generalized with confidence to the other types. We note that in their scrutiny of the applications for the Ethnic Minorities Achievement Grant, Gillborn and Mirza (2000: 7–11) found that all of the main minority ethnic groups came top of the league table for the GCSE (16+ examinations) in at least one Local Education Authority (LEA) and that the rank order of achievement by ethnic groups was by no means the same in each LEA. This, and other sources (e.g. Cline et al. 2002; Wilson et al. 2006), suggest that national averages obscure the diverse circumstances which give rise to them.

As an indication of this kind of diversity we note that Wilson et al. (2006: 54) found that in over 80 per cent of all schools in England, South Asian and Chinese pupils made more *progress* 11 to 16, than did white pupils in the same schools, some exceeding and some falling short of national norms of *achievement* for all pupils and/or for their group in particular. In between 50 per cent and 60 per cent of schools, 'black' pupils made more progress than their white school mates. For Black Caribbean pupils in particular, Strand (2010) found that this group made less progress than their white peers in the years 11 to 16. This is not necessarily inconsistent with the findings of Wilson et al. where the unit of reporting is the school not the individual.[11] But note also that the studies use different ethnic categories.

It might be true that, for particular minority groups, there are no empirical examples, or hardly any, of some of the types of school suggested in Table 4.2. This in itself would be an interesting finding. However, without some knowledge of the frequency distribution both of schools through these categories *and* of ethnic minorities across these kinds of school, any generalizations in this field based on a handful of case studies are of very uncertain validity. Yet much case-study work in this field has proceeded on the assumption that a study of students in a particular school can explain patterns of achievement at the national level without taking account of such variation.

Differential contributions to the aggregate

It might be argued that there are indeed some circumstances where this inference from case to aggregate would be sound. For example, if an ethnic minority group had a national mean well below that for the ethnic majority *and* we knew that the vast majority of this minority group of students went to schools of types 2.3, 2.4, 2.7 or 2.8 (in Table 4.2) then it might seem as if a study of school processes in a case-study school selected from one of those categories would illuminate the national pattern of achievement. However, this is still fallacious: what would be involved would be a comparison of the

---

11   See later remarks on Simpson's paradox.

Table 4.3 Variation in the performance of ethnic minority and ethnic majority pupils within a fictional local education authority: invented data

	School					
	1	**2**	**3**	**4**	**5**	**Total % ('No')**
Percentage of all majority ethnic students in each school	20%	20%	20%	20%	20%	100 (600)
Percentage of all minority ethnic students in each school	48%	31%	14%	6%	1%	100 (100)
Average GCSE score of ethnic majority students	20	23	29	41	65	**Mean score =35.6**
Average GCSE score of minority ethnic students	16	19	25	37	61	**Mean score =19.9**
Mean level of GCSE performance in each school	18.9	22.2	28.6	40.8	65.0	**Mean score all schools = 31**

achievements of *some* students concentrated in only *some types* of school with a national achievement level that is created by processes affecting all students and going on in *all types* of school. Table 4.3 provides a more detailed illustration of this point, using fictional data about an LEA made up of five schools.

These schools achieve very different mean scores at GCSE, ranging from 18.9 to 65.0.[12] Ethnic majority students are distributed evenly among the schools, but minority ethnic students are not. Forty-eight per cent of them are in the lowest achieving school. We have assumed, for the sake of argument, that in each school minority ethnic students score four points less than ethnic majority students, on average, in each school.

---

12 The scores express the combined results of all subjects taken in the year 16+ GCSE examinations, entered by most pupils in England and Wales. They are calculated by summing GCSE passes where each A* = 8 points, each A = 7 pts, B = 6 pts, and so on to G = 1 pt, with grades for vocational qualifications being scored as equivalents to GCSEs. This system of scoring was superseded in 2004. We have not used the new system because it weights lower grade passes disproportionately highly compared with higher grade passes, and exaggerates the difference between G grade and ungraded results and thus gives a very distorted picture. http://www.education.gov.uk/performancetables/schools_04/sec3b.shtml

Now, imagine that a case-study researcher in School 1 observes that minority group students are treated differently from majority group students, and concludes that this is to the disadvantage of the former. This might be thought to explain why it is that, at LEA level, minority ethnic students do less well than ethnic majority students. And, indeed, it may provide part of the explanation. But note that the difference in performance between the two groups in School 1 is four points, whereas at LEA level the difference is actually 15.7 points: this leaves another 12.7 points of difference to explain. And this would be true whichever of the schools was chosen as a case study, since the difference in performance between the two groups is four points in each of the schools. Thus, in this hypothetical LEA, only 25 per cent of the difference in performance at aggregate level could be accounted for by reference to any differential treatment of pupils of different ethnicity attending the same school. The remainder of the difference is explained by the uneven distribution of ethnic minority students between schools that have different overall performance levels for 'school effect' reasons, and/or because of differences between school-based cohorts of pupils with different levels of ability, motivation, material deprivation at home, and so on.[13]

Intuitively, it might seem that School 1 makes the greatest contribution to the gap between minority and majority group pupils at LEA level, because this is the school in which there are most minority ethnic pupils, and where such pupils have the lowest achievement level. But, on the contrary, the contribution this school makes to ethnic differences at LEA level is to *reduce* them marginally. If we deleted this school from the set, the ethnic gap at LEA level would increase from 15.7 points to 16 points. The reason for this is

---

13 To suggest that the situation shown in our invented data is not too wide of the mark, note that the Office for Standards in Education (OfStEd) investigation into the achievements of Black Caribbean pupils (2002) recorded 31.5 points for these pupils averaged across 47 schools where they made up more than 10 per cent of the roll, as against 36.2 points for pupils of all other ethnicities in the same schools. For that year (2001) the score of pupils of ethnicities other than Black Caribbean in England was 40.9. The Black Caribbean pupils in these 47 schools then were 9.4 points short of the national average for all pupils, but only half of that difference is available for attribution to differential treatment within the schools they attended (and that 'half' also has to accommodate any allowance for differences in prior achievement, deprivation, ill-health and other factors difficult for schools to ameliorate). The 47 schools would have contained around 16 per cent of all Black Caribbean pupils, but only a tiny percentage of pupils of all other ethnicities taken as one group.

that this school is pulling down the mean performance of the ethnic majority in this LEA.

The school that is contributing most to the gap is actually School 5. Even though it has only one minority ethnic pupil (albeit performing well above the LEA average for the majority studentship) this school is the one making the biggest contribution to the gap at LEA level. If we deleted it from the results, the ethnic gap would be almost halved to 8.8 points as against the previous 15.7. This is because this school raises the ethnic majority average at LEA level substantially while having little effect on the minority ethnic average. In real LEAs, no doubt, there are schools with no members of some particular ethnic minority group which, because of the performance of majority students therein, make an important contribution to increasing the LEA or national attainment gap between minorities and the majority. Given the highly asymmetrical distribution of minority ethnic pupils through schools in England and Wales and the very small numbers, or absence, of particular groups from some schools (Cline et al. 2002; Gillborn and Mirza 2000: 11), there is a strong probability that school processes most influential in creating ethnic achievement gaps are those going on in schools with few or no pupils from particular minority ethnic groups. For example, Cline et al. 2002 and Gillborn and Mirza 2000, found that where minority ethnic pupils made up a very small percentage of a school's roll – which was mainly in non-inner city areas – then both they and their white peers achieved more than pupils in the inner city schools where minority ethnic pupils tend to be concentrated, and these were schools in which a minority group was most likely to out-perform its white peers.

The contributions made by Schools 2 and 3 (Table 4.3) again are actually to reduce the gap at the level of our invented LEA, despite the fact that in both schools minority group pupils do worse than majority group pupils. So, a case study of how minority pupils were treated differently from majority pupils in Schools 2 and 3 could not possibly explain the gap at LEA level in any straightforward way, since the contribution of these schools is to make the gap smaller. Schools 1, 2 and 3 have the net effect of pulling down the majority group mean more than they pull down the minority group mean.[14] What

---

14 The presence of School 1 in the set reduces the majority mean for the LEA by 10 per cent compared with what it would be without School 1, but it reduces the minority mean by 15 per cent, while the presence of School 5 in the set enhances the minority mean by 2 per cent and the majority mean by 21 per cent. Such effects from particular schools will of course be smaller in real LEAs with much larger numbers of schools.

we are pointing out here is that, to a considerable extent, inequalities at LEA or national levels may be generated as much by differences between schools, including differences in the make-up of their pupil body, as by what goes on within any particular school or classroom.

To complete the picture it is important to note first, that the figures in Table 4.3 represent aggregations of aggregates and disguise much of the diversity there may be between ethnic groups within each school and between each school, *and* within ethnic groups within and between schools: for example both with regard to pupil characteristics such as gender ratios and socio-economic status and to different combinations of GCSE subjects taken and passed. Departments differ as much or more in effectiveness within and between schools than do the schools which contain them, so the distribution of ethnic groups through subjects may be an important matter. Second, the same considerations as apply with regard to the contributions schools make to LEA means apply to relations between LEA means and national means, such that an LEA where a minority ethnic group has a mean performance lower than that of the majority might be contributing either to the reduction or to the augmentation of an ethnic gap at national level, depending on the relationships between LEA means and national means. For example, had these fictional data been for 2003, then Schools 1, 2 and 3 had averages below the national average score for all pupils (which is very close to the average score for white pupils) and would have been dragging that national average down. And had the minority group been Black Caribbean boys then their averages in Schools 4 and 5 would have been pulling up the national average for this category of pupils.

What has been demonstrated above is an example of Simpson's paradox (a.k.a., the reversal paradox, amalgamation paradox, Lord's paradox, the suppression effect or the Yule-Simpson effect) where there are radically different, perhaps opposite, results derived from aggregate measures (such as percentages or means) compared with the several results from each of a number of sub-groups (Malinas and Bigelow 2009; Wainer and Brown 2004). The best-known example perhaps, is that of alleged sex discrimination at University of California at Berkeley where it was found to be concurrently true that a smaller percentage of women applicants were admitted to the university as a whole, and that in no faculty was there a bias against female candidates. Indeed four out of six admitted a higher percentage of female applicants, and in the remaining two the successful application rate for males was only slightly higher than for females (Bickel et al. 1975). By the same token it is possible that, as noted earlier, it is both true that in over 50 per cent of schools Black Caribbean pupils make more progress than their white peers, while overall Black Caribbean pupils make less progress. Simpson's paradox is not an uncommon phenomenon.

Small numbers and disproportional distributions

The small numbers of pupils of any particular ethnic minority background in a year group, and the even smaller numbers of each gender belonging to such minorities, bedevils research into differences in educational achievement. This problem is exaggerated by the way minority ethnic pupils are concentrated in particular schools and Local Education Authorities. For example, there are approximately 7,000 Black Caribbean pupils per year group in England, say 3,500 boys. Seventy-five per cent of these are to be found in only six per cent of schools – fewer than two-hundred schools at secondary level. That would be 13 per year per school, although, of course, some of these 200 schools have much larger numbers than others (see Table 4.4). Disproportionately distributed small numbers do constitute a problem for survey researchers, but this can be ameliorated by stratified random and booster samples.[15] Disproportionately distributed small numbers present even more difficulties for drawing inferences from case-study research as in the following example.

In their evaluation of the *Aiming High, African Caribbean Achievement Project*, Tikly et al. (2006) claim that Black Caribbean boys are disproportionately allocated to lower ability sets for maths and science, and disproportionately entered for only the lower tiers of GCSE[16] assessment. This they present as

---

15 For regression analyses, stratified random samples or booster samples are taken (e.g. Strand 2007 a and b, 2010, forthcoming a and b), or, in the case of the Youth Cohort studies, several sweeps (cohorts from different years) are combined (Connolly 2006; Rothan 2006). Without these strategies many categories would become too small for further analysis once already broken down by ethnic group and gender.

16 For Maths and Science in the 16 plus GCSE examinations taken by most pupils in England and Wales there are tiers of entry. Candidates entered for the lowest tiers are unable to attempt the more difficult questions, and hence unable to achieve the highest grades of pass.

Table 4.4 Two possible distributions of Black Caribbean boys' non-entries plus entries to lowest tier of maths assessment for KS3, (at 41.7% overall): school by school, bench-marked against all-school percentage for Pakistani boys (at 32.7%). Numbers in year group and percentages from Tikly et al. 2006: Table 6 for 2005 assessment. Other figures invented.

(a) School Number	(b) Number of Black Caribbean boys in year group (actual)	Distributed proportionate to school cohort size		Distributed more evenly	
		(c) Same % as Pakistani boys in numbers of pupils	(d) In excess of % for Pakistani boys in numbers of pupils	(e) Same % as Pakistani boys in numbers of pupils	(f) In excess of % for Pakistani boys in numbers of pupils
1	55	18	5	5	2
2	31	10	3	4	1
3	29	9	3	5	1
4	26	8	2	4	1
5	24	8	2	5	2
6	23	7	2	5	1
7	22	7	2	4	2
8	15	5	1	5	1
9	15	5	1	4	2
10	14	5	1	5	1
11	14	5	1	4	2
12	11	4	1	5	1
13 to 31*	141[1]	46[2]	13[3]	82[4]	21[5]
Totals	420	137	38	137	38
		(=32.7%)	(=9.0%)	(=32.7%)	(=9.0%)
	100%		=41.7%		=41.7%

Number of lowest-tier entries and non-entries for Black Caribbean boys, bench-marked against Pakistani boys (invented distributions)

*19 schools

[1] under 10 pupils in each of 19 schools

[2] Average 2 in each of 19 schools

[3] Average less than 1 in each of 19 schools

[4] Average 4–5 in each of 19 schools

[5] Average about 1 in each of 19 schools

a major explanation for the gap at Key stage 4 (KS4)[17] between Black Caribbean boys and most other pupil groups shown at national level. The claim is actually quite plausible, but the way it is made, seems to entail the division fallacy

---

17 In England results for the 16+ GCSE examination form 'Key Stage 4' of the scheme for the national monitoring of the educational achievement of individuals, schools, LEAs and England as a whole.

in so far as it requires the pattern shown when data are aggregated from the 31 schools of the study to be true for at least a substantial majority of them. If this is not so then, as we will demonstrate, it is unlikely that schools would be able to follow the evaluators' advice to implement fairer systems of allocating pupils to sets (tracks) or to adopt fairer procedures for deciding on entry levels at GCSE.

The *Aiming High Project* involved 31 schools chosen because 10 per cent or more of their year groups comprised African Caribbean pupils, and because these pupils were achieving less at KS4 than their peers nationally. We cannot examine the claims made by the evaluators with regard to allocation between ability sets (tracks), or entry to GCSE tiers since, for both, 50 per cent of the relevant data are missing. However, more or less complete data are available for tiered entry to KS3 assessment for maths and science. We shall focus on tiered entry for KS3 assessment for maths, though our remarks would apply to science assessment as well. Allocation to a lower tier of assessment at KS3 (age 14) limits the possibilities for higher scores. This is important for a pupil's KS4/GCSE (age 16) achievement in so far as the results influence the allocation of pupils to ability sets, and set membership influences entry level at GCSE and GCSE entry level influences GCSE results: though the authors do not actually demonstrate this causal chain.

The data for 2005 for all 31 schools show that whereas 41.5 per cent of Black Caribbean boys were either not entered or were entered at the lowest level, the corresponding figure for boys of all other ethnic groups was 30.5 per cent (Tikly et al. 2006: Table 6). As the evaluators say, it is to be expected that the percentage for Black Caribbean boys here should exceed that of most other boys because, they, together with Pakistani boys, had the lowest scores at KS2. However, they say:

> Black Caribbean boys and Pakistani boys had the same Key Stage 2 average point scores (24.6) but between 2003–2005 Black Caribbean boys were more likely than Pakistani boys to be entered for the lower tier Key Stage 3 papers (on average 42.5% of Black Caribbean boys were entered for the lower tier paper in mathematics compared to 35% of Pakistani boys). (Tikly et al. 2006: 23)

Earlier key stages are; KS1 age 7, KS2 age 11 and KS3 age 14, each marked by national assessments taken by almost all pupils and usually called 'SATs', but properly 'National Curriculum Tests'. As for KS4/GCSE, assessment for maths and science at KS3 was tiered (see FN16) until 2009 when KS3 tests were abolished.

Tikly et al. do not give us any indication of dispersion around the means for the two groups and, without this, their conclusion that the Black Caribbean/ Pakistani difference is unfair is not a convincing one, since it is quite possible, indeed usual, for two groups with the same mean to have different proportions above and below some threshold score. However, we will proceed as if this were no problem and concentrate instead on the relationship between what is shown in aggregate and what might be the situation school by school.

In the 31 schools there are 420 Black Caribbean boys in the year group, which would be 13 or 14 per school if they were evenly distributed. But this is not so. As Table 4.4 shows (column b), three of the schools contain nearly 30 per cent of the cohort and 60 per cent of schools have fewer than 10 each. Four hundred and twenty pupils is a substantial percentage of the national population in the year group: between 12 and 13 per cent: so this group is contributing substantially to the ethnically specific national aggregated figure compared, say, to white pupils, or indeed Pakistani pupils in the same schools.

If we took the percentage of Pakistani boys not entered or entered at the lower level as the benchmark of equitable treatment (32 or 33%), then 137 Black Caribbean boys were 'fairly' entered at the lower level (32.7%), and 38 (9%) were not entered when they should have been or were entered lower than they should have been: a 9 per cent disparity. If the comparison were with boys of all other ethnicities, then there were 47 extra Black Caribbean boys not entered or entered at the lowest level. However, because Black Caribbean boys (together with Pakistani boys) scored less than other groups of boys at KS2, not much of the excess of 47 over 38 is likely to be at variance with entry according to ability measured at KS2. However it is measured, this still leaves a question of how the 'excess' non-entry and lower-tier entries are distributed between schools. We are not told this. Table 4.4 gives just two of many possibilities. The first possibility (columns c and d) is where we have distributed the excess in proportion to the numbers in the cohort in each school, which is the same as each school having the same *percentage* excess. Think of this now from the viewpoint of case-study researchers. In none of the schools does the discrepancy between 'fair' and 'unfair' discrimination reach a statistically significant level, and in only one school should an observer have any confidence that the difference was not just due to chance, if he or she only had information for this school, this year. This is particularly so given the rather poor degree of year on year predictability of achievement data after controlling for ability (Gray et al. 2001, 2003; Pugh and Mangan 2003). However, beyond this, confidence in this being an *inequitable* difference would depend on (among other things) whether decisions depended stringently on some ability score, or whether they allowed for (say) progress since last assessment, responsiveness to parental undertakings to supervise home work, course work achievement in addition to a test, circumstances mitigating poor course work or mitigating a bad test result, suspicions of plagiarism or of parental assistance, and so on. The more factors taken into consideration the less confident we could be about the extent of the excess as evidence of unfair discrimination in any one school and about location of inequity among the 31 schools.

Discrimination could be more visible if it were more disproportionate. In Table 4.4 the three largest schools already account for a quarter of the excess in the hypothetical 'proportionate' distribution of unfairness. However, suppose they accounted for a half. Then, of course, some other schools would host no discrimination at all. The more visible the discrimination at school level, the less widespread it must be, and the more widespread it is, the less visible it will be at school level. If spread evenly (at one or two instances per school, say) it would be completely invisible to the ethnographic observer restricted to observation in one or a few schools. This is illustrated in the second distribution in Table 4.4 (columns e and f).

Attention must be drawn, however, to some simplifying assumptions made above. The first is that Black Caribbean pupils are only excessively entered at the lower level of assessment. But it is quite possible that some who might otherwise have been entered at the lowest level because of their low prior achievement will actually have been entered at a higher level. As calculated in Table 4.4 the aggregated figures will show the net figure for under and over entries. But note that this means counting as advantageous entry at a level higher than a measure of prior achievement suggests, whereas there must be pupils who would be disadvantaged by trying to work 'above their level'. Alternatively then, inequity might be calculated as under-entries *plus* (rather than minus) over-entries. Of course, if some pupils are advantaged and some disadvantaged by being entered at a higher level than would be indicated by a strict criterion, *and* some pupils are advantaged and some disadvantaged by being entered at a lower level, we would have to give up hope of measuring inequity unless we had some means of distinguishing between these types of pupil. And this seems impossible since it would involve ungrounded counterfactual reasoning to decide what would have happened to each pupil had they been entered differently.

Deciding what is equitable will be even more difficult with regard to actual pupils in actual schools, for a number of reasons. First, some schools may 'over-enter' Black Caribbean boys at higher levels, and some *different* schools may 'under-enter' them, as well as over- and under-entries occurring in the same school. Second, the same may be true also of other pupils whose entry patterns might contribute to the benchmark for judging equity. Third, the benchmark for equity is derived from an aggregate measure, but pupils of different ethnicities are combined in different proportions in different schools: each no doubt with different ability profiles. Comparing the proportions of Black Caribbean boys entered at the lowest level in a particular school with the proportions of (say) Pakistani boys entered at the same level in the same school, is not the same as the comparison with the average for all Pakistani pupils in all 31 schools. Given that there were only 120 Pakistani boys altogether, some schools with Black Caribbean pupils will have very few, or no, Pakistani boys to compare entry patterns with anyway. Fourth, the criteria for entry to particular levels may differ from school to school. There is no centrally set score of prior achievement to constitute eligibility for entry to levels of KS3 assessment (nor for GCSE tier level), nor rigid rules about how stringently any such scores should be utilized in such decision making. Some schools may be lenient, and some more stringent in their requirements. Even if stringency and leniency are exercised in each school in ways that do not disadvantage particular ethnic groups, members of different ethnic groups are distributed through schools disproportionately, and those disproportionately present in stringent schools may, in aggregate terms, be more confined to the lower level entry. In this eventuality it would be perfectly possible for a group showing what could be alleged to be an inequitable entry pattern according to criteria derived from the aggregate, nonetheless to be allocated to assessment levels allegedly equitably in each, or most schools, if judged on the basis of school-specific norms: another possible example of Simpson's paradox (*vide supra*).

In summary, then, the inference being drawn from an aggregate measure by Tikly et al. may well suffer from the fallacy of division in so far as it assumes that each case (each school) is a microcosm of the aggregate. Their recommendation for remediation is for schools – all of them in the group apparently, to devise fairer methods of entering pupils for tiered assessments.[18] But we have shown (for the set of 31 schools) that if inequity were visible it must logically occur only in a few schools; and correspondingly if it is widespread it will not often be visible, or indeed extant, at school level. Given that these 31 schools have bigger cohorts of Black Caribbean pupils than most others nationally, invisibility (or absence) at case level is the more likely on a national scale.[19]

Since the *Aiming High* evaluation study was published, Strand (forthcoming a and b) conducted a large-scale study of ethnicity and tiered assessment using data from the Longitudinal Study of Young People in England. He found that there was indeed widespread over-representation of Black Caribbean pupils (both genders) at the lower tiers of assessment at both KS3 and 4. And he found further that this was to a greater extent than could be predicted by measures of their prior achievement, and by measures of their socio-economic status, alone or finessed by a great many other measures as well.[20] Strand finds that the entry-tier patterns for ethnic/gender groups,

---

18 Tickly et al. are somewhat evasive about the measures which should be taken to implement a fairer system of allocation to teaching groups and to entry levels for assessment. Their complaint is that such allocations do not accurately reflect current or prior achievement, but they are evidently not recommending a strict use of such measures as placement criteria, since they see them as largely reflecting past discrimination. Their main recommendation seems to be that 'behaviour' should not influence placement. No guidance is offered on how teachers might solve the perpetual pedagogic dilemma of deciding how much past and future performance depends on 'ability' and how much on behaviour. Nor is it entirely clear why predictions of future behaviour should not influence such decisions. It is interesting for example, that the education systems of Japan, Taiwan and Singapore, which seem to produce high levels of achievement, group pupils explicitly by effort and motivation as much as by ability (Ireson and Hallam 1999: 353).

19 Two of the ethnographic case studies of ethnicity and differential treatment in secondary education allow for the estimation of the extent of inequitable allocation of ethnic groups to sets, streams or assessment tiers. That by Gillborn and Youdell (2000) suggests between three and five pupils misallocated in each of two schools, but no allowance is made for differences between groups in prior achievement. The Commission for Racial Equality study (1992, and see Troyna 1991, 1992; Toyna and Siraj-Blatchford 1993) does make some attempt at controlling for prior achievement and suggests three pupils misallocated to ability sets per year group (Gomm 1993, 1995 and see Troyna 1993). However, missing data and other matters make this estimate problematic, and here it is the South Asian pupils who as a group perform best at GCSE, although it is members of this ethnic group who are allegedly inequitably treated.

20 These included measures of home circumstances and pupil and parent attitudes and aspirations. But since differences here are strongly correlated with pupil gender and socio-economic status,

other than Black Caribbeans, are more or less the same for all pupils with the same prior ability and socio-economic status and other similarities. For Black Caribbean pupils the socio-economic dimension reduces, but does not eliminate what could be counted as 'racial' discrimination. Roughly speaking, white pupils were more likely to feature in the higher tiers of maths and science assessment than Black Caribbean pupils of *the same prior ability, similar socio-economic status and other similarities* by a ratio of 3 to 2. A ratio of 3 to 2 is a large ratio but it would not be distinguishable from random flutter in the vast majority of secondary schools with fewer than 10 Black Caribbean pupils in the year group. The aggregate might well include some schools with the reverse ratio, and will certainly include some schools where there are no Black Caribbean pupils, but which nonetheless contribute to the white benchmark against which Black Caribbean entry levels are being compared.

Mediated comparisons

Educational achievement might be criterion-referenced in terms of passes and grades, but the measures gain much of both their political importance (Hammersley 2006) and their academic interest from norm-referencing: from comparing the achievements of different groups, rather as if they were competing teams. The discussion so far has assumed norm-referencing, but here we want to consider it further.

In multi-level regression analyses such as Strand's, mentioned above, measures of educational achievement are made after adjusting for pupil-level differences in prior achievement, socio-economic status or the behavioural and attitudinal characteristics of both pupils and their parents and other pupil and contextual factors. Something like this is now a central part of the performance management of schools and LEAs in England. The calculation of both value added (VA) and contextual value added (CVA) scores adjust raw scores on the assumption that pupils vary in their capacity to benefit from education, and hence that only some of the differences in educational achievement can be attributed to the treatment they receive in schools. Value added

---

they do not effect much further differentiation between ethnic/gender groups. Although these characteristics appear to be more important in the study by Wilson et al. (2006) much depends on the sequence in which variables are entered into the analysis.

scores compute each pupil's prior achievements, via National Curriculum (or SATs) assessments, and re-express them as a metric comparing his or her score with that achieved by the average pupil nationally with the same level of prior achievement.

CVA scores adjust these VA scores to take account of gender, ethnicity, a number of socio-economic and other indicators both at the pupil and the neighbourhood level and the school's overall profile of achievement. The result provides a comparison between what has been achieved by the particular pupil and the average performance for pupils nationally with similar characteristics: for example, the expected average GCSE score for white male pupils, receiving free school meals, not in care, with prior achievements at KS2 and or KS3 at a particular level, living in a neighbourhood with a particular deprivation score (and other characteristics). The result is a set of benchmarks, based on the actual achievement of such sub-groups, against which the quality of education provided by a particular school is judged.[21] As a strategy for the official monitoring of school performance it remains controversial as to the extent to which pupil performance, measured via the comparisons can be attributed to the treatment received by pupils in their schools: in other words to 'the school effect'.

Here we do not wish to engage in a discussion of the strengths and weaknesses of multi-level modelling used in performance management or in explanatory research (Goldstein and Spiegelhalter 1996; Yang et al. 1999; Leckie and Goldstein 2009; Goldstein and Leckie 2008; Gorard 2005, 2006). Rather our immediate interest is in how measures of this kind relate to case-study research, and the relationship between what can be observed in the field and what is shown in aggregate measures. The important point here is that the use of VA and CVA measures involve what might be called 'mediated comparison', in the sense that the comparison of the performance of any two groups within a school, or between schools is made via comparing their performance, severally, with their peers nationally. Such measures do not facilitate a comparison between one local group of pupils and another local group in any straightforward way. Rather, saying that group A in a particular school has a mean CVA score above *its* national benchmark, while group B in the same school has a score below *its* national benchmark, is akin to pointing out that the girls' net ball team came top of their league, while the boys' soccer

---

21 For an explanation of how VA and CVA scores are calculated see www.education.gov.uk/performancetables/pilotks4_05/annex or http://nationalstrategies.standards.dcsf.gov.uk/node/170105

team came nearly bottom of theirs. It may be that this situation arose because of differential investment or more competent coaching in girls' as opposed to boys' sports in that school, but it is even more likely that it arose because of the composition, coaching, commitment, and so on of all other net ball teams in their league on the one hand, and all other soccer teams in their league on the other. In this sense the causes of ethnic differences in VA or CVA performance, as recorded in aggregate terms, cannot be 'seen' in local case studies. Putting this another way, and more generally, case-study researchers must be very careful in relating the activities which they can observe which might lead to local outcomes, to the activities they cannot observe which set the norms against which local outcomes are compared.

Putting case studies in context

Many of the case studies which have been cited as evidence of racially dis-criminatory behaviour by teachers were conducted at a time when it was difficult for researchers to obtain comprehensive pupil-level data on back-ground and performance for the school being studied, or data about the school itself which would enable it to be compared with other schools. So it is not surprising that case studies such as those cited by Gillborn and Gipps (1996: 48–62) provide scant information of the kinds which would enable them to be located in the context of the aggregated picture. However, it does seem that most of the studies are concentrated in schools with a substantial proportion of working-class pupils performing well below the national aver-age for pupils of all ethnicities at the time (type 1:4 in Table 4.1, type 2.8 in Table 4.2)[22] and or schools contributing much more to minority ethnic results nationally than to the national results of the ethnic majority. If this is so, then such case studies may not provide a good basis for generalization to all schools. Indeed, if the issue is one of differences in outcomes for different ethnic groups *compared with the national average for all pupils,* then, as we have seen, what goes on in schools with no members of a particular minority

---

22 Generalizations inferred from studies of cases with extreme values can be particularly misleading with regard to causal processes, as is demonstrated by Collier et al. 2004. This includes the risk of mistaking the statistical artefact of regression to the mean for change caused by some hypothesized substantive cause (Wainer and Brown 2004; Schagan 2008).

group will also be implicated among the causes of the *relative* performance of that group.

Similarly, the amount of information available at aggregate level, relevant to this topic has been limited until relatively recently. This has now changed with National Curriculum (or 'SATs') assessment[23] and with successively, the PND/PLASC/ School Census, providing a data base on the demographics and achievements of all pupils in all schools in England, together with the requirement for schools to make themselves publicly accountable via numerical data, as well as the advent of large-scale longitudinal studies such as LSYPE (ESDS 2011). In the past there has been an unfortunately antagonistic relationship between ethnographic researchers who have tended to claim that they are able to see school processes as they 'really' happen (Glaser and Strauss 1967: 40), and survey researchers who may claim that case-study researchers can't see the wood for the trees. But both approaches are needed. Census and survey work provides us with a matrix of associations between one thing and another which identifies patterns and tendencies which may best be investigated further through case-study research. The fallacy of division is a major risk with regard to the macro-sociological approach, especially if groups are thought of only in terms of group means and if within-group diversity and diversity among schools are ignored. Sample survey, or (better) census-based studies which enable comparisons of different kinds of pupil in the same schools are among the antidotes. Another is to model the different ways in which the same outcomes in aggregate might be produced by different constellations of factors at local level – rather as begun in Table 4.4. In other chapters of this book we canvas the merits of case-focused configurational analysis, as against, or in addition to, regression analyses.

Case-study research of the ethnographic kind may sometimes be capable of identifying the processes that result in measures which are accumulated to create the associations comprising the aggregate picture. But it may well happen that what are significant tendencies at the aggregate level are not clearly visible locally. This may be so with regard to our example of allegedly inequitable ethnic differences in set placement ('tracking') or tier of assessment. It is possible that such inequity as occurs is smeared thinly across a large number of schools such that it cannot be observed with much confidence in local

---

23 Although note the abandonment of national testing in England at KS3 in 2009, which may be an indicator of things to come and that national testing (apart from 16+ and 18+ examinations) is not practised in schools in Wales, Scotland or Northern Ireland.

cases, but is nonetheless significant in the aggregate. Further research will be needed to establish if this is so: research which at one and the same time enables the comparison of the treatment and achievement of pupils of known prior achievement in the same schools, and where such pupils constitute a representative sample of schools and pupils nationally.

For case-study research the fallacy of composition is a danger. That is the unwarranted assumption by case-study researchers that the case(s) they have studied are typical of all cases, or of a major sub-division of them when this is not actually so. What may appear very important in a local case, may not be so in other cases, or may only be important in a sub-group of cases. As we have seen, this is a dangerous neglect of diversity within aggregates. Stereotyping is a qualitative version of the fallacy of composition. Case studies of the ethnographic kind often present readers with memorable pen portraits of individuals and or classroom episodes which may form or reinforce stereotypes of particular kinds of school, pupil or teacher. Mirza (1992, 1997) for example, suggests that the depiction of 'rebellious' Black boys in anti-racist ethnographies, may have had this effect (see also Gomm 2001). So it is important that such researchers exercise more caution in the claims they make about the generalizability of their findings and that they find and report the kinds of information which would enable each case to be located in the aggregate concerned, in terms of the dimensions identified as important by larger-scale research.

References

Bickel, P., Hammel, E. and O'Connell, J. (1975) 'Sex bias in graduate admissions: data from Berkeley', *Science*, 187, 4175, pp. 398–404. doi:10.1126/science.187.4175.398. PMID 17835295.

Bradley, S. and Taylor, J. (2004) 'Ethnicity, educational attainment and the transition from school', *Manchester School*, 72, 3, pp. 317–46.

Burgess, S. and Wilson, D. (2003) 'Ethnic segregation in English Schools', CMPO Working Paper Series 03/086, Bristol: University of Bristol. Available at: <http://www.bristol.ac.uk/cmpo/publications/papers/2003/wp86.pdf>.

Cline, T., de Abreu, G., Fibosy, C., Gray, H., Lambert, H. and Neale, J. (2002) *Minority Ethnic Pupils in Mainly White Schools*, London: Department for Education and Skills.

Collier, D., Mahoney, J. and Seawright, J. (2000) 'Claiming too much: warnings about selection bias', in Bradey, H. and Collier, D. (eds) *Rethinking Social Inquiry: diverse tools, shared standards*, Latham MD: Rowman & Littlefield Publishers, Inc, pp. 85–102.

Commission for Racial Equality (1992) *Set to Fail? Setting and banding in secondary schools*, London: Commission for Racial Equality.

Connolly, P. (2006a) 'Summary statistics, educational achievement gaps and the ecological fallacy', *Oxford Review of Education*, 32, 2, pp. 235–52.

— (2006b) 'The effects of social class and ethnicity on gender differences in GCSE attainment: a secondary analysis of the Youth Cohort Study of England and Wales 1997–2001', *British Educational Research Journal*, 321, pp. 3–21.

DfCSF (2005) 'Ethnicity and education: the evidence on minority ethnic pupils', Research Topic Paper RTPO1-05. London: Department for Children Schools and Families. Available at: <http://www.dcsf.gov.uk/research/data/uploadfiles/RTP01-05.pdf>.

Drew, D. (1995) *'Race', Education and Work: the statistics of inequality*. Aldershot: Avebury.

Drew, D. and Gray, J. (1991) 'The black-white gap in examination results: a statistical critique of a decade's research', *New Community*, 17, 2, pp. 159–72.

Drew, D., Gray, J. and Sime, N. (1992) 'Against the odds: the education and labour market experiences of young black people', England and Wales Youth Cohort Study Report No 68, Sheffield: Department of Employment.

Eggleston, J., Dunn, D. and Anjall, M. (1986) *Education for Some: the educational and vocational experiences of 15–18 year old members of minority ethnic groups*. Stoke on Trent: Trentham Books.

ESDS (2011) 'A guide to the longitudinal study of young people in England', Economic and Social Data Service. Available at: <http://www.esds.ac.uk/longitudinal/access/lsype/l5545.asp>.

Foster, P. (1990) 'Cases not proven: an evaluation of two studies of teacher racism', *British Educational Research Journal*, 16, 4, pp. 335–48.

— (1993) 'Some problems in identifying racial/ethnic equality or inequality in schools', *British Journal of Sociology*, 44, 3, pp. 519–35.

Foster, P., Gomm, R. and Hammersley, M. (1996) *Constructing Educational Inequality*, London: Falmer.

— (2000) 'Case studies as spurious evaluations', *British Journal of Educational Studies*, 48, 3, pp. 215–30.

Freedman, D. A. (1999) Ecological inference and the ecological fallacy. Available at: <http://www.stanford.edu/class/ed260/freedman549.pdf>.

Gillborn, D. and Gipps, C. (1996) *Recent Research on the Achievements of Ethnic Minority Pupils*. London: Office for Standards in Education, HMSO.

Gillborn, D. and Mirza, H. (2000) *Educational Inequality: mapping race, class and gender*. London: Office for Standards in Education, HMSO. Available at: <http://www.ofsted.gov.uk/publications/docs/447.pdf>.

Gillborn, D. and Youdell, D. (2000) *Rationing Education: policy, practice, reform and equity*. Buckingham: Open University Press.

Glaser, B. and Strauss, A. (1967) *The Discovery of Grounded Theory*. Chicago: Aldine.

Goldstein, H. and Leckie, G. (2008) 'School league tables: what can they really tell us?', *Significance*, 5, 2, pp. 67–9.

Goldstein, H. and Spiegelhalter, D. (1996) 'League tables and their limitations: statistical issues in comparisons of institutional performance', *Journal of the Royal Statistical Society*, Series A, 159, pp. 385–443.

Gomm, R. (1993) 'Figuring out ethnic equity', *British Educational Research Journal*, 19, 2, pp. 149–65.

— (1995) 'Strong claims, weak evidence: a response to Troyna's, "Ethnicity and the organisation of learning groups" (Educational Research, 34, 1')', *Educational Research*, 37, 1, pp. 79–86.

— (2001) 'Unblaming victims and creating heroes: reputational management in sociological writing', *Discourse: studies in the cultural politics of education*, 22, 2, pp. 227–47.

— (2008) *Social Research Methodology: a critical introduction*, Second edition, Basingstoke: Palgrave.

Gomm, R., Hammersley, M. and Foster, P. (2000) *Case Study Method: key issues, key texts*. London: Sage.

Gorard, S. (1999) 'Keeping a sense of proportion: the "politician's error" in analysing school outcomes', *British Journal of Educational Studies*, 47, 3, pp. 235–46.

— (2000) 'One of us cannot be wrong: the paradox of achievement gaps', *British Journal of Sociology of Education*, 21, 3, pp. 391–400.

— (2006) 'Value-added is of little value', *Journal of Educational Policy*, 21, 2, pp. 235–43. [Education-*line* version (2005) http://www.leeds.ac.uk/educol/documents/143649.htm]

Gray, J., Goldstein, H. and Thomas, S. (2001) 'Predicting the future: the role of past performance in determining trends in institutional effectiveness at A level', *British Educational Research Journal*, 27, 4, pp. 391–405.

— (2003) 'Of trends and trajectories: searching for patterns in school improvement', *British Education Research Journal*, 29, 1, pp. 83–8.

Green, P. (1983) 'Teachers' influence on the self-concept of pupils of different ethnic origins', PhD thesis, University of Durham.

Hallam, S. and Toutounji, I. (1996) *What Do We Know About the Grouping of Pupils by Ability? A research review*, London: Institute of Education.

Hammersley, M. (2001) 'Interpreting achievement gaps: some comments on a dispute', *British Journal of Educational Studies*, 49.3, pp. 285–98.

— (2006) *Media Bias in Reporting Social Research? The case of reviewing ethnic inequalities in education*, London: Routledge.

House of Commons (2008) *Election Statistics: UK 1918–2007*, Research Paper 08/12, London: House of Commons. Available at: <http://www.parliament.uk/documents/commons/lib/research/rp2008/rp08-012.pdf>.

Ireson, J. and Hallam, S. (1999) 'Raising standards: is ability grouping the answer?', *Oxford Review of Education*, 25, 3, pp. 343–58.

Ireson, J., Hallam, S. and Hurley, C. (2005) 'What are the effects of ability grouping on GCSE attainment?', *British Educational Research Journal*, 31, 4, pp. 443–58.

Johnston, R. and Watson, J. (2004) 'Accelerating the development of reading, spelling and phonemic awareness skills in initial readers', *Reading and Writing: an interdisciplinary journal*, 17, 4, pp. 327–57.

Jussim, L. and Harber, K. (2005) 'Teacher expectations and self-fulfilling prophecies: knowns and unknowns, resolved and unresolved controversies', *Personality and Social Psychology Review*, 9, 2, pp. 131–55.

Leckie, G. and Goldstein, H. (2009) 'The limitations of using school league tables to inform school choice', *Journal of the Royal Statistical Society*, A 172, pp. 835–51.

Malinas, G. and Bigelow, J. (2009) Simpson's paradox, *Standford Encyclopedia of Philosophy*. Available at: <http://plato.stanford.edu/entries/paradox-simpson/>.

Mirza, H. (1992) *Young, Female and Black*. London: Routledge.

— (1997) 'Black female success: a new social movement', *Social Science Teacher*, 26, 3, pp. 2–5.

OfStEd. (2002) *Achievement of Black Caribbean Pupils: good practice in secondary schools*. London: Office for Standards in Education. Available at: <http://www.ofsted.gov.uk/Ofsted-home/Publications-and-research/Browse-all-by/Education/Inclusion/Minority-ethnic-children/Achievement-of-Black-Caribbean-pupils/(language)/eng-GB>.

Pugh, G. and Mangan, J. (2003) 'What's in a trend? A comment on Gray, Goldstein and Thomas (2001)', *British Educational Research Journal*, 29, 1, pp. 77–82.

Ragin, C. (1987) *The Comparative Method*, Berkeley: University of California Press.

Ragin, C. and Becker, H. (1992) *What is a case? Exploring the foundations of social inquiry*. Cambridge: Cambridge University Press.

Robinson, W. (1950) 'Ecological correlation and the behaviour of individuals', *Annual Review of Sociology*, 15, pp. 351–7.

Rogers, C. (1982) *The Social Psychology of Schooling*. London: Routledge and Kegan Paul.

Rollock, N. (2007) 'Legitimising black academic failure: deconstructing staff discourses of academic success, appearance and behaviour', *International Studies in Sociology of Education,* 17, 3, pp. 275–87.

Rothan, C. (2006) 'The importance of social class in explaining the educational achievements of minority ethnic pupils in Britain: evidence from the Youth Cohort Study', University of Oxford Sociology Working Papers No 2006-02. Oxford: University of Oxford. Available at: <http://www.sociology.ox.ac.uk/research/workingpapers/2006-02.pdf>.

Schagan, I. (2008) 'A simple guide to voodoo statistics', *Education Journal*, 112, pp. 33–6. Available at: <http://www.nfer.ac.uk/publications/55501/>.

Smith, D. and Tomlinson, S. (1989) *The School Effect: a study of multi-racial comprehensives*. London: Policy Studies Institute.

Strand, S. (2007a) 'Minority ethnic pupils in the longitudinal study of young people in England', Research report 851/2007. Nottingham: Department for Education and Skills.

— (2007b) 'Minority ethnic pupils in the longitudinal study of young people in England (LSYPE)', Warwick: Warwick Centre for Educational Development Appraisal and Research, University of Warwick (for the Department for Children, Schools and Families). Available at: <http://www.dcsf.gov.uk/research/data/uploadfiles/DCSF-RR002.pdf>.

— (2010) 'Do some schools narrow the gap? Differential school effectiveness by ethnicity, gender, poverty and prior achievement', *School Effectiveness and School Improvement*, 21, 3, pp. 289–314.

— (forthcoming a) 'The limits of social class in explaining ethnic gaps in educational attainment', *British Educational Research Journal*, forthcoming.

— (forthcoming b) 'The White British-Black Caribbean achievement gap: tests, tiers and teacher expectations', *British Educational Research Journal*, forthcoming.

Strand, S. and Lindsay, G. (2009) 'Evidence of ethnic disproportionality in special education in an English population study', *Journal of Special Education*, 43, 3, pp. 174–90.

Sukhnandan, L. and Lee, B. (1998) *Streaming, Setting and Grouping by Ability: a review of the literature*, Berkshire: NFER.

Tikly, L., Haynes, J., Caballero, C., Hill, J. and Gillborn, D. (2006) 'Evaluation of Aiming High: African Caribbean Achievement Project', Department for Education and Skills Research Report RR801, Bristol: University of Bristol. Available at: <http://www.standards.dfes.gov.uk/ethnicminorities/resources/ACAPevalrsrchreportoct06.pdf>.

Torgerson, C., Brooks, G. and Hall, J. (2006) 'A Systematic Review of the Research Literature on the Use of Phonics in the Teaching of Reading and Spelling', Department for Education and Skills Research Report 711, Nottingham: University of Sheffield for Department for Education and Skills. Available at: <http://www.education.gov.uk/publications//eOrderingDownload/RR711_.pdf>.

Troyna, B. (1991) 'Underachievers or underrated? The experience of pupils of South Asian origin in a secondary school', *British Educational Research Journal*, 17, 4, pp. 361–76.

— (1992) 'Ethnicity and the organization of learning groups: a case study', *Educational Research*, 34, 1, pp. 45–55.

— (1993) 'Underachiever or misunderstood? A reply to Roger Gomm', *British Educational Research Journal*, 19, 2, pp. 167–74.

Troyna, B. and Siraj-Blatchford, I. (1993) 'Providing support or denying access? The experiences of students designated as ESL and SN in a multi-ethnic secondary school', *Educational Review*, 45, 1, pp. 3–11.

Wainer, H. and Brown, L. (2004) Three statistical paradoxes in the interpretation of group differences: illustrated with medical school admission and licensing data. Available at: <http://www.statlit.org/pdf/2004Wainer_ThreeParadoxes.pdf>.

Wilson, D., Burgess, S. and Briggs, A. (2006) 'The dynamics of school attainment of England's ethnic minorities', CASE paper 105, Centre for Analysis of Social Exclusion, London: London School of Economics. Available at: <http://sticerd.lse.ac.uk/dps/case/cp/CASEpaper105.pdf>.

Wright, C. (1986) 'School processes: an ethnographic study', in Eggleston, J., Dunn, D. and Anjall, M. (eds) *Education for Some: the educational and vocational experiences of 15–18 year old members of minority ethnic groups*. Stoke on Trent: Trentham Books.

— (1992) 'Early education: multiracial primary school classrooms', in Gill, D., Mayor, B. and Blair, M. (eds) *Racism and Education,* London: Sage.

Yang, M., Goldstein, H., Rath, T. and Hill, N. (1999) 'The use of assessment data for school improvement purposes', *Oxford Review of Education*, 25, 4, pp. 469–83.

Part II
Exploring Case-Focused
Approaches to Causal Analysis

Analytic Induction versus Qualitative Comparative Analysis

5

Martyn Hammersley and Barry Cooper

Chapter Outline

In this chapter we will examine two approaches that are qualitative – and, more specifically, case-focused – in character, but are also explicitly concerned with causal analysis: analytic induction (AI) and Qualitative Comparative Analysis (QCA). We believe that it is worth comparing them for what they can tell us about the task of social science explanation, and how this task can best be pursued, since they share some important features in common while also differing in significant respects. We should note, however, that they have very different histories. AI was given its name in 1934 by Florian Znaniecki, in his book *The Method of Sociology*; though various elements of it can be traced back within philosophy through the work of Cassirer, Mill, Whewell, and Bacon to Aristotle.[1] It emerged in the context of Chicago

---

1 For a discussion of the philosophical background to analytic induction, see Hammersley 2009a.

sociology, being influenced primarily by the work of W. I. Thomas, though it also drew on Znaniecki's earlier philosophical studies in Poland (Bierstedt 1969; Markiewicz-Lagneau 1988; Kwilecki and Czarnocki 1989; Halas 2000). Znaniecki presented AI as capturing the logic of science in a way that statistical method, increasingly influential in US sociology at the time, failed to do. AI came to be applied, primarily, in studies of crime and deviance: it was central to Sutherland's critique of multiple factor explanations of delinquency (see Laub and Sampson 1991), and the classical applications of it are Lindesmith's study of opiate addiction, Cressey's work on financial trust violation (Lindesmith 1937, 1947 and 1968; Cressey 1950 and 1953), and Becker's investigation of marihuana use (Becker 1953 and 1955; see Hammersley 2011a).[2] While AI is still sometimes advocated today (see Becker 1998), it is seriously at odds in significant respects with the trends that are currently dominant within much qualitative research in many parts of social science: notably, in its commitment to science, its realist orientation, its concern with hypothesis-testing, and its pursuit of universal laws.

QCA appeared much more recently, though it too has roots that go back at least into the nineteenth century, notably to the work of Mill and Boole.[3] It was first fully presented in Ragin's book *The Comparative Method*, published in 1987, and has been further developed in subsequent articles and books (notably, Ragin 2000 and 2008). This approach came out of US political science and historical sociology, where quantitative research had become dominant but where there also existed a longstanding qualitative comparative-historical case-study tradition that had turned into a minority pursuit in the third quarter of the twentieth century.[4] QCA is presented as an alternative to conventional forms of quantitative analysis, but at the same time as providing a more rigorous basis for case-study work. Ragin has proposed that it can

---

2 A key role was played here by Lindesmith, who converted Sutherland to this view of scientific method (Gaylord and Galliher 1988: 124–6), and supervised Cressey's dissertation. AI was also used by Angell (1936) in his study of variations in the responses of families to the great depression, though the form it took here was rather different (Angell 1954). Later, it was applied in Bloor's (1978) work on doctors and in a study of lawyers, see Katz 1982, 1983 and 2001.

3 Ragin uses a variety of terms as partial synonyms for QCA, such as 'case-oriented approach', 'diversity-oriented approach' and 'Boolean approach' and, most recently, 'configurational comparative method' (Rihoux and Ragin 2009).

4 Some of the relevant background here is provided by King et al. 1994 and Brady and Collier 2004. See also Eckstein 1992; Kalberg 1994: 3–9 and Mahoney and Goertz 2006.

serve as a bridge between the two (Ragin 2000: 28–30; Rihoux 2003).[5] In the past few years it has gained considerable influence within political science and beyond, and its fortunes seem to be on the rise.

We will begin by briefly outlining the assumptions about the logic of social inquiry characteristic of AI and QCA. We will then look at their similarities and differences, and conclude with an assessment of what lessons can be drawn from the comparison.[6]

Analytic induction

Like many other terms used in the methodological literature, 'analytic induction' does not have a single, stable meaning: it is used in a variety of ways. Becker (1998: 194–212) distinguishes between 'classical' or 'rigorous' and 'less rigorous' versions of AI, and here we will focus on the former because this provides the sharpest picture of what is involved. On this interpretation, AI has often been presented formally as a set of steps designed to produce a theory that explains some type of outcome. Here is our own attempt to formulate it in these terms[7]:

1. An initial description of the type of outcome to be explained is formulated.
2. One or a few cases where this outcome occurs are investigated.
3. Data from these are analysed in order to identify common elements, and to generate an explanatory hypothesis (one which relates to necessary conditions).
4. Data from further cases are collected and/or analysed in order to test this hypothesis. There may be an attempt to maximize the diversity of cases studied where the outcome occurred, and perhaps also cases where the outcome did not occur but where at least some of the components of the candidate cause, and other potentially relevant factors, were present (thereby attempting to identify jointly sufficient conditions).

---

5 There are other formulations as well, for example: the notion of a 'middle path', one which is not a 'compromise', 'rather it transcends many of the limitations of both' (Ragin 2008: 71).

6 It is of some significance that these two approaches were developed in separate subfields of social science, and were designed to address rather different sorts of explanatory task. However, their comparison can be fruitful despite this. Becker (1998: 194–5 and 212) claims that they resemble one another, along with the kind of property space analysis developed by Lazarsfeld, in their underlying logic. This is illuminating in some ways but misleading in others.

7 For a discussion of the relationship between this formal account and how Lindesmith and Cressey seem to have gone about their work, see Hammersley 2009a.

5. If the hypothesis is not confirmed, there are two options available. Most obviously, the hypothesis can be revised. However, there is an alternative: the definition of the outcome type, of what is to be explained (the explanandum), can be revised in such a way as to exclude discrepant cases. This is done only where it seems likely that the original outcome category contained instances generated by different causal processes. The aim is to identify a type of outcome that is causally homogeneous.

6. This process of modification – of hypotheses and/or of outcome definitions – continues until the explanatory hypothesis fits all the data from new cases, as well as that from previous ones. While it can never be proved that there are not other cases, not yet investigated, that would force a revision, at this point the explanation can be put forward as highly credible, even though still necessarily fallible (as is all knowledge).[8]

We noted earlier that AI was presented as an alternative to statistical method, which was dismissed by Znaniecki as failing to conform to a properly scientific approach. And this opposition persisted throughout the first half of the twentieth century. A good illustration of what was at stake can be gained from examining Sutherland's critique of the Gluecks' study of the causes of delinquency (Laub and Sampson 1991). There were several themes in this criticism.

---

8 Note that this is a rational reconstruction of what is involved: it is a slightly modified version of that provided by Cressey 1971: 16. There are a couple of areas of variation or ambiguity as regards this procedure. The first concerns whether the initial hypothesis is generated out of the analysis of cases or is developed prior to the data collection. For example, in his listing of the steps involved in AI, Cressey presents the production of a hypothesis as prior to the investigation of cases. This matter relates to a contentious issue in the history of philosophical discussions about scientific method, regarding the role of hypotheses: see Losee 1993. What is involved here is not usually an all-or-nothing matter, but rather differences in view about the importance of the role of hypotheses. Neither Mill nor Bacon denied that they can play a key role, but Whewell placed much greater emphasis on their role. Moving into the twentieth century, Popper seems to reject the role of empirical investigation in the development of hypotheses; though this could be read as a denial that there is any '*logic of discovery*', rather than a denial that empirical data may be fruitful in stimulating hypotheses. The second variation or ambiguity concerns the number of cases that must be studied and the role of comparative analysis. Znaniecki sometimes gives the impression that what is involved is the analysis of a single case, or a very small number of cases, to discover the essential features, but both Lindesmith and Cressey collected data on a relatively large number of cases *alongside* their progressive specification of what they were trying to explain and their development and testing of hypotheses.

First, Sutherland insisted that there is no fundamental difference between the causal processes that generate crime and delinquency and those that produce lawful behaviour; since the former are not a product of evil or badness but of ordinary social processes. In effect, this was an argument against attempts to explain crime and delinquency as products of individual abnormality, whether by appealing to genetics or to early child-rearing practices. More radically, of course, it also rules out the idea of social pathology (see Sutherland 1945).

Second, Sutherland insisted that any causal explanation of crime and delinquency must identify a coherent system of factors, rather than listing a disparate collection of contributory causes. This seems to have been closely bound up with the idea that crime and delinquency must be explained primarily in terms of currently operating *social* factors, rather than by biological or individual psychological factors alone. The task, then, was to build a *sociological* theory of crime and delinquency that identified a systematic causal process.[9]

Third, Sutherland rejected the idea that causal analysis is aimed at identifying factors that are *associated with* the commitment of criminal offences, where what is involved is a matter of *degree*: for example, a *tendency* for delinquents to be more likely to come from 'broken homes' than those children who do not engage in delinquency.[10] Instead, he insisted that the aim should be to discover universal not probabilistic laws, such that where a cause is operating the relevant outcome will always (and only then) occur. The task, in other words, is to discover that set of factors which, when they are all present, always results in the outcome; whereas, when this complete set of factors is not present, the outcome never occurs. In short, to specify necessary and jointly sufficient conditions of occurrence.

Finally, Sutherland argued that building a general theory of this kind requires careful comparative analysis of particular cases, rather than the collection of data on a small number of variables across a large number of cases. The reason he put forward for this was that the aim should be the development as well as the testing of a causal explanation. In-depth knowledge of particular cases is required to identify common features that could account

---

9 For a discussion of this, see Cressey 1964: 38–41.

10 In fact, Sutherland's own initial theory of crime had been a multiple factor theory; his views seem to have changed in the mid-1930s under the influence of Lindesmith.

for the type of outcome to be explained, and/or to revise the definition of that outcome type if it does not seem to be causally homogeneous.

Qualitative Comparative Analysis

As already noted, QCA arose in the field of political science during the 1980s in the US. Within that field at that time we can identify two broad traditions of work. On the one hand there was comparative historical work. Initially this began under the influence of the structural functionalism that was dominant in the 1950s and 1960s, Eisenstadt's (1963) *The Political Systems of Empires* being an example (see Hamilton 1984). Later there were studies like those of Moore and Skocpol that retained use of the comparative method but employed very different theoretical resources (Moore 1966; Skocpol 1979). The other main tradition was much more quantitative in methodological approach: it was concerned, for example, with investigating relationships among macro-societal level variables, such as between level of economic growth and level of democratic development (see, for example, Lipset 1981).

The starting point for QCA seems to have been Ragin's dissatisfaction with multivariate statistical analysis of the kind that had become the staple method in this quantitative tradition.[11] Working on the assumption that much social scientific theorizing is inherently set-relational in nature (Ragin 2008: 2), he argues that there are important social science questions that correlational forms of analysis are not well-suited to address, notably where relatively complex causal processes are involved, comprising conjunctions and perhaps also disjunctions of causal factors. While conventional forms of statistical analysis can address these to some extent, through the investigation of interaction effects among causal factors, this is not possible unless very large datasets are available. Moreover, in political science the unit of analysis is often quite large, for example whole countries, the result being that the number of extant cases is often relatively small (in statistical terms).[12] Furthermore, because conventional statistical analysis requires

---

11 QCA has developed considerably over time, and has been applied in a variety of ways. As a result, it is not possible to make unequivocal statements about all aspects of it. As far as possible, we have tried to take account of variations and qualifications without losing sight of what seems to be the core logic of the approach.

12 See Ragin 1987: vii and 2000: xiii–xiv.

a large number of cases in order to operate, there is a tendency to frame research questions broadly, by seeking generalizations across what may be highly relevant variations in context, and in the process obscuring crucial causal relations. Ragin also raises questions about some of the assumptions built into the use of conventional statistical analysis, for example about what count as cases of the same general kind. Can all nation-states be treated as belonging to the same population, irrespective of the particular focus of analysis, or are more subtle categorizations of *types of* nation-state required? He also challenges what he regards as simplistic assumptions about causation that are built into much statistical analysis in social science – notably, that the contributions of different causal factors are additive in a linear fashion (Ragin 2006).

In its crisp set version, QCA works with categorical variables and is specifically designed to explore what combinations of the presence or absence of causal factors generate an outcome. So, data are collected relevant to these factors across a set of cases, documenting whether these factors are present or absent when the outcome to be explained occurs, and when it does not occur. More specifically, a 'truth table' is constructed in which each row includes the cases characterized by a particular combination of causal factors as well as the proportion of these cases achieving the outcome (see Chapters 6 and 7 for more detail). Taken together these rows exhaust all the logically possible combinations of the presence or absence of the chosen factors; though, in practice, there may, empirically, be no cases or few cases appearing in some rows. Boolean algebra is then used to simplify the patterns appearing in this truth table so as to identify those combinations that capture necessary and/or sufficient conditions for the occurrence of the outcome concerned, within the dataset being examined.

While QCA originally addressed conditions and outcomes represented as crisp sets, that is sets in which a case could be only either a full member or a full non-member, with respective membership values of one and zero, Ragin (2000) subsequently utilized fuzzy set theory to develop a version of QCA that allows conditions and outcomes to have values other than those of one and zero. Here a value, for example, of 0.5 for a condition would indicate that a case was 'as much in as out' of the fuzzy set representing this condition. We will leave the discussion of the more complex fuzzy QCA to a later section. In the first part of this chapter we will compare analytic induction with crisp set QCA.

Similarities and differences

We can list some significant *similarities* between AI and QCA as follows:

1. They share a focus on generating and testing explanatory theories that are designed to account for the occurrence of a specific type of outcome. This marks them off from much qualitative analysis, including grounded theorizing (see Chapter 3), and from some quantitative work too; since these are often concerned, instead, with documenting the perspectives of a set of people, the strategies employed in a particular situation, the set of principles governing the *whole range of behaviour* of some type of social phenomenon, and/or the distribution of some type of attitude or form of behaviour in a population.
2. Both AI and QCA are committed to employing Mill's methods of agreement and difference, rather than his method of concomitant variation, or any of the other methods he outlines.[13] This aligns them with the use of comparative method in history and social science, and marks them off from much contemporary statistical analysis.
3. As a result of 1 and 2, both approaches adopt a case-focused, rather than a variable-oriented or aggregate-focused, approach (see Introduction).[14] For our purposes here, we take this to mean one or more of the following:

---

13 The method of agreement involves seeking cases where an outcome of the type to be explained is displayed but other things are as different as possible, in order to discover what else is common to all of them, this being taken to be the candidate cause. The method of difference requires comparing cases that are instances of the outcome type with those that are not, the cases on each side being as similar to one another as possible, so as to facilitate identifying those features (taken to form the likely cause) that are present when the outcome occurs and absent when it does not. The method of concomitant variation is concerned with detecting co-variation, positive or negative, between two quantitative variables. Mill identifies four 'methods of experimental inquiry', though strictly speaking there are five in the section of his book that has this heading. The method of residues is the main other one, but there is also the joint method of agreement and difference or indirect method of difference. This involves examining cases where the outcome is absent so as to discover whether the candidate cause identified through the method of agreement is also absent (effectively, a less rigorous version of the method of difference). It is worth noting that in the chapters on 'the logic of the moral sciences' Mill denies that these methods are applicable in the social field and explores others which we will not be examining here (see Mill 1843–72). We should also note that Ragin (1987) spells out the problems arising from multiple and conjunctural causation for those wishing to employ Mill's methods.

14 As noted earlier, at one point Ragin (1987: 168–9) describes QCA as a middle road between variable-oriented and case-focused approaches, but most of his discussion implies that it belongs in the latter category.

a. The starting point for theory-development is the identification of features,[15] found through analysis of a relatively small number of cases, that could explain the outcome of interest and/or its absence.

b. Data about a relatively large number of features of each case are examined.

c. There is a focus on identifying how these features may combine with one another in causing the outcome, rather than on their separate, additive contributions to the likelihood or degree of the outcome.

In each of these respects, there is a contrast with most non-experimental quantitative research.

4. Both approaches work with categorical or qualitatively structured rather than with continuous or quantitatively structured variables. This distinguishes them from much quantitative analysis.[16]

5. AI is concerned with deterministic rather than with probabilistic causal relations: in other words with finding combinations of causal factors that *always* produce the outcome if they are present and without which the outcome never occurs. This is also true of QCA on some accounts, especially those where relatively small numbers of cases are the focus of study; where a larger number of cases is investigated, Ragin recognizes that in practice *tendencies* are likely to be discovered rather than *all or nothing relations*. This results from the effects of random causal processes, factors omitted from the theoretical model, and measurement error (Ragin 2000: 108).

6. An important consequence of Point 5 is that both forms of analysis require detailed investigation of deviant cases, on the grounds that this is essential for developing and testing theories effectively.[17]

While the similarities listed above are very important, making these two approaches distinctive by comparison with the orientation of most qualitative

---

15 Features are, of course, scores on variables, though generally speaking these are categorical variables.

16 As noted earlier, for the moment we are leaving on one aside the more complex case of fuzzy QCA. Here, continuous variables, via a process of 'calibration' (see Chapters 6 and 7), are transformed into fuzzy sets, allowing the researcher to retain finer distinctions, but within a set theoretic and configurational framework.

17 Conventional forms of statistical analysis do not require this, and it remains rare to find it; though Lazarsfeld recommended it, and the notion of outliers, popularized by Tukey, encourages it (see Kendall and Wolf 1955; Tukey 1977). There has been some useful recent discussion of deviant case analysis in the context of how one might select cases for in-depth study (e.g. Seawright and Gerring 2008).

and quantitative work, there are also several significant methodological differences *between* QCA and AI, and these will require detailed discussion in the remainder of the chapter.[18] In summary, they are as follows:

1. AI is concerned with identifying a causal system that *always* generates some type of outcome *and which is the only system generating this type of outcome*. Thus, the set of causes identified must constitute the necessary *and* jointly sufficient conditions for the occurrence of an outcome of the relevant type.[19] By contrast, QCA seeks to discover which combinations of causal factors generate a particular type of outcome, accepting that several combinations may do this. In other words, it is primarily concerned with identifying sufficient conditions. While there is sometimes also an interest in specifying what may be necessary conditions (Ragin 2000: ch8 and 2003), there is no requirement to focus entirely on discovering *necessary and jointly sufficient* sets of factors.

2. A key feature of AI is that there will often be a requirement to reformulate the definition of the phenomenon to be explained – in other words, the outcome variable – since only by doing this will it be possible to reach a causally homogeneous definition, one which *only* includes instances caused by the set of causal factors identified, ones that are *never* caused by anything else. While Ragin (2000: 46–9) stresses that all researchers need to pay very careful attention to what is or is not a case of their outcome variable, since the results depend on the decision, his position does seem to differ from that characterizing AI. The motive for his concern seems to be to distinguish sub-types of the original outcome category produced by different conjunctions of causal factors. In a paper addressing causal complexity (Ragin 1999: 1227), he recognizes the value of the AI approach, but goes on to argue that the *same* outcome may result from different combinations of causal conditions.

3. There is another potential difference that may follow from Point 2. Ragin sometimes presents case-oriented comparative analysis as concerned with understanding 'specific historical outcomes in a small number of cases or in an empirically defined set of cases' (1987: 17), rather than being aimed at producing a *universal* theory about what always generates some type of outcome, other things being equal. So, QCA seems to allow here for the possibility that social science theories

---

18 In one place, Ragin (1994: 93–8) contrasts AI and QCA on the grounds that the former is concerned with identifying commonalities while the latter is focused on discovering differences. In fact, restricting the discussion to 'rigorous' AI, both approaches are generally concerned with analysing both similarities and differences in order to identify causal relations.

19 As noted earlier, in practice, the classic studies using AI tend to place most reliance upon the method of agreement, which only allows the discovery of necessary conditions, but they do also make some use of the method of difference, direct and indirect.

may identify causal processes that are not universal but instead specific to particular times and places; albeit perhaps to long periods and to broad areas of the world. By contrast with this, AI is explicitly concerned with producing universal laws that explain the occurrence of types of phenomena *whenever and wherever instances of these occur.*[20]

4. AI involves an iterative process of data collection and analysis in which the collection of data from new cases plays a key role at each stage of the analysis.[21] This does not seem to be a central feature of QCA, even though not incompatible with it.[22]

5. AI requires the examination of particular cases in considerable depth (Znaniecki 1928: 316), whereas QCA seeks to preserve 'the essential features of case-oriented methods' *in the development of techniques for dealing with a larger number of cases than is common with case-study work* (Ragin 1987: x). The result is that it usually operates with less in-depth knowledge, or less open exploratory investigation, of particular cases than AI demands.[23]

---

20 Note that this is a different sense of 'universal' from 'deterministic'.

21 In this respect, and some others, it is similar to grounded theorizing (GT). But note that it does not explicitly require the kind of interaction between data collection and data analysis demanded by GT: it could operate entirely *within* the analytic process – in other words, analysis of the initial cases could be followed by analysis of data on further ones that have already been collected.

22 It is worth noting that Ragin believes that the production of a truth table, outlining combinations of causal factors in terms of their production or non-production of instances of an outcome type, provides the basis for searching for new cases that would fill cells that are currently empty (Ragin 1987: 118).

23 In fact, in practice, there is probably no systematic difference between AI and QCA in terms of number of cases studied. Lindesmith carried out interviews with 50 addicts (in one place the figure reported is around 70), gained through the assistance of Broadway Jones whose life history Sutherland had published (Sutherland 1937; see Lindesmith 1937: ch1 and Lindesmith 1988: x–xi); though Lindesmith notes that a small number of these interviews played a much more important role in developing the analysis than the rest. He also drew on other cases mentioned by these informants, besides their own addiction, and on published sources, so that the number of cases used was probably much larger than this. Cressey carried out interviews with 133 inmates in penitentiaries who had engaged in financial trust violation: see Cressey 1953: 25. In fact, he lists over 300 'cases' some of which come from probation reports and other documents. At one point he also mentions that Sutherland had given him access to his 'file of unpublished material on embezzlement' (Cressey 1953: preface). Note too that, because of the different areas of social science in which AI and QCA developed, the sort of data used often varies. The kind of case-study work that Ragin refers to is generally located in political science, and usually relies upon historical documents rather than the generation of data through the research process in the manner of *most* qualitative research in the rest of the social sciences.

6. QCA systematically explores the logically possible combinations of causal factors through the construction of truth tables. This is necessary in order to bring to light the assumptions that are involved when examining the causal combinations that actually occur in the data. Researchers using AI have not usually examined all possible combinations of the elements of the theories they have developed, and so do not normally assess their emerging theory against other potential combinations of causal factors. They are concerned simply with whether it fits the evidence (that which they have already collected and that coming in from new cases).[24]

7. QCA takes account of the absence of features as well as of their presence in the causation of outcomes. This has not generally been done in the use of AI, though it is not ruled out.

We will look more closely at these differences in the next section.

Assessing the differences

Points 1 and 2: on whether 'cause' should be defined as a set of necessary and jointly sufficient conditions or, instead, more broadly as any necessary condition or contributory factor; and on the requirement that what is to be explained may need to be redefined

The first issue here concerns how restrictive we should be in defining the term 'cause'.[25] The difference, in this respect, between AI and QCA is quite a fundamental one. The notion of cause that underpins AI is one whose history can be traced back, in various forms, at least to Aristotle. Here, a cause is all and only what is necessary and jointly sufficient for the production of instances of a specific outcome type. By contrast, the main conception of causation employed by QCA defines a cause as a set of factors that, taken together, are sufficient to produce instances of the relevant type of outcome, although as already noted there is

---

24 There is an issue about whether what is involved here is potential invalidation of the theory or the discovery that it is 'incomplete' in some respect. See Mill 1843–72: 393–4.

25 Mill (1843–72: 328–9) notes that in everyday life we often apply the word 'cause' to particular necessary features or even to contributory factors. He writes: 'Nothing can better show the absence of any scientific ground for the distinction between the cause of a phenomenon and its conditions than the capricious manner in which we select from among the conditions that which we choose to denominate the cause' (p. 329).

sometimes an interest in necessary conditions as well (Ragin 2003). The explicit model here is Mackie's (1974: see, especially, pp. 61–2; Ragin 2008: 154) analysis of causation in terms of 'insufficient but non-redundant parts of an unnecessary but sufficient condition' (INUS condition); so that, for example, the causes of a fire might include an electrical short-circuit and the proximity of flammable material, neither of which is sufficient on its own to cause the fire, furthermore neither separately nor together are they necessary for fires to occur, but together they could be sufficient for a fire to occur in a particular context.

Several considerations are relevant in opting for one or other of these positions. First, there is the ontological issue of whether causal relations of the kind assumed by AI are available for discovery in the social world. Second, there is the methodological question of whether, even if they *are* present, social scientists have the means available for discovering them, given that they are usually unable to employ experimental method. Third, we need to consider whether there is any pragmatic justification for restricting what can be adjudged an adequate causal proposition to the narrow definition used by AI.

As regards the first issue, it seems clear that, as with some kinds of realist philosophy, such as Critical Realism (Bhaskar 1997), AI assumes a distinction between underlying, relatively determinate causal processes that can be discovered by science and the superficial, more contingent, processes that are apparent in everyday experience and represented in commonsense understandings of the world. There seem to be at least two aspects to this distinction. First, by contrast with scientific concepts, because of their pragmatic nature commonsense categories will, at best, only imperfectly grasp natural kinds, and the causal relations intrinsic to them (see Bird 2008). An example of such a commonsense concept in relation to the natural world would be a category of 'fish' that includes whales and dolphins. Using such imperfect categories, we would often only be able to identify probabilistic relations even if the underlying causal processes were deterministic; though, in the case of evolutionary biology, it seems that they are probabilistic anyway. Second, even if *some* commonsense concepts actually capture relations based on underlying natural kinds, most will not do so because they are concerned with local tendencies rather than universal causal relationships; attention to these local relations being essential for practical purposes.[26]

---

26 This follows automatically from the fact that the primordial commonsense categories are evaluative in character. Only if the values underpinning human evaluations were built into the very constitution of the universe, in the manner assumed by Aristotle, would evaluative categories pick

This distinction between science and commonsense was central to the original formulation of AI: Znaniecki sharply opposed his approach to statistical method specifically on the grounds that the latter was content to work with commonsense categories that do not capture real underlying causal processes.

For some advocates of AI it follows from this that, on the model of, say, physics, the sole task of social science should be to identify causal systems.[27] However, Turner (1953) has argued that, in order for it to operate, any causal system must depend upon non-systematic forms of causation. For example, while Lindesmith claims to have identified the necessary and jointly sufficient conditions for opiate addiction to occur, by contrast non-systematic causal processes lead to particular people taking opiates, some of them recognizing that the symptoms they experience are a product of withdrawal from the drug, and some of them using the drug to eliminate those symptoms. These causal processes are 'historical' in character: by their very nature they cannot be specified in terms of necessary and jointly sufficient conditions. Thus, people can arrive *by a variety of different routes* at the point where they meet each of the necessary conditions that Lindesmith identified as jointly sufficient for opiate addiction to occur.[28] Some may have been given opiates in hospital to reduce pain, while others were introduced to the recreational use of heroin by friends or partners, and so on.[29] Several questions arise here: do systematic causal systems actually operate in the social world, as well as among physical

---

out causally homogeneous sets of phenomena. The key point is that, generally speaking, commonsense categories will not gather things together or differentiate them on criteria that are primarily concerned with cause, but rather for example with the implications or consequences for human concerns and activities, and causal force is only one such consideration.

27 See, for example, the discussion in Lindesmith et al. 1978: ch1; though the model of science used here, as with Lindesmith 1981, is not physics but medicine – in particular, the example of explaining malarial infection.

28 The distinction between systematic and historical causation is made in Lewin (1936), and is appealed to by Cressey 1953. Lindesmith seems to take the view that all causation is systematic rather than historical, and this may also be true of Becker (1953), in line with his Meadian argument that outcomes are a product of situational rather than background factors: see Hammersley 2009c. However, Cressey appears to accept that both systematic and historical causal relations need to be examined (Cressey 1953: 13), perhaps as a result of the influence of Turner (Cressey 1971: 6 of Preface to the Wadsworth edition; see also Cressey 1960), though he also attributes this view to Lewin.

29 Of course, it might be argued that what are involved here are various causal systems interacting with one another, some bringing people into contact with opiates, others generating recognition of withdrawal symptoms, and so on. On this argument, there is no 'historical' causation.

phenomena? If they do, but some causal processes are 'historical', should the latter be included within the focus of social science? Judgements about these matters will depend, in part, upon how successful it is believed studies using analytic induction have been, and whether we think that application of this approach can be extended to other topics. These are issues we discuss below.

By contrast, as already noted, QCA does not rely upon a distinction between systematic and historical causation. It is interested in how instances of a particular type of outcome have occurred, and any sort of outcome is treated as open to explanation through comparative analysis. Moreover, QCA assumes that different configurations of factors can produce the same type of outcome. So, whereas the focus of AI is on identifying natural kinds, QCA involves no such commitment, and therefore does not draw such a sharp distinction between scientific and commonsense categories. In this specific respect it is similar to the sort of correlational approach that is common in quantitative social science, and also in much qualitative research (see Chapter 3).

As regards the viability of the search for causal systems or natural kinds in the social world, there are some grounds for doubt about this. One is theoretical: we might question whether natural kinds are to be found at the level of either psychological or social phenomena (see Ellis 2008). Indeed, it could be suggested that the sort of symbolic interactionist social psychology which shaped Lindesmith's and Cressey's studies itself rules out the operation of deterministic, and perhaps even probabilistic, causal systems in the social world. After all, this psychology insists that human action is contingent in character: courses of action can be suspended and redirected at any point, on the basis of symbolic re-interpretation of situation or self (see Blumer 1969).

A second reason for doubt about the viability of AI is methodological. This concerns whether it is possible to identify causal systems effectively without the use of experimental control of variables, which is frequently not available in social science. Experimental research has, indeed, usually been directed towards discovering systematic causal relations, and it does this by allowing the manipulation and control of background factors so that a causal system can be revealed if it exists. A central plank of the argument for AI is that it constitutes a non-experimental means of identifying causal systems, but is this true?

We should note that Mill (1843–72: 881–2) argued at some length against this possibility, insisting that the method of difference is essential to causal analysis and denying that it could be used in social science. He argues that while there are exact laws of the mind that psychology can identify, there are no exact laws of social life, only inexact ones that are relative to what he calls collocations: basic facts about how the world happens to be. Furthermore, he argues that there are problems with the data that *are* available: 'the circumstances [. . .] which influence the condition and progress of society, are innumerable, and perpetually changing; and though they all change in obedience to causes, and therefore to laws, the multitude of the causes is so great as to defy our limited powers of calculation' (p. 878). This problem arises, in large part, from the fact that (given Mill's methodological individualism) the laws and causes operate on multiple individual human beings as units. Mill's argument here is not that social processes are entirely contingent – to the contrary, as just indicated he views them as subject to causal laws – but rather that if we are to be able to explain and predict social patterns of behaviour we must take account of multiple factors operating upon a large number of individual actors, and this defies our capabilities. Moreover, in such complex fields even the implications of exact psychological laws can only amount to tendencies, not absolutely determinate predictions based upon necessary and jointly sufficient conditions.

It is perhaps worth examining Znaniecki's position against this sceptical background, since he believed both that closed – in other words determinate, causal – systems operate in the social world and that these are open to investigation through observation rather than experiment. The clearest exposition of his point of view is in a paper on 'social research in criminology', published in 1928. He writes:

> In [criminological] research [. . .] while the nature of our facts precludes material experiment, it does not prevent us from applying in our field the same logic which the physicist and the biologist use in their experiments. The logic of the experiment consists in simplifying the conditions in which certain facts occur; the scientist builds a definite and limited system of objects cut off from irrelevant external influences, and investigates the changes which are going on in this system, trying to determine their causal relations. The sociologist can do something similar with less difficulty, for he does not need to build closed systems artificially; he finds them readymade in social life. Man in his individual and collective behaviour is continually constructing and reconstructing limited systems of objects which he intentionally tries to keep undisturbed by external influences. All the scientist needs to do is to determine by exact observation and analysis what these systems are, and to study by comparative method the processes which occur within them.
> (Znaniecki 1928: 310–11)

Znaniecki goes on to examine two of what he sees as the simplest social systems relevant to criminology: the crime as a social action, and the social personality of the criminal. In the case of the former, he outlines the elements which the agent seeks to keep in an ordered relationship and which define one another in pursuit of the goal. He writes:

> the subject tries to maintain this system such as it is against all disturbing influences until the action is achieved; that is, while acting he keeps as far as possible his tendency, his object, his expected result, his instrumental process free from any changes except those which the very course of his action is meant to produce. He suppresses other tendencies which may interfere with the satisfaction of the present one; he avoids, or overcomes, unexpected external conditions which prove an obstacle to the solution of the practical problem as it has been defined. In so far the action, as long as it lasts, is a closed system like the laboratory experiment of a physicist or a biologist.
>
> Nevertheless, it often happens that unexpected outside factors do influence certain elements of the action, either at its very beginning or in the course of its achievement. In this case certain other elements of the action undergo a change. Particularly important are such changes of the situation as produce changes of the tendency. It is possible to determine exactly and to express in the form of a causal law the effect which in a certain kind of action a definite change of the situation will produce upon the tendency. (pp. 312–13)

As an illustration of different action systems, Znaniecki contrasts a revengeful act that is the product of unusual provocation with one that someone has long nursed but waited for the opportunity to carry out.[30]

It is not at all clear whether Lindesmith's and Cressey's theories fit this Znanieckian model; or, indeed, whether that model is viable. Moreover, the kinds of causal system that Lindesmith and Cressey claim to have identified are also somewhat different from one another. In the case of Lindesmith, causal closure seems to be brought about primarily by the physiological effects of opiates, specifically the very unpleasant results of withdrawal. Without these effects, it is doubtful that the pattern of behaviour which Lindesmith claims to explain would be so stable. This is illustrated by the case of Becker's (1953) analysis of marihuana use, which is explicitly modelled on Lindesmith's work. In so far as Becker is seeking to identify the necessary conditions for people to find smoking marihuana enjoyable, the outcome shares much the same stability as the craving for opiates that Lindesmith defines as addiction.

---

30 It is worth noting here that Znaniecki recognizes that countervailing factors may operate in a way that obscures the effect of the cause being investigated.

However, when Becker shifts to explaining regular use of marihuana (Becker 1955), there is much less stability in the phenomenon being explained: 'Unlike opiates, marijuana does not produce addiction. People use it much more casually, sometimes a lot, sometimes not at all' (Becker 1998: 204). So, whether or not people continue smoking marihuana on a regular basis seems to depend upon a variety of contingencies, in a manner that, arguably, the behaviour of opiate addicts does not (Hammersley 2011a); in the terms used earlier, it perhaps should be seen as involving historical rather than systematic causation.[31]

By contrast, if we look at Cressey's theory, closure seems to be achieved here through the specification of a rational model: if people have a personal problem that they must deal with on their own, can see a way of resolving it through financial trust violation, and can persuade themselves that this is a legitimate means, then they will embezzle. A question that arises about this, and perhaps about some of the other theories produced by AI, is whether it amounts to tautology. Turner (1953) has argued that: 'What the method of universals [in other words AI] most fundamentally does is to provide definitions' (p. 608). It should be noted that what he has in mind here are real, rather than conventional or stipulative, definitions (see Robinson 1954). Thus, he comments that 'In Lindesmith's presentation he has outlined the essential stages in becoming addicted by the time that he has arrived at his full definition of the phenomenon. The essential stages are implicit in the concept of addiction as he presents it' (p. 608). So, these theories: 'serve chiefly to delimit a causally homogeneous category of phenomena, the so-called essential causes of the phenomenon being deducible from the definition' (p. 609). And Turner concludes:

> It is, of course, not accidental but the crux of the method that these generalizations should be deducible. It is through the causal examination of the phenomenon that its delimitation is effected. The operation in practice is one which alternates back and forth between tentative cause and tentative definition, each

---

31 The issue here is complex because, of course, all causal systems rely upon what Mackie (1974) refers to as the causal field: all those many background factors that must be present for the operation of the mechanism to occur. In the case of Lindesmith's explanation, these would include: the existence of human beings who have more or less the same physiology as currently; an available supply of opiates; non-interference of anything that would undermine the capacity to recognize the onset of withdrawal symptoms, for instance psychosis; and so on.

modifying the other, so that in a sense closure is achieved when a complete and integral relation between the two is established. Once the generalizations become self-evident from the definition of the phenomenon being explained, the task is complete. (p. 609)

As this indicates, Turner is not claiming that the definitions are reached by deduction; to the contrary, they are achieved by a process of induction during which the formulation of both explanans and explanandum may be altered. However, once this process is completed, what is produced is a deductive system that corresponds to the causal system that it captures, and that can be used deductively to explain any occurrences of the outcome.[32]

This analysis certainly fits Lindesmith's theory if it is taken to define 'addiction' in behavioural terms – as the use of opiates to ward off withdrawal symptoms – since this behaviour is also a component of the identified cause. But it is less clear that Turner's analysis fits Lindesmith's theory if we interpret it as being concerned with explaining the craving that underlies addict behaviour: while appeal to the conscious use of opiates to avoid withdrawal distress would be tautological, Lindesmith argues that what is involved is a craving for opiates produced by an unconscious anxiety that withdrawal distress is about to begin. By contrast, it is hard not to see Cressey's theory as tautological, on almost any interpretation.

Turner also suggests that circularity is involved in practical terms: because it would be impossible to determine, for example, whether people 'are able to apply to their own conduct [. . .] verbalizations which enable them to [retain] their conceptions of themselves as trusted persons [. . .]' (Cressey 1953: 30) independently of whether people had actually violated financial trust. Similar problems seem to arise with elements of Becker's theory of marihuana use: how could we know that people have successfully managed to find a means of defending their self-conception from the idea that those who smoke marihuana are 'dope fiends' independently of the fact that they regularly use marihuana?

Since neither Lindesmith nor Cressey responded to Turner's article in print, it is hard to know what attitude they would have taken towards it. At face value, though, his arguments raise doubts about the epistemic status of the theories produced by AI. Moreover, even if we put such doubts on one

---

32 This is similar, in some key respects, to Aristotle's theory of scientific method (see Losee 1993) and in others to that of Mill (see Skorupski 1989).

side, there are questions about the validity of these theories. The best test case here is probably Lindesmith's work; since it became extremely influential in academic, if not in policy, circles.[33] In formal terms, Lindesmith certainly produces a causal system of the kind that analytic induction intends. He specifies necessary and jointly sufficient conditions: taken together they constitute a mechanism which, other things being equal,[34] will always produce opiate addiction, and which must operate if this is to result. However, his theory has been subject to some criticism. The most illuminating critique for our purposes here is that of McAuliffe and Gordon (1975).[35] These authors argue that he was wrong to suggest that euphoric effects resulting from taking opiates are restricted to initial usage, and wrong to claim that the only cause of continued use of opiates after habituation, in other words the only cause of addiction, is the desire to avoid withdrawal symptoms. These authors argue that sustained use of the drug takes two relatively stable forms, one involving very frequent usage, the other less frequent usage; that these are generated by desire for the 'high' produced by the drug as well as by concern to avoid withdrawal symptoms; and that the reason why people fall into one pattern of use rather than the other is largely down to the availability of supply plus the effects of other commitments, including the demands of work.

While the revised theory that McAuliffe and Gordon present can still be seen as identifying a causal system which always generates addiction – it identifies a distinctive pattern of positive and negative reinforcement as generating a stable drug habit (of one or other of the two kinds they identify) – there is a qualification that needs to be made here. This is that their methodological approach is a statistical one, in the sense that they do not seek to demonstrate that desire for the euphoric effect of opiates is necessary if addiction is to result. Rather, they try to show that most of the addicts they studied did experience and desire the euphoric effect, and they argue that this motivated them to take more of the drug than was necessary solely to ward off withdrawal symptoms. McAuliffe and Gordon's data come from a survey and a set of interviews carried out by participant observers engaged in studying heroin addicts in Baltimore, and it amounts to frequency

---

33   It was subjected to public attack by Federal drug authorities (see Keys and Galliher 2000).

34   This *ceteris paribus* clause is necessary to deal with Mackie's (1974) background causal field.

35   For a different set of criticisms, see Weinberg 1997.

patterns.[36] At the same time, they do use one argumentative strategy that is closer to the sort of theory-testing characteristic of Lindesmith's work: they report that methadone was available cheaply or free, that it blocks withdrawal symptoms while not producing euphoria, but that few addicts used it. If true, this would count as convincing evidence against Lindesmith's theory and in favour of their own.

Even if we were to accept Lindesmith's claim to have identified a causal system, we might nevertheless retain some doubts about how far his study can provide a model for work on other topics. What is crucial here is the distinctive role that physiological processes play in the phenomenon he is investigating. As already noted, the causal power involved in the generation of withdrawal symptoms seems to be what produces the stability of the causal system that Lindesmith claims to identify. A more general point is that all the classic examples of analytic induction have been social psychological, or micro-sociological, in character. The mechanisms studied have been psychological ones that bring about particular types of behaviour on the part of individual actors. By contrast, QCA has generally been applied at the level of macro-social processes, and of course much social science has this focus. There are questions, then, about whether, even if they are to be found at a micro level, causal systems of the kind assumed by AI operate at the macro level too.

As we have already noted, QCA does not seem to be tied to a sharp contrast between scientific and commonsense categories, or to the idea that causes relate to the essential features of natural kinds. Indeed, for all its differences from conventional correlational analysis, in many ways it appears largely to share the same broad philosophical position: there is no assumption here that we can *only* find causal relations among natural kinds, or any strong assumption that there *are* such kinds within the social world. This is why QCA involves no requirement that the notion of cause be restricted in its reference to sets of factors that always *and only* produce some specified type of outcome. Moreover, even though in some formulations there is an insistence upon universal causal relations, in the sense that an identified

---

36 As Lindesmith (1975: 149) points out in his response, their sample of addicts is restricted to intravenous heroin users who are 'members of a drug subculture in a particular cultural setting at a particular time'. Lindesmith's own 'sample' has also been criticized as 'unrepresentative': see Keys and Galliher 2000: 70–5. However, the relevant issue here is not representativeness but rather the extent to which there is sufficient diversity included in order to overcome spurious inferences about what are necessary and sufficient conditions.

causal configuration must always be sufficient to produce the outcome, in other places, and often in practice, this is relaxed in favour of the specification of a 'probabilistic' threshold: a configuration of factors must generate the outcome for a high proportion of the cases within the data analysed in order to deserve the label of a candidate cause (Ragin 2000 and 2006; Cooper 2005; Cooper and Glaesser 2008).[37]

So, whereas the justification for AI seems to place primary reliance upon a particular conception of scientific method, and an associated ontology, the case for QCA is generally presented in much more pragmatic terms: that conventional correlational analysis cannot enable us to answer some sorts of question, and that conventional qualitative analysis needs improving so as to make it more rigorous. This seems to us to be a more satisfactory view, as regards both theory and practice, than the one enshrined in AI. The preferred aim in QCA, even in dealing with relatively large datasets, has usually been to resolve fully any contradictory rows in truth tables by including more conditions (Ragin 1987: 113). However, Ragin has argued from the beginning (e.g. Ragin 1987: 117; see also Ragin 2000) that, when analysing larger numbers of cases, a 'probabilistic' approach may be needed. Here, we cannot expect fully to resolve contradictions and the researcher must employ thresholds for *quasi*-sufficiency, such as 90 per cent of the cases characterized by some combination of causal conditions achieving the outcome, in order to analyse sufficiency and/or necessity.[38]

Point 3: explaining versus theorizing

There is a longstanding distinction within the philosophy of social science between an idiographic and a nomothetic approach to social research. The first is concerned with understanding some specific set of actually existing phenomena in their unique characteristics – or at least within some relevance framework that is *not* concerned with drawing general conclusions about

---

37 Even where full sufficiency is insisted upon, it is sufficiency within the dataset: there usually seems to be little attention to whether this set is representative of some larger population, such as that defined by the scope conditions of a theory.

38 We have illustrated this approach in Chapter 6, where we showed how introducing, serially, new conditions improved our analysis of the sufficient and/or necessary conditions for educational achievement. In the context of such 'large n' studies, issues obviously arise about what degree

what types of factor produce what types of outcome, and why, *wherever they occur*. By contrast, a nomothetic approach is directed exclusively towards reaching such general conclusions.[39] It is important to recognize that this is not a contrast between descriptive and explanatory orientations. Idiographic work may be concerned with *why* a particular event or feature occurred, and/ or with its *consequences*. But this is different from, even though it may draw on ideas about, what produces events *of this type* or what are the consequences of events *of this type*, generally speaking. We will use the labels 'explaining' and 'theorizing' to capture this distinction between two kinds of work, these implying quite different kinds of inquiry, even though what they produce may well be complementary.

AI is explicitly nomothetic in its orientation, and could (though perhaps need not) involve the assumption that the theories produced would be adequate for explaining any particular occurrence of the type of outcome concerned, whatever the context. This would imply erasure of any distinction between explaining and theorizing: all explaining would be theorizing. As we noted, QCA seems more ambivalent on this issue. Sometimes, it is presented as a way of clarifying (via comparison) the causal processes involved in a particular case (or set of cases) that is of primary interest; in other words, sometimes it seems to be idiographic in character. And this is compatible with the idea that cases have been selected as having something in common, or as differing in some significant respect, on the basis of interest or value relevance, and that the explanatory conditions considered have been selected similarly. For example, it seems beyond doubt that it might be illuminating in seeking to understand what happened in one socio-political revolution to compare it with one or more others (for instance, why did the French Revolution of

---

of tendency should be taken as strong evidence in any particular case. Even when a defendable threshold has been set for quasi-sufficiency, if the cases being studied can be seen as samples from some population, the additional issue of sampling error arises. Ragin (2000) proposed ways of dealing with this problem, and early versions of the fsQCA software incorporated some statistical significance testing procedures. Ragin (2000) also proposes various ways of dealing with measurement error, a second problem for those hoping to find perfect relationships between various combinations of conditions and the presence or absence of an outcome.

39 Note that while the nomothetic orientation is usually formulated in terms of the pursuit of universal laws, this is unhelpful since many of those who seek general explanations or theories would deny the possibility of universal laws, perhaps because they assume that these imply the specification of necessary and sufficient conditions.

1789 succeed, whereas that of 1848 did not?). The primary aim here would be to understand the main case of interest, and investigation of the other cases would be limited to what is useful for this purpose.[40] However, in practice, QCA generally focuses on a set of cases each of which is given equal priority, so *in fact* the aim seems to be to produce general knowledge about some *type* of phenomenon, for example socio-political revolutions, rather than to illuminate particular ones. Thus, at one point Ragin writes: 'the challenge comes in trying to make sense of the diversity across cases in a way that unites similarities and differences in a single, coherent framework' (1987: 19), and he implies that this is the aim of QCA. From this it would appear that it is aimed at general rather than idiographic knowledge.[41]

However, there seem to be two versions of such general knowledge in discussions of QCA: we can distinguish the goal of producing a causal generalization about how a particular type of outcome arose in a specified set of cases from that of producing a theory that identifies causal relationships among types of phenomena wherever and whenever they occur, only the latter being a purely nomothetic approach.[42] In places, Ragin appears to link QCA with the first of these options, for example he writes:

> Because of limited diversity, statements about causation (in the absence of simplifying assumptions) are necessarily restricted to the combinations of causally relevant conditions that actually exist. If an analysis were to show, for example, that rapid commercialization combined with traditionalism in peasant societies

---

40 See, for example, Agevall's (2005) use of QCA to illuminate Weber's explanation for the rise of rational capitalism in the West.

41 In fact, ambivalence over an idiographic or nomothetic focus is characteristic of much social scientific research, both qualitative and quantitative. What are actually put forward, often, are explanations for particular events, patterns of action, distributions of attitudes, etc. that occurred in a particular time/place-specified locale or population, but with the implication that the same explanation would apply in other similar situations/populations. Yet most of the evidential work carried out typically relates to trying to show that the explanation fits the case(s) studied, rather than showing that it is a sound general theory. There is a sharp contrast here with experimental research designed to develop and test social psychological theories. This very different orientation is exemplified by Cohen's (1980) book *Developing Sociological Knowledge*, where an attempt is made to apply this experimental model to social science generally, and conventional social scientific practice is criticized for failing to adhere to it.

42 There is an ambiguity in what the word 'generalization' means here that parallels the issue of the meaning of 'induction', as discussed by Mill (1843–72: Book 3, ch ii).

causes peasants to revolt, the general statement would be limited to existing peasant societies with known combinations of causally relevant features. It is entirely possible that peasant societies with different configurations of causally relevant features may have existed in the past or may exist in the future (or were simply overlooked) and that these peasant societies experience revolts for entirely different reasons. Rapid commercialization and traditionalism might be irrelevant in these cases. *This, of course, would not change the results of the analysis*, but it is important to have some sense of the limitations on diversity. (Ragin 1987: 105 emphasis added)

Elsewhere, however, he seems to imply that the production of general theories applying beyond the cases studied is the goal, in other words that the approach is truly nomothetic, as for example in his invoking the example of Harris's explanation for meat taboos (Ragin 1987: 45–6), and his repeated appeals to Mill's methods of agreement and difference.

We should note that the two orientations between which QCA seems to be torn would imply rather different research designs. The first might require that only the cases in the set being studied need be given attention, since any 'generalization' applies only to them. The second demands that cases be selected in such a way as to provide a test of the likelihood that the theory produced will apply to all cases of the relevant type. This would demand that we maximize diversity in cases studied where the outcome occurs, and seek to minimize differences between cases studied where the outcome occurred and those where it did not. As we will indicate in the next section, this sort of strategic selection of cases does not seem to be a central feature of QCA as it is typically practised.

Besides this issue of procedure, though, there are also some questions about the viability of both these enterprises. As regards the first, we need to consider whether or how it is possible to come to conclusions about what caused what in the cases being studied without relying upon counterfactual assumptions that might need to be tested by examining cases that approximate to those assumptions. As regards the second, truly nomothetic, task, as we saw in the previous section, there are questions about whether human social life is governed by causal principles that operate in a deterministic or even a predictably probabilistic fashion, and also about whether the means are available for discovering them even if they do exist (given that experimental control, random allocation and double blinding are often inapplicable). These, however, are problems that relate to all social science methods committed to a nomothetic goal, they are not specific to AI and QCA.

Points 4, 5 and 6: differences in strategy

At face value, in terms of its formal specification, AI involves producing an initial definition of what is to be explained, collecting data on a few examples, developing a hypothesis, testing it against data from new cases, and so on, in an iterative process. By contrast, QCA seems to operate simultaneously on a whole set of cases, about which data have already been collected, systematically examining all combinations of potential causal factors, taking into account their absence as well as their presence.

What we appear to have here are two rather different ways of carrying out research. The first is what we might call a developmental approach, in which ideas generated on the basis of the analysis of data from initial cases are continually tested out against data from new cases, and modified, until the point at which no further revisions seem to be necessary.[43] This is similar in many ways to programmes of experimental research. Here, an initial hypothesis is tested, this usually fails and has to be reformulated, the new hypothesis is then tested, and perhaps also fails; and the process is continued until a hypothesis has been discovered that stands up to further tests. Note that this may involve an iterative relationship over time between data collection and analysis, each informing the other. It might be argued that this facilitates theory development and testing in the most effective manner possible.[44]

By contrast, QCA is more similar to survey research in its overall strategy, where all the data are collected and then subjected to simultaneous analysis. A similar approach is also more or less demanded where the number of cases actually available in the world is sharply limited, and their characteristics already known, as for example in the study of socio-political revolutions. There are some specific advantages to this approach. One is that it allows us to explore all the logically possible combinations of factors, many of which are likely to be overlooked and not subjected to investigation by a developmental approach; though, of course, there will be limits operating on which

---

43   Here, AI relies upon an idea that parallels what in the context of grounded theorizing is referred to as 'theoretical saturation': the investigation of new cases should continue until no new information is being generated, and should only be re-continued if reasons arise for believing that there are cases that would force a revision of the theory.

44   Thus, on Becker's (1998: 196) account, in AI the data collection process is modified over time so as to better develop and test the emerging theory. It seems very likely that this was also a key feature of the other classic examples of AI; though, as we noted earlier, this is not essential to the approach.

of these can actually be studied empirically, since there will usually be no examples of some possible combinations. A second advantage is that Boolean algebra can be used to find the most economical account of the combinations that generate the outcome (see Ragin 2000: 139–44).

One attitude towards these different strategies, developmental versus non-developmental, would be just to accept them as alternatives, each being treated as fruitful in different circumstances. As already noted, a developmental approach will sometimes not be possible because new cases are not available or because the costs of gaining information about them are excessive. However, it may also *sometimes* be possible to combine these approaches.[45] AI could perhaps employ the Boolean analysis characteristic of QCA recurrently, in order to systematically check the relationships among causal components and outcomes in cases about which data have been collected up to that point in the investigation; after all, AI studies have in practice collected data on relatively large numbers of cases (by the standards of most qualitative research, and even in comparison with many QCA studies). Similarly, in QCA studies it might be possible to collect data on new cases, and then to redo the analysis to discover whether the new information forces revisions to the findings. Indeed, outlining combinations of causal factors, in terms of their production or non-production of instances of an outcome type, could provide an especially productive basis for searching for new cases that would fill cells that are currently empty (Ragin 1987: 118). So, here too a pragmatic attitude seems to be advisable.

Point 7: taking account of the absence as well as the presence of causal factors

QCA is distinctive in that it is concerned with the impact not just of the presence of particular factors in causal configurations but also of their absence. This is not a feature of AI, and it may be at odds with the kind of realist stance which that approach takes; in other words, it is concerned with the causal factors that must exist or operate if an outcome of the specified type is to occur. This feature of QCA points usefully to what we might call

---

45 See Becker 1998: 206, who notes how Ragin (1994: 94–8) sought to re-analyse the data generated by Katz's (1982) study of lawyers, this study having originally employed an analytic inductive approach.

the pragmatic character of explanation: that we are not simply concerned with documenting what happened, why it occurred, and what it led to in indiscriminate terms, but rather with understanding what factors of relevant kinds are implicated in causal processes that produce the type of outcome in which we are interested. However, this is not a feature of explanation that is given much attention in QCA studies. Quite the reverse, there is a tendency for the theories produced to be treated as simply representing what causes what, rather than the conclusions being explicitly located within value-relevance frameworks.[46]

The implications of fuzzy QCA

There has been much development of QCA since it was originally introduced. The most significant aspect of this has probably been the creation of a fuzzy set version (fsQCA). Here, in place of a sharp distinction between membership and non-membership of a set, the concept of '*degree* of membership' is introduced. So what is now being compared is not membership of different sets but the *degree to which* various items belong to two or more sets. This may appear to remove one of the main similarities between AI and QCA: their reliance upon 'categorical variables'. By contrast with most quantitative analysis, AI and crisp set QCA (csQCA) are both concerned with whether or not some type of outcome occurs, not with measurements on a scale representing *the degree to which* the outcome variable is present.[47] Similarly, in the case of each component causal factor they are concerned with the presence/absence of that factor, not with variations in the level of that factor. By contrast, in terms of what it aims to do, though not in how it achieves this, fsQCA seems closer to standard forms of quantitative analysis. Indeed, it might be inferred that fsQCA effectively marks a move away from the use of Mill's methods of

---

46   On the need for this see Hammersley 2011b.

47   It is probably true that there is still a greater affinity with categorical thinking in fsQCA than in conventional quantitative analysis. The possibility of full membership or non-membership (and therefore thinking in underlying categories) is implied with fuzzy sets, but not necessarily with conventional interval scales. However, here, as in conventional quantitative analysis, it is important to maintain a distinction between the degree to which particular cases possess some characteristic and the frequency with which some specified degree of a property is possessed across some sample or population.

agreement and difference, which seem to underlie both AI and csQCA, to what he called the method of concomitant variation. It must be emphasized, however, that the non-additive and non-compensatory characteristics of the operations employed in fsQCA, especially the use of the minimum operator for fuzzy set intersection (see Chapter 6), mean that fsQCA retains important differences from a correlational approach.

It is quite clear that many (perhaps all) sociological categories do not match what has been called the Aristotelian model of classification, in which a definition can be produced that identifies a set of essential features shared by all members of the category and displayed by no cases falling outside that category. Znaniecki and Lindesmith argued that this is because sociologists have not yet managed to generate scientific concepts that iden-tify deterministic causal relations; and, indeed, that social scientists have a predilection for sticking with commonsense categories which, because of their pragmatic origins, are necessarily fuzzy, because causally heteroge-neous.[48] However, there are some reasons to doubt this diagnosis. One of these is: how, if commonsense categories are necessarily fuzzy, can socio-logical theories incorporate reference to them – so as to take account of their role in guiding human actions – without making *themselves* concep-tually fuzzy?[49] From this point of view, it seems likely that many, if not all, social scientific concepts cannot but be fuzzy. This is over and above any more fundamental ontological argument about whether deterministic, or relatively closed, causal systems operate at the social, or even the psycho-logical, levels (Ellis 2008).

This would seem to suggest that both AI and csQCA face a fundamen-tal difficulty, and that the shift to a fuzzy set version of QCA is essential. However, there are questions about how far this move deals with the prob-lem. It is important to note that fsQCA operates with a notion of *degree* of membership, which assumes that, for each category, there would be one ideal member, even if in practice examples fully matching this might never be found. This ideal would presumably have all of the features essential to the category. Along with this, it seems to be assumed that degree of mem-bership is unidimensional (or, if there is more than one dimension, the

---

48 For a similar argument in the field of political science, see Eckstein 1992.

49 There has, of course, been much work done by Rosch 1999 and others on the fuzzy nature of eve-ryday categories. For an elaboration of the argument here, see Hammersley 2009b.

dimensions are taken to vary in tandem, or in such a way that variation in one can compensate for variation in the other).[50] Yet much of the research on everyday concepts or categories suggests that they do not involve a single ideal exemplar, that members of a category share only family resemblances, so that what is involved is a complex kind of vagueness (more complex than the traditional examples in philosophy, for example that of how little hair a man must have to be adjudged bald, which are closer to the fsQCA model).[51] Moreover, the suggestion in this literature is that this kind of complexity is irremediable (Lakoff 1987).

In practical terms this may not be an impassable obstacle, it may be possible in most cases to make judgements about whether a case is an instance of a category; indeed, about whether a case is a *clear* instance of a category, a *borderline case* or a *non-instance*. Note, however, that fsQCA seems to go beyond this, to claim that set membership can be calibrated in a more delicate and rigorous fashion, the implication being that it is analogous to true measurement on a scale. Yet there are questions about whether this is possible; and, if it is not, then it may be hard to apply fuzzy set theory appropriately.

There is a further concern about the recognition of fuzziness in categories, one that would probably have been voiced by the original advocates of AI. This is that it will effectively allow the survival of category differentiations that ought to have been abandoned because they do not adequately capture the differences, or the natural kinds, in the world that they are intended to map. To illustrate, take an example provided by Smithson and Verkuilen (2006) in their introduction to fuzzy set theory. They argue that since the letter 'y' in the English language is sometimes pronounced as a consonant and sometimes as a vowel, it should be judged to be a partial member of these two sets. But it seems likely that a more productive approach would be to recognize the discrepancies between the sounds used in oral English and standard orthography, and, where this is important (e.g. in linguistic transcription), to move to use of a phonetic alphabet that differentiates 'y' into two or more letters.

---

50 Usually, it is only when these sets are combined, using the operations of union and intersection discussed in later chapters, that fsQCA explicitly addresses more complex concepts, such as types of welfare state (see, for example, Kvist 2007).

51 For a useful discussion of philosophical approaches to vagueness, see Hookway 2002: ch5.

Problems that AI and QCA share

There are a number of other important issues that relate to *both* AI and QCA. A first one concerns what *sorts* of cases must be studied before we can reasonably judge that a theory is true or false (albeit even then only 'until further notice'). Many rational reconstructions of AI, in terms of the steps it involves, place little emphasis upon the strategic selection of cases for study. Indeed, while Cressey makes much of the search for negative cases as an essential feature of AI (see also Denzin 2006), he does not draw a strong distinction between studying further cases in order to find out whether there are any exceptions and *strategically selecting cases that are most likely to open up the theory to challenge*. For example while, in his formal account of the method of AI, he lists as a seventh step 'for purposes of proof, cases outside the area circumscribed by the definition are examined to determine whether or not the final hypothesis applies to them' (Cressey 1953: 16), this is very unspecific. In much the same way, while accounts of QCA emphasize the importance of taking account of negative cases, there is little emphasis on how cases are to be selected, other than that (where the concern is sufficiency) these should include both those where the outcome occurs and those where it does not.

We can identify a number of different sorts of case selection strategy that could be important. In his discussion of the methods of agreement and difference, Mill emphasizes that differences between cases must be maximized in using the first method, while in the second differences between cases should be minimized. This is, of course, the standard methodological concern with controlling the effects of factors outside the theory that might influence the outcome to be explained. The aim of this is to avoid spuriously reporting accidental relations as causal ones, *and* to eliminate the (approximately random) effects of factors that operate as overdetermining or countervailing forces in particular cases.[52]

---

52 The concept of the 'accidental' is a problematic one. What we are referring to here are the two widely recognized forms of 'spurious correlation': a) where both the outcome and the factor that is believed to explain it are in fact the result of some third factor that has not been investigated, and where the candidate explanatory factor has no effect on the outcome apart from this; and b) the situation where, in the set of cases studied, the candidate factor happens to be strongly associated with another one (included or not included in the investigation) which is the actual causal factor, the hypothesized explanatory factor having no, or little, causal power of its own.

Interestingly, in practice, Lindesmith did seek to build diversity into the cases of addiction he studied; and while it is less clear that Cressey was able to do this to any extent, the large number of cases he studied should certainly have introduced some relevant diversity. Furthermore, both these researchers made some use of the method of difference, and did so in a way that would have eliminated at least a few sources of diversity. Both examined data about the experiences of their informants before the outcome occurred: times when they had used opiates but not become addicted, or had been in a position of financial trust but had not violated it.[53] Of course, studying the same subjects at different times will not have eliminated all of the differences between the occasion when the outcome did occur and those when it did not, since some of these will not be tied to stable characteristics of the person concerned. Furthermore, there is the related, and serious, problem that both authors relied upon retrospective accounts, which cannot but have been affected by the subsequent experience of addiction or trust violation.

In many QCA studies, there is investigation both of cases where the outcome occurred and those where it did not. However, strictly speaking, in Mill's terms, this amounts to what he calls the indirect method of difference, since there is not usually much minimizing of diversity in the cases. This weakens claims to have found sufficient conditions because there is only weak control over potentially confounding variables.[54] In fact, what would strengthen both AI and QCA studies is investigation of cases where it was known that one or more of the identified causal components are present but where it is unknown to the researcher whether the outcome has actually occurred, or (in the case of a longitudinal study) whether it *will* occur. For instance, in the case of Cressey it would have been much more convincing if people in positions of financial trust had been investigated to see whether

---

53 Lindesmith also used documented cases in the literature, for example of the use of opiates in medical settings, and Cressey used a large number of additional cases from legal files.

54 Two rows of a truth table – representing configurations of causal conditions – that differ only on one condition, that is only in respect of the presence or absence of some particular feature, might allow something like counterfactual reasoning to be undertaken about the causal importance of this feature and, in Mill's terms, whether it is an indispensable part of the cause of the outcome. However, unless the theoretical model underlying the truth table has succeeded in including all the causally relevant conditions, and this is very unlikely to be achieved in practice, the problem of unmeasured selectivity will remain as a threat to any reasoning based on such pair-wise comparisons.

at any times all the factors identified had been present but no offence had occurred.[55]

There is another strategy of theory development and testing that might be mentioned. This is the idea that other implications should be derived from the theory besides the main explanatory hypothesis, and these investigated so as to provide a test of its validity. Lindesmith supplies an example of this, though it is implicated in an important ambiguity in his theory. One of his aims was to show that addiction cannot be explained entirely in physiological terms, and in this context he stresses the role of significant symbols in people recognizing the physiological effects of withdrawal and anticipating how these could be avoided. On this interpretation, as Lindesmith notes, animals and young babies cannot become addicted. So, he looks at experimental evidence about the effects of opiates on animals; though there is some dispute about his treatment of these (McAuliffe and Gordon 1975; Lindesmith 1975). At the same time, on a more behaviouristic interpretation of his theory, which he seems to present in responding to McAuliffe and Gordon, it is less clear why we would expect differences between human and non-human animals in this respect.

The weaknesses as regards strategic selection of cases in both AI and QCA studies mean that the validity of the findings could be quite sensitive to the particular set of cases actually studied; and, in particular, to how these relate to what is possible, in terms of the relevant causal processes that operate in the social world. The ambiguity, in the case of QCA, about whether the orientation is nomothetic or idiographic may serve to obscure this issue. In the case of AI, the failure to distinguish between treating a single negative case as refutation of the hypothesis and actively searching for cases that put the hypothesis under severe test, as regards both necessity and sufficiency of the conditions identified, does the same.

A second issue follows on from this: both AI and QCA, in its more deterministic usages, tend to run together three ideas that are separable:

1. That deviant cases or counter-instances must be examined with a view to determining their implications for the hypothesis they count against and/or for the current definition of what is to be explained;

---

55 Another approach would be experimental investigation. While this would raise questions about drawing inferences from the experimental situation to what happens in the world more generally, such studies could be a useful complement to more 'naturalistic' investigations. Thus, Cressey sought to test his argument about the significance of non-shareability of problems through asking his subjects what they would do in a case that was framed as a shareable financial problem (Cressey 1971: 71–5).

2. That exceptions must always be treated as refutations of the hypothesis; and
3. That the goal must be to produce theoretical conclusions that have the form of universals.

There are good reasons for keeping these three ideas separate, and indeed for abandoning the second, and perhaps also the third. As Ragin (2000: 108) and others have noted, descriptive errors will often be present and these may generate spurious exceptions. On top of this, in comparative analysis of extant cases there is always the potential for noise from confounding variables that cannot be controlled, and this too may generate spurious exceptions. As regards the issue of whether theoretical conclusions must be universals, distinctions need to be drawn between different senses of 'universal'. The word can be employed to refer to the contrast between: deterministic and probabilistic claims; claims about the behaviour of all human beings as against what happens, say, in particular types of society; and between empirical regularities and causal relationships that are only visible under very unusual circumstances. It would probably be sensible to allow investigation of causal claims that are both universal and non-universal in all three of these senses.

A third issue concerns what we might call the functional and temporal structuring of causal relations. Factors may play various roles in bringing about an outcome. QCA recognizes this in part by drawing a strong contrast between necessary and sufficient conditions (see also Mahoney 2008; Mahoney et al. 2009), a distinction not really addressed by writers on AI even though it is implicit in their approach. However, there are other sorts of functional variation often highlighted by historians, for example between pre-disposing and trigger factors, and there may also be factors that operate as catalysts. The issue of temporal structuring is foregrounded by Abbott (2001), and is also given attention in historical explanations (see Roberts 1996). Here the potential significance of the *sequence* in which different factors impact, and the *pacing* of the impacts, is highlighted. It seems to us that these are issues that may sometimes need to be taken into account, though it should not be assumed that they are always crucial to the task of sociological explanation.[56]

---

56 For one attempt to incorporate temporal relations into QCA, see Caren and Panofsky (2005). In a critical response to this paper, Ragin and Strand (2008) show how the existing software for fsQCA can be used to incorporate simple sequence data.

Another issue is that both approaches tend to give primacy to finding relationships in the data, rather than to theoretical work designed to identify the causal processes that could produce the outcome, processes in which the components of the causal configuration identified play a role. The nature of the explanations offered by AI imply the need for this kind of theoretical work, given the systemic nature of the causal process, but in accounts of this approach *in use* the emphasis tends to be on generating hypotheses out of the data.[57] Similarly, the emphasis of QCA is on exploring the possible combinations of factors, identifying those that produce the outcome and then simplifying the combinations. While Ragin (1987) mentions the need for theoretical and substantive knowledge, this is primarily in relation to making sense of what is found in the data.[58] There is not much discussion of the range of theoretical ideas about social processes that might be drawn on. For example, there is no equivalent to the lists of types of 'basic social process' offered by Glaser (1978: chs 4 and 6), in the context of grounded theorizing.

This is an issue that is of particular significance in relation to one of the philosophical resources to which Lindesmith and Cressey appeal: Lewin's distinction between Aristotelian and Galilean modes of science (Lewin 1931). Lewin takes this distinction from Cassirer, and the latter's constructivist epistemology places primary emphasis on the role of conceptual schemes in constituting phenomena. In particular, modern natural science is portrayed as applying mathematical frameworks that give primacy to the meta-concept of relation rather than to that of substance (Cassirer 1923). The model here is the notion of functional relations that is central to algebra. In other words, Cassirer's conception of modern science is resolutely anti-inductivist: it places great emphasis on the role of constructing theories which then organize phenomenal content. It is not entirely clear from his account on what basis, aside from coherence, theoretical schemes should be selected, but his work does provide a salutary reminder of the importance of theoretical work.

Finally, there is a deep question, raised earlier, about the nature of causation in the social world. Both AI and QCA assume that a relatively strong form of productive relation operates between cause and effect; such that, for

---

57 However, note that Cressey (1971: 4 of Preface to the Wadsworth edition) did draw on the work of Mills (1940) and others in developing the idea that rationalization plays a key motivational role in financial trust violation: it allows a course of behaviour that would not otherwise be possible.

58 He also stresses, of course, in later work on fsQCA, the role of such knowledge in calibrating the fuzzy sets that enter into analyses.

example, under given conditions the occurrence of a particular set of factors will always be sufficient to produce an instance of the specified outcome. While QCA recognizes that different sets of factors could produce 'the same' outcome, it does not acknowledge the possibility that the same set of factors could produce different outcomes; in other words, that causation in the social world may be only weakly determinate. This is a point that comes out of some theoretical approaches in the social sciences. One example mentioned earlier is the symbolic interactionism on which AI purportedly relies. Another is complexity theory, in which new forms of organization are seen as emerging out of 'lower' types of activity; though here deterministic relations are assumed even though the outcomes are not predictable (see Byrne 1998).[59]

Conclusion

Our goal in this chapter has been to compare AI with QCA in terms of the 'logics' of inquiry that guide them. Part of our interest is that there are important similarities between these two approaches, for example that they are concerned with identifying necessary and/or sufficient conditions, and differ from most quantitative and other qualitative work in this respect. However, as we have seen, there are also some important differences between them. Both the similarities and differences raise interesting issues, which we have discussed in detail.

It is our view that there are fundamental problems with much current qualitative and quantitative analysis, and that AI and QCA may point in more promising directions. In particular, a great deal of qualitative research, and methodology, fails to get to grips with the task of causal analysis, even though in practice it is inevitably concerned with identifying causal relationships. Similarly, much quantitative analysis is not only weak in its capacity to identify causal processes, but there are some fundamental problems with its basic principles (Ragin 2008). Of course, while AI and QCA may offer a better prospect, we are not under any illusion that they are a complete solution. Indeed, our main focus has been on some of the problems. So, in this chapter we have sought both to show the value of these approaches and to consider the difficulties they face.

---

59 What seems to be implied here is what Mill referred to as chemical, rather than mechanical, composition.

Advocates of AI claim that it specifies the character of scientific method with which all social science must comply. In effect it demands that qualitative and quantitative research be re-formed, in ways that require radical modifications to the former as much as to the latter. By contrast, as we saw, QCA is often put forward as a bridge between qualitative and quantitative approaches, though it sometimes also seems to be offered as a third way that transcends them (Ragin 2008: 1–2). Another interpretation, not incompatible with some of Ragin's discussion, is that it amounts to a third approach that complements the other two, each being more or less appropriate depending upon the nature of the explanatory task being addressed. We are inclined to adopt this third position, and to see both AI and QCA as among several useful approaches that are available to social scientists. While it is important to examine the epistemological and ontological assumptions on which they rely, their value cannot be determined entirely through philosophical or conceptual analysis. Rather, a more pragmatic attitude is required, in which we try to learn from past experience how to improve the effectiveness of future work.

References

Abbott, A. (2001) *Time Matters*, Chicago: University of Chicago Press.

Agevall, O. (2005) 'Thinking about configurations: Max Weber and modern social science', *Etica & Politica/Ethics & Politics*, 2, 2005. Available at (accessed 7.08.09): <http://www.units.it/etica/2005_2/AGEVALL.htm>.

Angell, R. C. (1936) *The Family Encounters the Depression*, New York: Scribner.

— (1954) 'Comment on discussions of the analytic induction method', *American Sociological Review*, 19, pp. 476–7.

Becker, H. S. (1953) 'Becoming a marihuana user', *American Journal of Sociology*, 59, 3, pp. 235–42.

— (1955) 'Marihuana use and social control', *Social Problems*, 3, 1, pp. 35–44.

— (1998) *Tricks of the Trade*, Chicago: University of Chicago Press.

Bhaskar, R. (1997) *A Realist Theory of Science*, Second edition, London: Verso.

Bierstedt, R. (1969) 'Introduction', in Bierstedt, R. (ed.) *Florian Znaniecki on Humanistic Sociology*, Chicago: University of Chicago Press.

Bird, A. (2008) 'Natural kinds', *Stanford Encyclopedia of Philosophy*. Available at (accessed 14.07.09): <http://plato.stanford.edu/entries/natural-kinds/>.

Bloor, M. (1978) 'On the analysis of observational data: a discussion of the worth and uses of inductive techniques and respondent validation', *Sociology*, 12, 3, pp. 545–52.

Blumer, H. (1969) *Symbolic Interactionism*, Englewood Cliffs NJ: Prentice-Hall.

Brady, H. E. and Collier, D. (eds) (2004) *Rethinking Social Inquiry: diverse tools, shared standards*, Lanham MD: Rowman and Littlefield.

Byrne, D. (1998) *Complexity Theory and the Social Sciences*, London: Routledge.

Caren, N. and Panofsky, A. (2005) 'A technique for adding temporality to Qualitative Comparative Analysis', *Sociological Methods and Research*, 34, 2, pp. 147–72.

Cassirer, E. (1923) *Substance and Function*, Chicago: Open Court.

Cohen, B. P. (1980) *Developing Sociological Knowledge*, Englewood Cliffs NJ: Prentice-Hall.

Cooper, B. (2005) 'Applying Ragin's crisp and fuzzy set QCA to large datasets: social class and educational achievement in the National Child Development Study', *Sociological Research Online*, 10, 2. Available at (accessed 27.05.09): <http://www.socresonline.org.uk/10/2/cooper.html>.

Cooper, B. and Glaesser, J. (2008) 'How has educational expansion changed the necessary and sufficient conditions for achieving professional, managerial and technical class positions in Britain? A configurational analysis'. *Sociological Research Online*, 13, 32. Available at <http://www.socresonline.org.uk/13/3/2.html>.

Cressey, D. (1950) 'The criminal violation of financial trust', *American Sociological Review*, 15, pp. 738–43.

— (1953) *Other People's Money*, Glencoe ILL.: Free Press.

— (1960) 'Epidemiology and individual conduct: a case for criminology', *Pacific Sociological Review*, 3, 2, pp. 47–58.

— (1964) *Delinquency, Crime and Differential Association*, The Hague: Martinus Nijhoff.

— (1971) *Other People's Money*, Second edition, Belmont CA: Wadsworth.

Denzin, N. K. (2006) 'Analytic induction', in Ritzer, G. (ed.) *Blackwell Encyclopedia of Sociology*, Oxford: Blackwell.

Eckstein, H. (1992) 'Case study and theory in political science', in Eckstein, H. (ed.) *Regarding Politics: essays on political theory, stability, and change*, Berkeley: University of California Press.

Ellis, B. (2008) 'Essentialism and natural kinds', in Psillos, S. and Curd, M. (eds) *The Routledge Companion to Philosophy of Science*, London: Routledge.

Gaylord, M. and Galliher, J. F. (1988) *The Criminology of Edwin Sutherland*, Brunswick NJ: Transaction Books.

Glaser, B. G. (1978) *Theoretical Sensitivity*, Mill Valley CA: The Sociology Press.

Halas, E. (ed.) (2000) *Florian Znaniecki's Sociological Theory and the Challenges of the 21st Century*, Frankfurt am Main: Peter Lang.

Hamilton, G. (1984) 'Configuration in history: the historical sociology of S. N. Eisenstadt', in *Vision and Method in Historical Sociology*, ed., Theda Skocpol. Cambridge: Cambridge University Press.

Hammersley, M. (2009a) 'On the process of analytic induction in the work of Lindesmith and Cressey', unpublished paper.

— (2009b) 'Is social measurement possible, or desirable?', in Tucker, E. and Walford, G. (eds) *The Handbook of Measurement: how social scientists generate, modify, and validate indicators and scales*, London: Sage.

— (2011a) 'On Becker's studies of marihuana use as an example of analytic induction', *Philosophy of the Social Sciences*, forthcoming.

— (2011b) 'Can social science tell us whether Britain is a meritocracy? A Weberian critique', unpublished paper.

Hookway, C. (2002) *Truth, Rationality, and Pragmatism*, Oxford: Oxford University Press.

Kalberg, S. (1984) *Max Weber's Comparative-Historical Sociology*, Cambridge: Polity Press.

Katz, J. (1982) *Poor People's Lawyers in Transition*, New Brunswick NJ: Rutgers University Press.

— (1983) 'A theory of qualitative methodology: the social system of analytic fieldwork', in Emerson, R. M. (ed.) *Contemporary Field Research*, Boston: Little, Brown.

— (2001) 'Analytic induction revisited', in Emerson, R. M. (ed.) *Contemporary Field Research*, Second edition, Prospect Heights ILL: Waveland Press.

Kendall, P. L. and Wolf, K. M. (1955) 'The two purposes of deviant case analysis', in Lazarsfeld, P. F. and Rosenberg, M. (eds) *The Language of Social Research*, Glencoe ILL: Free Press.

Keys, D. P. and Galliher, J. F. (2000) *Confronting the Drug Control Establishment: Alfred Lindesmith as a public intellectual*, Albany NY: State University of New York Press.

King, G., Keohane, R. O. and Verba, S. (1994) *Designing Social Inquiry*, Princeton: Princeton University Press.

Kvist, J. (2007) 'Fuzzy set ideal type analysis', *Journal of Business Research*, 60, pp. 474–81.

Kwilecki, A. and Czarnocki, B. (eds) (1989) *The Humanistic Sociology of Florian Znaniecki: Polish period 1920–1939*, Warsaw-Posnan: Polish Scientific Publishers.

Lakoff, G. (1987) *Women, Fire, and Dangerous Things: what categories reveal about the mind*, Chicago: University of Chicago Press.

Laub, J. H. and Sampson, R. J. (1991) 'The Sutherland-Glueck debate: on the sociology of criminological knowledge', *American Journal of Sociology*, 96, 6, pp. 1402–40.

Lewin, K. (1931) 'The conflict between Aristotelian and Galileian modes of thought in contemporary psychology', *Journal of General Psychology*, 5, pp. 141–7. [Reprinted in Lewin, K. (1935) *A Dynamic Theory of Personality*, New York: McGraw Hill, and in Gold, M. (ed.) (1999) *The Complete Social Scientist: A Kurt Lewin Reader*, Washington D.C.: American Psychological Association.]

— (1936) 'Some social-psychological differences between the United States and Germany', *Character and Personality*, 4, pp. 265–93.

Lindesmith, A. (1937) *The Nature of Opiate Addiction*, Chicago: University of Chicago Libraries.

— (1947) *Opiate Addiction*, Evanston ILL: Principia Press.

— (1968) *Addiction and Opiates*, Chicago, Aldine.

— (1975) 'A reply to McAuliffe and Gordon's "A test of Lindesmith's theory of addiction"', *American Journal of Sociology*, 81, 1, pp. 147–53.

— (1981) 'Symbolic interactionism and causality', *Symbolic Interaction*, 4, 1, pp. 87-96.

— (1988) 'Foreword', in Gaylord, M. S. and Galliher, J. F. (eds) *The Criminology of Edwin Sutherland*, New Brunswick NJ: Transaction Books.

Lindesmith, A., Strauss, A. and Denzin, N. (1978) *Social Psychology*, New York: Holt, Rinehart and Winston.

Lipset, S. M. (1981) *Political Man*, Second edition, Baltimore MD: Johns Hopkins University Press.

Losee, J. (1993) *A Historical Introduction to the Philosophy of Science*, Third edition, Oxford: Oxford University Press.

Mackie, J. L. (1974) *The Cement of the Universe*, Oxford: Oxford University Press.

Mahoney, J. (2008) 'Toward a unified theory of causality', *Comparative Political Studies*, 41, 4/5, pp. 412–36.

Mahoney, J. and Goertz, G. (2006) 'A tale of two cultures: contrasting quantitative and qualitative research', *Political Analysis*, 14, pp. 227–49.

Mahoney, J., Kimball, E. and Koivu, K. L. (2009) 'The logic of historical explanation in the social sciences', *Comparative Political Studies*, 42, 1, pp. 114–46.

Markiewicz-Lagneau, J. (1988) 'Florian Znaniecki: Polish sociologist or American philosopher?', *International Sociology*, 3, 4, pp. 385–402.

McAuliffe, W. E. and Gordon, R. A. (1974) 'A test of Lindesmith's theory of addiction: the frequency of euphoria among long-term addicts', *American Journal of Sociology*, 79, 4, pp. 795–840.

— (1975) 'Issues in testing Lindesmith's theory', *American Journal of Sociology*, 81, 1, pp. 154–63.

Mill, J. S. (1843–72) *A System of Logic Ratiocinative and Inductive*. (Edition used: Volumes VII and VIII of *Collected Works of John Stuart Mill*, Toronto: University of Toronto Press, 1974.)

Mills, C. W. (1940) 'Situated actions and vocabularies of motive', *American Sociological Review*, 5, pp. 904–13.

Moore, B. (1966) *Social Origins of Dictatorship and Democracy: lord and peasant in the making of the modern world*, Boston: Beacon Press.

Ragin, C. (1987) *The Comparative Method: moving beyond qualitative and quantitative strategies*, Berkeley CA: University of California Press.

— (1994) *Constructing Social Research*, Thousand Oaks CA: Pine Forge Press.

— (1999) 'Qualitative Comparative Analysis and Causal Complexity', *Health Service Research*, 34, pp. 1225–39.

— (2000) *Fuzzy-Set Social Science*, Chicago: University of Chicago Press.

— (2003) 'Fuzzy-set analysis of necessary conditions', in Goertz, G. and Starr, H. (eds) *Necessary Conditions: theory, methodology, and applications*, Lanham MA: Rowman and Littlefield.

— (2006) 'The limitations of net effects thinking', in Rihoux, B. and Grimm, H. (eds) *Innovative Comparative Methods for Policy Analysis*, New York: Springer.

— (2008) *Redesigning Social Inquiry: fuzzy sets and beyond*, Chicago: University of Chicago Press.

Ragin, C. and Strand, S. I. (2008) 'Using Qualitative Comparative Analysis to study causal order: comment on Caren and Panofsky' (2005), *Sociological Methods and Research*, 36, pp. 431–41.

Rihoux, B. (2003) 'Bridging the gap between the qualitative and quantitative worlds? A retrospective and prospective view on Qualitative Comparative Analysis', *Field Methods*, 15, 4, pp. 351–65.

Rihoux, B. and Ragin, C. (2009) (eds) *Configurational Comparative Methods: Qualitative Comparative Analysis (QCA) and related techniques*, London: Sage.

Roberts, C. (1996) *The Logic of Historical Explanation*, University Park PA: Pennsylvania State University Press.

Robinson, R. (1954) *Definition*, Oxford: Oxford University Press.

Rosch, E. (1999) 'Reclaiming concepts', in R. Nunez and W. J. Freeman (eds) *Reclaiming Cognition: the primacy of action, intention and emotion*, Exeter UK: Imprint Academic. Published simultaneously in *The Journal of Consciousness Studies*, 6, 11–12, pp. 61–77. Available at (accessed 19.02.08): <http://psychology.berkeley.edu/faculty/profiles/erosch1999.pdf>.

Seawright, J. and Gerring, J. (2008) 'Case selection techniques in case study research: a menu of qualitative and quantitative options', *Political Research Quarterly*, 61, pp. 294–308.

Skocpol, T. (1979) *States and Social Revolutions: a comparative analysis of France, Russia, and China*, Cambridge: Cambridge University Press.

Skorupski, J. (1989) *John Stuart Mill*, London: Routledge.

Smith, J. K. (1989) *The Nature of Social and Educational Inquiry*, Norwood NJ: Ablex.

Smithson, M. and Verkuilen, J. (2006) *Fuzzy Set Theory: applications in the social science*s, Thousand Oaks CA: Sage.

Sutherland, E. (1937) *The Professional Thief, by A Professional Thief*, edited and interpreted by E. Sutherland, Chicago: University of Chicago Press.

— (1945) 'Social pathology', *American Journal of Sociology*, 50, 6, pp. 429–35.

Tukey, J. F. (1977) *Exploratory Data Analysis*, Reading MA: Addison-Wesley.

Turner, R. H. (1953) 'The quest for universals', *American Sociological Review*, 18, 6, pp. 604–11.

Weinberg, D. (1997) 'Lindesmith on addiction: a critical history of a classic theory', *Sociological Theory*, 15, 2, pp. 150-206.

Znaniecki, F. (1928) 'Social research in criminology', *Sociology and Social Research*, 12, pp. 307–22.

— (1934) *The Method of Sociology*, New York: Farrar and Rinehart.

Set Theoretic versus Correlational Methods: The Case of Ability and Educational Achievement

Barry Cooper and Judith Glaesser

Introduction

Much existing empirical research on social class and educational outcomes often takes the form of either large sample quantitative work employing some form of regression analysis or small to medium sample qualitative work employing some form of narrative or inductive analysis.[1] The former genre – which we will be examining here – addresses correlations between variables and, in regression modelling, the predictive relationship between one or more variables and some outcome variable. Individual cases, the carriers of the variables, usually remain in the background. In so far as causal claims are made, the variables themselves often seem to act through having effects on a dependent outcome variable. In a common form of multivariate study, the purpose is to report the net (usually average) contribution of each independent variable to the level of the outcome variable, i.e. its contribution when other variables are 'controlled'. The underlying mathematics is matrix algebra and the basic tool is a symmetric measure of correlation. A typical paper will contain a table setting out a list of all the examined independent variables and, for each, a coefficient allowing its relative net contribution to be assessed.[2] A typical question examined might be whether it is cognitive or social variables, treated as independently contributing factors, that explain more of the variance in educational achievement.

It is assumed in this predominant model that these 'independent' variables do indeed act independently of one another. As Ragin (2006a) argues, in this 'net effects' approach,

> . . . estimates of the effects of independent variables are based on the assumption that each variable, by itself, is capable of producing or influencing the level or probability of the outcome. While it is common to treat 'causal' and 'independent' as synonymous modifiers of the word 'variable,' the core meaning of 'independent' is this notion of autonomous capacity. Specifically, each independent variable is assumed to be capable of influencing the level or probability of the outcome *regardless of the values or levels of other variables* (i.e., regardless of the varied contexts defined by these variables). Estimates of net effects thus assume *additivity*, that the net impact of a given independent variable on the outcome is the same across all the values of the other independent variables and their different combinations. (pp. 14–15)

---

1   The strengths of the qualitative tradition are its focus on meaning and interpretation, its concern to understand sequences of events and outcomes in context and its holistic treatment of individual cases. Notwithstanding the use of quantitative indicators in the not so distant past (Lacey's (1970), Hargreaves' (1967), Ball's (1980) and others' studies of ability grouping in schools all employed these long before 'mixed methods' became a focus of discussion), much recent case-based work in the sociology of education has eschewed numbers and formal analytic procedures.

2   See, for example, all four papers in the October 2008 issue of *Sociology of Education*.

Such causal homogeneity across cases is often, though not always, *assumed*. The contribution of, say, measured ability to educational achievement is commonly reported, net of the contributions of competing variables, in terms of a single coefficient applicable to all cases in the sample or, by inference, in the population. For those who regard such simple regression models as more than description, these assumptions – actually assumptions about the causal structure of the social world – allow the prediction of an outcome for a new case from the same population to be made simply by adding the effects due to the values of various independent variables for that case. Of course, more sophisticated forms of regression modelling, employing such methods as multilevel modelling (Goldstein 1995), can address aspects of causal heterogeneity. Dummy variables and interaction terms can be employed to move beyond the additivity assumption, though there are various technical difficulties inherent in that move.[3] In this chapter, however, we deliberately focus on the basic building block of the regression approach, symmetric linear correlation, in order to bring out key differences between regression approaches based in linear algebra and an alternative approach based in set theory.

The regression approach has received considerable critical discussion over a long period, and not only from those 'qualitative' writers who regard its being 'positivist' as an adequate reason to dismiss it (see also the relevant discussion of quantitative approaches in Chapter 2). Turner (1948), long ago, raised serious worries about the assumption of 'a causally homogeneous universe' and of linearity in his discussion of statistical logic in social science. Meehl (1970) raised major problems about the conceptualization and adequacy of 'control' variables. There is also interesting relevant discussion in Abell (1971). Lieberson (1985), in a book that deserves much greater attention, developed such critical points in a number of fruitful directions. Freedman (e.g. 1991) focused critical discussion on regression used as a causal modelling procedure. Pawson (1989) offered an incisive critique of the weaknesses of the variable analytic tradition. Abbott (2001) unpacked many of the fundamental but often unrealistic assumptions of the linear modelling approach in social science and explored some case-based alternatives. Byrne (e.g. 2002) employed complexity theory to draw attention to analytic weaknesses that

---

3   For example, a multiplicatively constructed interaction term such as $X_1 X_2$ will tend to be highly correlated with both of X_1 and X_2, leading to the problems of standard error estimation that can result from high collinearity.

flow from the central assumptions of conventional quantitative analysis. In this chapter, though, we will focus our comparative discussion on the key points raised by Ragin in the earlier quotation: the default assumptions of independence, additivity and net effects.

The crucial difference between the linear algebraic approach and an alternative that drops these assumptions is summarized by Mahoney and Goertz (2006) in their discussion of the set theoretic alternative to regression and the way in which it addresses causal complexity via the language of necessity and sufficiency. Set theoretic (Boolean) equations have a functional form different from the regression equations with which social scientists are familiar. Here is their illustrative (and deterministic[4]) example:

$$Y = (A^*B^*c) + (A^*C^*D^*E) \qquad (1)$$

In these equations the symbol * indicates Logical AND (set intersection), + indicates Logical OR (set union), upper case letters indicate the presence of factors and lower case letters indicate their absence. In this fictional example of causal heterogeneity, the equation indicates that there are two causal paths to the outcome Y. The first, captured by the causal configuration A^*B^*c involves the conjoined presence in the case of features A and B, combined with the absence of C. The second, captured by $A^*C^*D^*E$, requires the joint presence of A, C, D and E. Either of these causal configurations is sufficient for the outcome to occur, but neither is necessary, given the other.[5] The factor C behaves differently in the two configurations. The factor B in this equation is an example of what are termed INUS conditions. An INUS condition is 'an *insufficient* but *non-redundant* part of an *unnecessary* but *sufficient* condition' (Mackie 1980: 62).

Wanting to move away from a purely critical stance on regression modelling, Ragin (1987, 2000, 2008), in the context of political science, has developed both an account of and tools for this set theoretic analytic approach, building on the assumptions of qualitative case study but coupling these with an avowedly 'scientific' approach to social science not, in recent years,

---

4   This illustrative example assumes no empirical exceptions. Such a strong assumption does not have to be made. See, for example, Ragin 2000, which includes extensive discussion of non-deterministic models.

5   The factor A is, on the assumption that all paths to Y have been captured in the model, a necessary one.

usually associated with that tradition. Ragin has argued that a concern with net effects has severely limited the progress of social science and he has shifted his attention to complex configurational causation, to INUS conditions, to necessity and sufficiency. In his *Qualitative Comparative Analysis* (QCA), which draws on Mill's logic as developed by Mackie, combinations of the presence and/or absence of usually *non-independent* factors are seen as the necessary and/or sufficient conditions for outcomes to occur. Multiple causal paths to outcomes are seen as characterizing much of the social world. Causal heterogeneity across types of case is something to be expected, with the effects of particular causes depending on the configurations of other factors characterizing the case (George and Bennett 2005; Mahoney 2008).

In the context of education, for example, the causal role of cognitive ability might be expected to differ not only in relation to the social class and gender of an individual, but also by the type of educational regime within which the child's career is played out, and perhaps by the interaction between these. More generally, much theoretical argument in the sociology of education implicitly, and sometimes explicitly, addresses non-linearity and/or relations of necessity and sufficiency. For example:

- Boudon (1974a) accounts for the social distribution of educational achievement in terms of the primary and secondary effects of stratification. The primary effects of social class create some part of the differences in measured achievement early in a child's career while secondary effects, arising from the ways in which the perceived costs and benefits of subsequent educational decisions vary by class origin, lead to further class differentiation of outcomes, even among those with similar levels of early achievement. This account has a clear affinity with a description of the form, 'a high level of achievement in early episodes of assessment, e.g. at the end of elementary school, is necessary but not sufficient for a high level in assessments later in an individual's educational career'.
- Bourdieu's theory of capitals has included, at various times, the claim that academic capital, 'a converted form of cultural capital' (Bourdieu 1974), has to be combined with other forms of capital to receive its full economic and social return. Here, academic capital in the form of diplomas is not sufficient for certain outcomes unless conjoined with other forms such as social capital (Bourdieu 1974).
- Turner's (1960) classic ideal typical account of the then school systems in the US and England implies that educational success is a function of the interaction of the stratification regime with an individual's characteristics.
- Lacey's (1970) *Hightown Grammar* included the claim that the reaction of boys to their being ranked in the pressurized academic environment of the grammar

school was a function of their class origin and relevant family resources rather than simply linear.

- Cooper and Dunne (2000), in their sociological analysis of quantitative and qualitative data on national testing in mathematics in England, showed how, given class differences in semantic orientation, particular forms of test item could, for children from particular class backgrounds, render mathematical knowledge necessary but not sufficient for success, while other forms could even render such knowledge unnecessary (see Cooper and Harries (2009) for further evidence).

None of these theoretical accounts of causal processes is simply linear. The ideal typical relation for linear regression has the same form as Hooke's Law describing the effect of increased force on the extension of a spring. None of these examples has an affinity with this ideal typical case of a causally homogeneous linear relation. They do seem, on the other hand, to have an affinity with the set theoretic, configurational, approach.

Elsewhere, we have used the configurational set theoretic approach in analysing survey data on class, education and mobility (e.g. Cooper 2005a, b, 2006; Cooper and Glaesser 2007, 2008a, b, 2010a, b; Glaesser 2008; Glaesser and Cooper 2010). In this chapter, we will draw on this experience to make some general critical arguments concerning the over-reliance on symmetric correlational ways of thinking in quantitative educational research and to illustrate how set theoretic methods can provide a fruitful alternative approach. We have chosen to focus our discussion on one running example: the varying relationship between measured ability[6] and eventual educational achievement across types of case.

In this chapter, rather than focusing on the differences between these two approaches as they appear in the equations that summarize analyses of datasets, we concentrate on the properties of the basic building blocks of the two competing approaches. As we noted earlier, for most regression analyses, the basic building block is linear correlation. For the configurational approach it is the set theoretic concept of a sufficient and/or necessary condition.[7] Our strategy will be to begin with a discussion of an artificially created dataset

---

6 Or early attainment, if some readers prefer that interpretation.

7 While *conjunctural* analyses will involve combinations of such conditions, the set theoretic approach might, both in principle and in practice, focus on just one condition (e.g. is 'high intelligence' a necessary condition for gaining entry to a university education). We should also note that, while the basic building block for regression is the linear correlation between two variables, actual work may involve partial correlations, multiple correlations, etc.

of 194 cases for whom we have invented data on ability, later achievement and social class. The discussion of these fictional cases will allow us to bring out some clear differences between the correlational and the set theoretic approaches. First, we show that there are features of this dataset that correlational methods might miss. Since these missed features – by our design – concern relations of sufficiency and necessity, we need a set theoretic approach to describe them. We therefore interrupt our discussion to introduce the basic elements of the set theoretic approach as developed mainly by Charles Ragin. We then use this approach to make sense of the 'anomalies' that arose in our correlational analysis of the invented dataset. Having shown that the set theoretic approach can make better sense of the invented dataset than the correlational approach, we then move to present some comparable real world results, drawing on some illustrative analyses of data from the National Child Development Study (NCDS). We will make considerable use of graphical representation.

The artificial dataset: a correlational analysis

We have several reasons for including this simulation:

1. To highlight the causal homogeneity assumption and illustrate the ways in which it can mislead.
2. To provide a reminder that correlations can be improved by modelling causal heterogeneity,[8] i.e. by taking account of types of case.
3. To show that linear correlation coefficients of the same size can arise from different *forms* of relationship.
4. To indicate that these different forms of relationship sometimes can be described better and/or more readily in terms of set theoretic models than linear algebraic models.

The invented dataset for our discussion comprises 194 cases, organized into three types of case, differentiated by a respondent's belonging to one of three

---

8   This can be addressed in a regression framework too, of course, but in a correlational rather than a set theoretic manner, i.e. in a way that assumes that 'net effects' of individual variables are meaningful. See Clark et al. (2006) for an interesting relevant discussion of how interaction terms can be used to model *simple* cases of sufficiency and necessity.

social classes of origin. The two other variables are each respondent's (early) cognitive ability and (later) educational achievement. These two variables are scaled from zero to one to facilitate our subsequent comparison of the correlational approach with a set theoretic analysis of these invented data. In constructing the dataset, we have chosen values for ability and achievement for each case, taking social class into account, in order that our analysis of the dataset will be able to demonstrate one particularly important point. This is simply that conventional correlational analyses of data may not bring out the existence of important relations of sufficiency and/or necessity in a dataset. That the relations between the variables in our invented dataset are not only 'pedagogically' useful but also happen to have some affinity with empirical relations in the social world will become clear later in the chapter, when we turn to analyse data from the NCDS.

Our discussion of the invented dataset will be organized around simple scatterplots of achievement by ability. Figure 6.1 is the basic scatterplot of achievement against ability for these 194 cases, with the size of each rhombus indicating the number of cases at any point. A linear regression line has been fitted.

Many elementary textbooks, we think, would describe this, by inspection, as a moderate to strong relationship with possible outliers. The correlation between achievement and ability, with all cases taken together, is 0.601, with unadjusted variance explained therefore of 0.36.[9]

Our next step is to introduce the data on class origin for these cases, i.e. to explore whether there might be causal heterogeneity across our three types. First, though, in Table 6.1 are the means and variances for ability and achievement by class, with class 1 having the highest mean scores for both ability and achievement. The greater variance for ability than for achievement in classes 1 and 3 should, for someone reflecting carefully on these parameters, indicate something important that requires further examination.

Table 6.2 provides the correlations of achievement and ability by class, with the fact that they have each risen above the overall correlation (from 0.601 to 0.739) suggesting that there is some sort of causal heterogeneity across classes needing to be addressed here. A regression of achievement on ability for each

---

9 A visual examination of the residuals plotted against the predicted value of achievement suggests no major problems with the regression model. It is always possible, of course, to play at (descriptive) curve fitting to improve variance explained. If we do this, using SPSS, we can raise the variance explained from 0.36 by using either a power curve (to 0.44) or an S curve (to 0.46).

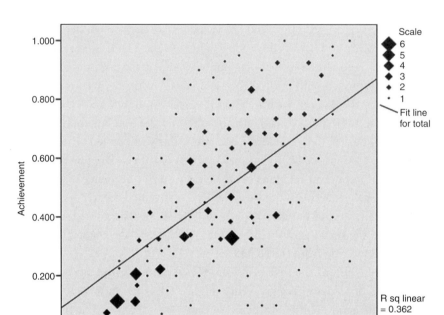

Figure 6.1 All cases (invented data, n = 194)

Table 6.1 Ability and achievement: means and variances by class (for the invented data)

Social class of origin		N	Minimum	Maximum	Mean	Variance
Class 1	Ability	43	.150	.960	.536	.043
	Achievement	43	.350	1.000	.751	.031
Class 2	Ability	78	.150	.870	.497	.033
	Achievement	78	.200	.890	.497	.032
Class 3	Ability	73	.100	.960	.481	.058
	Achievement	73	.050	.800	.303	.035
All cases together	Ability	194	.100	.960	.499	.045
	Achievement	194	.050	1.000	.480	.061

class taken separately would give, for each, an unadjusted variance explained of 0.739 squared, i.e. 0.546, against the figure for the dataset taken as a whole of 0.361. Something clearly was lost when the cases were considered together. Recognizing causal heterogeneity here – i.e. the existence of three types of case – improves the predictive power of the regression models considerably.

Table 6.2 Correlations between achievement and ability by class (for the invented data)

	Pearson correlation	N
Class 1	0.739	43
Class 2	0.739	78
Class 3	0.739	73
All cases	0.601	194

The three coefficients are, by design of our dataset, identical. The question remains, though, what their being identical does or does not signify. Though many introductory textbooks forget to remind their readers of the fact, Pearson's correlation coefficient is designed for linear relationships. Since many relationships are not linear, we cannot simply assume that our identical coefficients indicate that the functional form of the relationship between ability and achievement is of the same nature within each of our three classes.

In this case, does linear correlational modelling capture the functional form of the achievement/ability relationship equally well in the three class contexts? With this question in mind, in Figures 6.2–6.4 we show the scattergrams for the relation on which we are focusing broken down by class (with $y=x$ lines added to facilitate our later discussion of an alternative set theoretic analysis). Those readers familiar with regression modelling will have observed that the three scatterplots in Figures 6.2–6.4 are not of the same type. Indeed, of the three plots of residuals by predicted achievement (not shown here) only that for class 2 shows no problems with the linear regression model. Each of the other two – for classes 1 and 3 – show a pattern[10] 'indicative of "abnormalities" that require corrective attention', to quote a classic SPSS manual (Nie et al. 1975: 342, our emphasis).

Now, an 'abnormality' is only such within some set of modelling assumptions. Rather than address the 'abnormalities' represented by the patterns for classes 1 and 3 within a regression framework, we are now going to turn to an alternative framework – the set theoretic approach – which has an intrinsic

---

10 The plots for classes 1 and 3 have a conical/funnel shape indicating that the variance of the residuals varies with the value of ability, undermining one of the assumptions on which the significance tests used in regression analysis depend (Nie et al. 1975: 341).

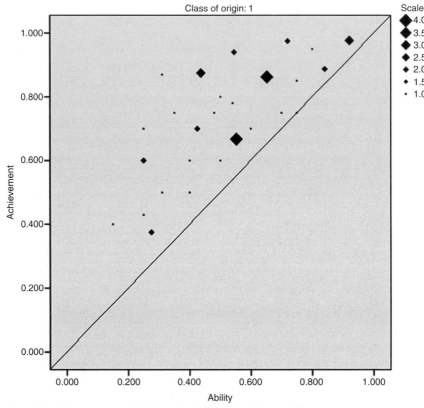

Figure 6.2 Achievement by ability for class 1 (invented data, *n* = 43)

affinity with the relationships between achievement and ability in classes 1 and 3. In doing so, we will, by shifting our underlying mathematical approach from the linear algebraic to the set theoretic, effectively transform what are perceived as 'abnormalities' under a linear correlational description to 'normalities' under a set theoretic one.

Because we are working with scaled, i.e. non-dichotomous data, we will need to employ a fuzzy set theoretic approach. Given the unfamiliarity of this approach we will now interrupt our discussion of these 194 cases in order to introduce the basic features of the set theoretic approach. Having done that, we will return to these three relationships between achievement and ability by class, treating them in terms of fuzzy sets, and reinterpreting them in the set theoretic language of necessary and/or sufficient conditions.

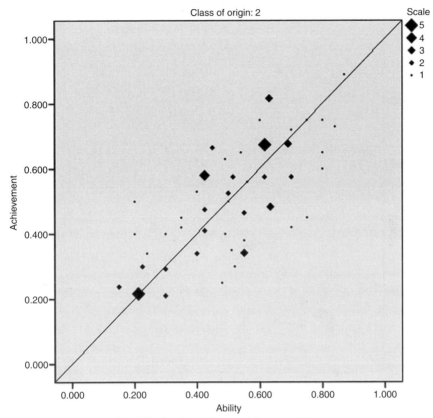

Figure 6.3 Achievement by ability for class 2 (invented data, $n = 78$)

Basics of the set theoretic approach

Conventional sets are not, of course, fuzzy. Cases are either in or out of any set. If we were to dichotomize our two scales we could, for example, create sets of high ability and of high achieving individuals. Forgetting our 194 cases for the moment, let us instead imagine some other artificial datasets for which we have this information. The Venn diagram in Figure 6.5 shows a case of perfect sufficiency (logical and, plausibly, causal). The condition set, that containing cases with high ability, is a subset of the outcome set, containing all cases achieving highly. It is important to note that while high ability is sufficient for high achievement here, it is not necessary. There are members of the set of high achievers who are not of high ability (the paler grey subset). In this imaginary world there are other routes, or potentially causal paths, to high achievement. Of course, in

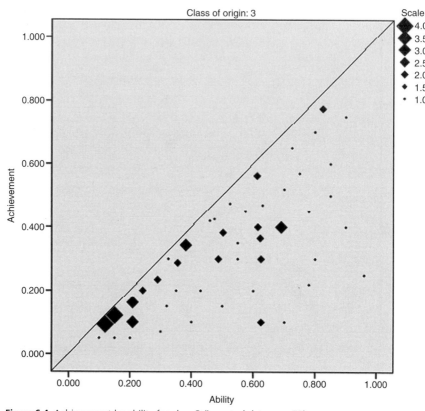

Figure 6.4 Achievement by ability for class 3 (invented data, $n = 73$)

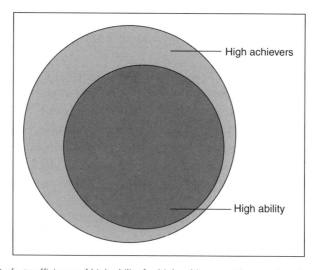

Figure 6.5 Perfect sufficiency of high ability for high achievement in some imaginary world

the real social world there are not likely to be many relationships as simple and apparently deterministic as this. The next example addresses this problem.

Figure 6.6 is only slightly different, but the difference is a crucial one. Here, in another entirely imaginary world, a small proportion of the membership of the high ability set (shown in black) is not contained within the set of high achievers. We do not have a relationship of perfect subsethood and therefore of perfect sufficiency. We do, however, have something that approaches it: what is termed in the literature 'quasi-sufficiency', 'near sufficiency' or 'probabilistic sufficiency'. Clearly, there can be degrees of this. The proportion of the condition set that is contained within the outcome set can be used as a simple measure of the *consistency* of the relationship with one of perfect sufficiency, i.e. of the degree to which perfect sufficiency is approximated (Ragin 2006b).

In one strand of the qualitative tradition of case study – one where causes are still happily discussed – and also in the literature on QCA, a likely next analytic move for Figure 6.6 would be to identify some other causal factor which, combined with high ability, would characterize just these cases that are within the set of high achievers (i.e. the darker grey subset). Perhaps they are of high ability **and** not from a lower class background, for example. We would then have a simple example of a conjunctural or configurational cause: being of high ability and not of lower class origin, conjoined, would be sufficient for the outcome.

While we are examining these diagrams we should also mention the concept of explanatory *coverage* (Ragin 2006b). In Figure 6.5 the proportion of

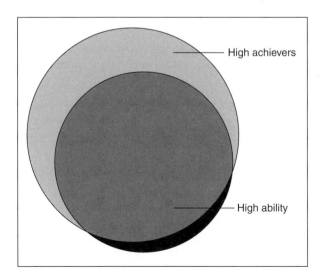

Figure 6.6 Quasi-sufficiency of high ability for high achievement in another imaginary world

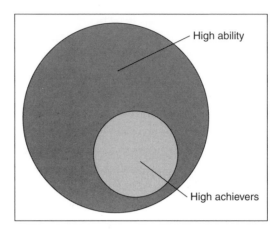

Figure 6.7 Perfect necessity of high ability for high achievement in yet another imaginary world

the high achievers set that is overlapped by the high ability set is clearly the proportion of those with the outcome 'explained' by their having high ability (subject to this claim making theoretical sense). Coverage in the set theoretic approach is analogous to variance explained in the regression approach and can be partitioned similarly in more complicated set theoretic models where there are multiple causal paths to an outcome (Ragin 2008).

We have shown that sufficiency, in the set theoretic context, is equivalent to a subset relationship. The condition set must be a subset (or near subset) of the outcome set. In the case of necessity, this is reversed, and the outcome set must be a subset of the condition set.[11] Figure 6.7 shows a situation in which the high achievers are a subset of those with high ability. Here, high ability is necessary (logically and, plausibly, causally) for high achievement, but it is not sufficient. Again, the analyst might want to explore factors that, combined with high ability, created combinations of conditions that were also sufficient. Being of high ability and from a high social origin might be a candidate configuration.

These subset relationships can also be discussed in the context of crosstabulations of membership in two sets (Boudon 1974b; Ragin 2000). In the tradition of correlational analysis, there is a concern with symmetry. For a high correlation we would want cases mainly in both of cells 2 and 3 of Table 6.3.[12] However,

---

11 In these simple bivariate cases, the proportional measure of the extent to which ability is necessary for achievement is equal to the explanatory coverage of ability for achievement when the sufficiency of ability for achievement is assessed.

12 Or, alternatively, but less realistically, given the example being used, in 1 and 4.

Table 6.3 Membership in the sets 'high achiever' and 'high ability'

	Not high achiever	High achiever
High ability	Cell 1	Cell 2
Not high ability	Cell 3	Cell 4

a concern with sufficiency (or necessity) moves us away from this concern with symmetry. To test whether high ability is sufficient for high achievement, we only need to look at the first row, containing cells 1 and 2. The crucial thing is that there be no (or very few) cases in cell 1, since these contradict the claim that being of high ability is sufficient (or quasi-sufficient) for high achievement. Similarly, for necessity of high ability for high achievement, we only need to look at cells 2 and 4, and we don't want to see cases in cell 4. If we were testing for joint sufficiency and necessity of high ability for achievement, we would, of course, want to see no (or few) cases in cells 1 *and* 4.

So far, we have discussed crisp sets – those where a case simply is either in or out of a set, i.e. whose set membership is numerically given as either one or zero. Those familiar with the history of mathematics will not be surprised to learn that mathematicians have developed an account of sets, usually termed fuzzy sets, where membership is allowed to vary between these limits of zero and full membership. An example often used to illustrate partial membership is that of adulthood (Kosko 1994). While most judges would agree that an age of 10 would rule out adulthood (giving a membership score of 0) and one of 30 would rule it in (giving a membership score of 1), there would be much less certainty about the age range 15–21. Here it would seem inappropriate to allocate a score of either zero or one – the only possibilities available in the crisp set context. In fuzzy set based descriptions of cases a score of 0.9 might be used for the 20-year-old to indicate almost full, but not quite full, membership of the set of 'adults'. A 19-year-old might be allocated a score of 0.8.[13]

The operations of conventional set theory (intersection, union, negation, subsethood, etc.) all have equivalents in fuzzy set theory (Goertz 2006; Ragin 2000; Smithson and Verkuilen 2006). There is considerable ongoing debate

---

13 A crucial difference from an interval scale measure for age should be noted. All ages over some threshold will here receive a score of one, indicating full membership of the set. From the set theoretic perspective, differences over this threshold are not relevant ones. Whether this calibration decision is actually appropriate in any particular context is a matter, of course, of the relevant kinds that exist in the social world and of their causal properties.

within mathematics about the best way to define some of these operators in the fuzzy set context. We will use some commonly agreed and fairly intuitive versions. For example, the simplest way of assessing fuzzy subsethood uses an arithmetic approach. If the membership of a case in set A is less than or equal to its membership in set B, then this case passes the test for fuzzy subsethood (also called fuzzy inclusion). The proportion of cases *with non-zero membership* in the condition set A passing such a test can be used as a simple test of consistency with a relationship of sufficiency for some outcome set B, i.e. of the degree to which perfect sufficiency is approximated. To begin with, we will employ this test for subsethood but, later in the chapter, having noted its limitations, will use a more sophisticated measure (for a fuller account of the development of more complex measures of consistency with sufficiency and necessity in Ragin's work, see Cooper 2005b). We will introduce other definitions as and when required.

We will now return to our 194 invented cases. From this point we will assume that our 0–1 scales for ability and achievement have arisen from a fuzzy calibration of these two factors, i.e. they are measures of partial membership in two fuzzy sets.[14]

The artificial dataset: a fuzzy set theoretic analysis

First, we need to look again at the scatterplots (Figures 6.2–6.4). Simple inspection shows that the three graphs by class have different forms. Figure 6.2, for class 1, has all cases above or on the diagonal $y = x$ line and is usually called an upper triangular plot (Ragin 2000). Figure 6.4, for class 3, has all cases below or on the $y = x$ line and is usually called a lower triangular plot. Figure 6.3, for class 2, is characterized by a degree of reflective symmetry around the $y = x$ line.

What, within a set theoretic approach, do these features indicate? We have already explained the simple arithmetic test for fuzzy subsethood. If we take Figure 6.2 for class 1, we can see that, for each case, the membership in ability is less than or equal to its membership in achievement. In fuzzy set terms, the

---

14 In employing correlation coefficients and, later, the second more sophisticated set theoretic measure of consistency we are implicitly assuming these are interval measures (see Smithson and Verkuilen 2006, for more discussion of measurement properties and fuzzy sets).

ability set is a subset of the achievement set. Ability is sufficient for achievement. More intuitively, across the whole range of ability, a case's partial membership in the ability set is an effective floor below which its membership in the achievement set doesn't fall. However, ability is not necessary for achievement. This must be so, within the rules of fuzzy set theory, since the relevant test cannot be passed (for necessity, y scores must be lower to or equal to x scores). More intuitively, this can be seen by noting that high membership scores in achievement can be gained – in this imaginary world – with fairly low membership scores in ability. The upper triangular plot represents, then, a sufficient but not necessary relationship. In this imaginary world, there must be other causal paths to high achievement than simply ability alone (involving, one might speculate, such enabling conjoined factors as private tuition, private schooling, support from highly educated parents, etc.).

Similar reasoning shows that Figure 6.4, for class 3, represents a necessary but not sufficient relationship. Here membership in ability sets a ceiling for achievement, but there are cases where achievement does not seem to reflect ability as strongly as in others. Here, we can speculate, there must be other conjoined constraining factors that explain these cases' positions away from the diagonal (perhaps such conjoined constraining factors as poverty, etc.).

Clearly, we invented our 194 cases so that these two graphs would show perfect triangular plots. The simple arithmetic index of consistency with sufficiency (the proportion of cases with ability less than or equal to achievement) has its maximum value of 1 for class 1, and the analogous measure of necessity here is near 0. The pattern is reversed for class 3. What about class 2 (Figure 6.3)? This looks more like a textbook scatterplot, of course. The simple measure of sufficiency is 0.59 and that of necessity is 0.54.[15] Even allowing quasi-sufficiency, we would not want to argue that, for class 2, ability is either sufficient or necessary for achievement. It might be, of course, when conjoined with some additional factors, but we have not designed our dataset set to explore such complexities. We can, however, note that the relation for class 2 is more-or-less symmetric. These results, together with those for the 194 cases taken as one group, are set out in Table 6.4.[16]

---

15 Given some cases are on the $y = x$ line, these don't add to one.

16 An analysis using a more sophisticated measure of consistency (Ragin 2008: 52) produces the same pattern of results, though, depending on where thresholds for quasi-sufficiency are set, can allow class 2 and the overall sample to be described as showing quasi-sufficiency and quasi-necessity. We return to this later in the chapter.

Table 6.4 Set theoretic testing of the ability => achievement relationship (*n*=194, invented data)

Simple inclusion algorithm	Sufficiency	Necessity	Result: ability is . . .
All classes together	0.459	0.598	Neither sufficient nor necessary
Class 1	1.000	0.023	Sufficient but not necessary
Class 2	0.590	0.539	Neither sufficient nor necessary
Class 3	0.000	1.000	Necessary but not sufficient

By presenting the analysis separately by class – in order to bring out the phenomenon of causal heterogeneity – we have moved the configurational nature of this analysis temporarily offstage. However, an examination of Table 6.4 allows us to write this simple example of a configurational set theoretic equation concerning sufficiency:

$$CLASS\_1*ABILITY => ACHIEVEMENT$$

where capital letters indicate membership in the sets and the asterisk indicates set intersection. Ability, then, is sufficient for achievement – in this imaginary world – just when it is conjoined with membership in class 1.

We created this example to illustrate an important point. A correlational approach, because it assumes linearity as a default, is not well-suited to describe relationships, causal or otherwise, in terms of necessity and sufficiency. Indeed, we have shown how three identical correlation coefficients can be associated with three different forms of set theoretic relationship.

There are, however, some limitations associated with the simple measure of subsethood we have employed up to this point. Consider the data in Figure 6.4. We can see that a small change in the fuzzy set calibration of the achievement variable could have the effect of moving cases, systematically, either upwards or downwards. If a change in calibration were to move cases upwards, we would see a rise in the index for sufficiency from its current value of zero (and a fall in the index for necessity). The degree of sensitivity to calibration is clearly a weakness of the simple measure of inclusion, especially for cases near the $y = x$ line. A similar point can be made about measurement error for cases near the $y = x$ line (Ragin 2000).[17]

---

17 Systematic errors would be particularly damaging. Changes in calibration might have a similar effect to these.

A further point can be noted by considering Figure 6.2. Here, were all of the cases to have smaller achievement scores (but not small enough to take them below the $y = x$ line) then our simple proportional measure of sufficiency would remain unchanged. A correlational measure would, of course, change since it, unlike the simple subsethood measure, takes account of distances from the means of y and x. Now, it could be argued that the lack of any change in the index of sufficiency is not a problem here, since both the original Figure 6.2 and the imagined changed Figure 6.2 both meet the formal requirements for perfect sufficiency embodied in the simple subsethood measure. We have some sympathy for this view. However, it is also the case that our intuitions tell us distances would matter were we to consider a set of cases similar to those in Figure 6.2 except that some cases were below the diagonal. Comparing two below-the-diagonal cases that wouldn't count positively for the simple measure of sufficiency with x and y values say of (0.70, 0.65) and (0.70, 0.20), we might prefer a measure that lets the second count more strongly against a sufficiency relation than the first. A variety of measures that do, in this sense, take account of distances exist in the literature (Cooper 2005b; Ragin 2000, 2006b; Smithson and Verkuilen 2006). We will briefly explain the rationale for the one we intend to use later in the chapter in addition to the simple measure employed thus far.

Consider again the two crisp sets in Figure 6.6. We pointed out that the proportion of the condition set that is contained within the outcome set provides a simple (and intuitive) measure of the degree to which high ability is sufficient for high achievement. We are actually focusing here on the relative sizes of two sets, one the intersection, or overlap, of the set of high achieving cases and the set of high ability cases (in darker grey), the other the set of high ability cases (the black and darker grey subsets taken together). Taking the condition and outcome sets, more generally, to be x and y respectively, the measure of the consistency with sufficiency we have used so far is formally:

$$\frac{|X \cap Y|}{|X|} \tag{2}$$

where $\cap$ indicates set intersection and the double bars the cardinality or size of the sets in the numerator and denominator.

Basically, via the numerator and denominator here, we compare the sizes of two sets. What we want is a fuzzy set analogue of this measure. In the crisp set context, we get our measure of the size of a set by counting the number of members in it. Clearly this won't work for a fuzzy set, where cases have partial membership. An 'obvious' intuitive measure of the size of a fuzzy set is given by summing the partial membership for all cases in a set. Formally, if m_x represents the degree of membership of each case i in the set x, a measure of the size of x is given, if we sum over all the members i of the set, by:

$$\sum_i m_x \tag{3}$$

This provides us with a way of calculating the denominator of expression (2). To calculate the numerator, we need, in addition, a fuzzy analogue of crisp set intersection. A commonly employed (but not the only[18]) operation for the intersection of two (or more) fuzzy sets involves taking the minimum of the cases' membership in each set. Ragin (2000) argues this definition of intersection is consistent with everyday experience and provides an illustrative example:

> . . . Consider the set of people who are young *and* blond. An excess of blondness cannot compensate for very low membership in the set of young people, just as an excess of youth or 'youngness' cannot compensate for very low membership in the set of people with blond hair. In either case, the resulting membership score in the set of people who are young *and* blond is ruled by the minimum. (Ragin 2000: 173)

Taking this approach (see Ragin 2006b), we have, for evaluating the fuzzy set sufficiency of x for y, the following expression for the consistency of the relation with one of sufficiency, where the intersection in the numerator is operationalized as the minimum of m_x and m_y for each case:

$$\frac{\sum_i m_{x \cap y}}{\sum_i m_x} \tag{4}$$

This expression does, of course, give the conventional result for two crisp sets since, in this case, the two summations reduce to counting the members

---

18   See Smithson and Verkuilen (2006) for some others.

Table 6.5 Set theoretic testing of the ability =>
achievement relationship: using the overlap
algorithm (n=194, invented data)

	Sufficiency	Necessity
All classes together	0.825	0.858
Class 1	1.000	0.713
Class 2	0.898	0.898
Class 3	0.630	1.000

of the two sets. A parallel argument gives us this fuzzy set expression for coverage[19]:

$$\frac{\sum_i m_{x \cap y}}{\sum_i m_y} \tag{5}$$

The consistency results produced by these expressions tend to be higher than those produced by the simple measure used earlier, since cases that contribute nothing to the first contribute something to the result here. For example, considering sufficiency, the case (0.6, 0.5) contributes nothing to the simple measure (since x is not less than or equal to y) but it does contribute something when expression (4) is used. In this respect, these measures partially address the problems associated with changes in calibration and/or measurement error for cases near the $y = x$ line.

The results of using expressions (4) and (5) to analyse the invented data are shown in Table 6.5. The *pattern* of results is the same as that when the simple measure was employed (Table 6.4). However, given the fairly high results for necessity for class 1 and for sufficiency for class 3, we clearly would want to set correspondingly high thresholds for quasi-sufficiency and quasi-necessity when verbally interpreting such tables. Our focus in this chapter will mainly be on the patterns of the consistency indices within tables, rather than on absolute values.

What about real social data? How might we apply these ideas and techniques to bring out any complex asymmetric causality that characterizes the social world? In the next section we will provide an illustration, drawing on

---

19 Note that, for two sets, expression (5) is equivalent to an index of the degree to which y is necessary for x.

the NCDS. In the remainder of this chapter, we will employ both the simple and the sophisticated measures of subsethood.

Social class and educational achievement in the NCDS: an illustration of the set theoretic analytic approach

Our purpose here is illustrative. We compare the merits of set theoretic and correlational descriptions of the ability/achievement relationship across types of case, with the latter appearing as conjunctions of features. The relationship between these variables seems likely, given the claims of such sociologists as Boudon and Bourdieu, to vary, non-linearly, across types of classed and gendered cases. As we have shown above, a set theoretic approach should be an appropriate and fruitful way to elucidate any such causal complexity.[20] Specifically, we assess the set theoretic quasi-sufficiency and quasi-necessity of ability for achievement over types of case defined by configurations of the conditions, for each case, of sex, father's class and grandfathers' class. We demonstrate that causal heterogeneity characterizes the ability/achievement relationship, and that it has the same form as that described for our invented dataset.

Data and variables

The NCDS is an ongoing longitudinal study of individuals born in one week in March 1958. We use a sample of 5,272 cases from the NCDS with no missing values on the variables we employ here.[21] Measured ability (variable n920) is

---

20 In this discussion we are, of course, using 'summarizing' variables. The actual mechanisms and/or processes by which 'class' produces its causal effects are not our focus in this chapter. Instead, we are attending to competing forms of description that might have greater or less affinity with the sorts of regularities, or tendencies towards them, that underlying causal mechanisms and processes produce.

21 We have omitted members of the military for father's class. We have also omitted the few cases where the ability score is given as zero. As is common in analyses of these data, our sample is much smaller than the original cohort, partly through attrition, partly because of missing values on our chosen variables.

taken at age 11. The measure of achievement, highest qualifications obtained, is taken at age 33 and includes both academic and vocational qualifications (derived variable HQUAL). Because of the ways each grandfather's class was recorded we will be using the categories of the Registrar General's scheme for these, but we will be using an approximation to Goldthorpe's class scheme for the respondent's father's[22] class (at the respondent's age of 11). Given the illustrative nature of the analysis here, this mixing of categories, though undesirable, is of no consequence, we believe, for our arguments. We have, of course, to calibrate, as fuzzy sets, the original distribution of scores for the measures of highest qualification and ability. For highest qualifications we have used the calibration employed for another purpose in Cooper (2005a) which ranges from a membership of zero for no qualification to one for a degree or higher.[23] For measured ability, we have employed a very simple calibration (a linear transformation) which just rescales the original scores (0–80) to 0–1.[24]

Causal heterogeneity: how does the ability/achievement relation vary by class background?

Before presenting evidence of causal heterogeneity in these data, we provide the summary picture for all of the cases taken together. Figure 6.8 shows the distribution of achievement by ability for the 5,272 cases, with the size of each rhombus indicating the number of cases at any point. A linear regression line has been fitted. The correlation coefficient is 0.534, with variance explained of 0.285. The scatterplot looks, at this global level, like a textbook example of a linear relation with a moderately sized correlation coefficient.

---

22 There are no data on grandmothers. In addition we use paternal class for the family to avoid the loss of many more cases that would arise were we to add a maternal measure.

23 This is calibrated as a fuzzy set thus: No qualification: 0; CSE 2–5/equivalent to NVQ1: 0.17; O Level/equivalent to NVQ2: 0.42; A Level/equivalent to NVQ3: 0.67; Higher qualification NVQ4: 0.83; Degree/higher NVQ5, 6: 1.0.

24 Cooper (2005a) used a more complex calibration in line with the particular purposes of that paper. Here, our purpose is to illustrate the potential of the set theoretic approach as transparently as possible and, for this reason, we have chosen this simple approach. On the crucial importance of calibration, see Ragin (2006a, 2008).

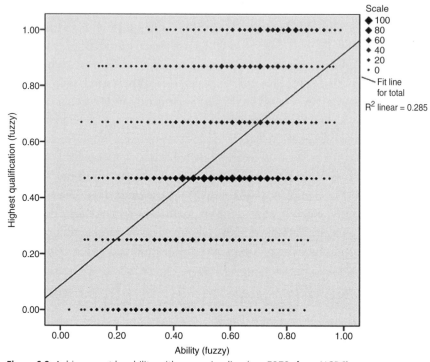

Figure 6.8 Achievement by ability with regression line (*n* = 5272, from NCDS)

We can begin our exploration of heterogeneity with a hypothetical argument about likely relations. If we consider two contrasting sets of cases (i.e. configurations of factors), males with a class of origin at the top of the social class distribution who also had grandfathers towards the top of this distribution, and then, by contrast, females who had fathers at the bottom and grandfathers towards the bottom of the distribution, we can hypothesize, from the literature on class, gender and schooling in the relevant period, that ability might have tended towards being a sufficient condition for achievement for the former group (but perhaps not a necessary one) and towards being a necessary condition for the latter group (but perhaps not a sufficient one). As explained earlier, if this is so, we should expect an upper triangular plot of achievement against ability in the first case and a lower triangular plot in the second.

Taking these two subsets identified for our initial exploration, the two contrasting graphs in Figures 6.9 and 6.10 show the relevant scatterplots. In Figure 6.9 the cases are 62 males whose fathers were in Goldthorpe's class 1

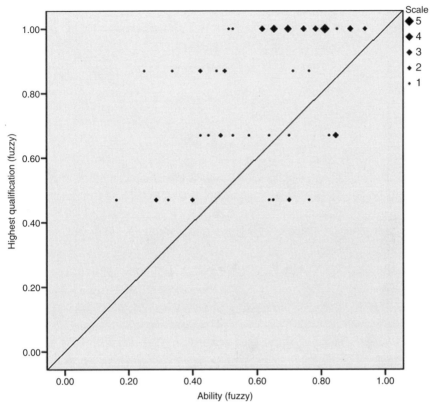

Figure 6.9 62 males from high class origins

(the upper service class) and whose grandfathers were both in either Registrar General's social class I or II. In Figure 6.10 the cases are the 100 females whose fathers were in Goldthorpe's class 7 (the semi and unskilled manual working class) and whose grandfathers were both in RG class IV or V. The correlation between achievement and ability for the 62 males with the configuration capturing higher social origins here is 0.466 and for the 100 females with lower origins it is 0.481. These linear measures of the relationship suggest no important difference. However, an inspection of the scatterplots suggests that there is an important difference and that it is as predicted, with tendencies to triangular plots being clear to see.

We cannot, of course, expect perfect triangular plots to turn up in an exploration of relations in the social world. Why not? The adequacy of the fuzzy set calibrations will be a contributory factor, as well as measurement error, plus the fact that this is a very simple model omitting many factors, and also the role of

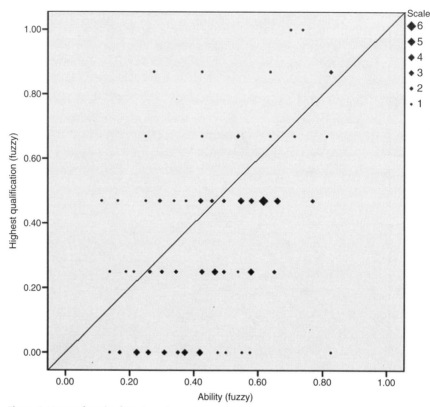

Figure 6.10 100 females from low class origins

'chance' in social life, however understood. Nevertheless, Figure 6.9 tends to the form of an upper triangular plot (sufficient, but not necessary) and Figure 6.10 to the form of a lower triangular plot (necessary, but not sufficient). If we calculate the simple fuzzy inclusion indices[25] of consistency with sufficiency and necessity we obtain, for Figure 6.9, values of 0.839 and 0.161 respectively. For Figure 6.10, the pattern is reversed, and we obtain 0.280 and 0.730. These values (on a 0–1 scale, recall) bear out the results of the visual inspection. If we employ the more sophisticated measures of subsethood, we obtain, respectively, figures of 0.954 and 0.742 for the 62 cases and 0.615 and 0.855 for the 100 cases. Taking account

---

25 It is important to note that these are calculated only for cases with non-zero membership in the condition set (sufficiency) or in the outcome set (necessity) respectively, while the correlation coefficient is calculated for all cases. Since we have omitted the few cases with zero scores on the ability measure, we actually have here the same *n* for both analyses of sufficiency.

of the higher values that arise from the use of the more sophisticated measure, we can see here a pattern of quasi-sufficiency and quasi-necessity being reversed as we move from the higher class males to the lower class females.

Summarizing, the clear *tendencies* are that

- For the configuration HIGH_GRANDFATHERS'_CLASS*HIGH_FATHER'S_CLASS* MALE, ABILITY is sufficient, but not necessary, for later ACHIEVEMENT.
- For the configuration LOW_GRANDFATHERS'_CLASS*LOW_FATHER'S_CLASS*male, ABILITY is necessary, but not sufficient, for later ACHIEVEMENT.

Before moving on, we can note that a possibly fruitful next stage here would be to zoom in on the cases in order to explore what it is about those in Figure 6.9, for example, that puts some on one side of the sufficiency line and some on the necessity side. To some extent very individual factors will be involved (e.g. a bout of bad health, parental disputes, etc.) but there are also likely to be factors that split these 62 cases into meaningful subtypes (secondary school type and/or social composition of school attended, etc.). An issue that arises very quickly – and one that tends to be glossed over in regression studies – is that of limited diversity (Ragin 2006a). Even with large samples, a study employing more than a handful of factors soon encounters cells with few or even zero cases.

Any such zooming-in, we should note, does not take the form of seeking to control for other independent variables in the way the 'net effects'/'average effects' regression approach does. Instead, it further specifies the nature of a type of case by expanding the configurational description or specification of its type. Here, the factors in the configuration are – subject to theoretical meaningfulness – seen as operating conjuncturally rather than additively to produce their effects. For example, a well-off grandfather may have helped with the fees necessary to put a son of moderate measured ability who had failed to win a selective grammar school place through a private school. Here, the grandfather's decision may have acted as an (enabling) switch, moving the child from a non-selective secondary modern school future where academic examinations may not have been available at all to one where they were, and hence *allowing* ability to produce its (perhaps moderate) effects.

We have obviously, for illustrative purposes, chosen two clearly contrasting examples. We can note, in passing, that from the point of view of theory development and testing, this is often an appropriate strategy (Seawright and Gerring 2008). These two graphs would count against any simple theory that claimed that ability operated causally in the same manner across contexts of

Table 6.6 The ability => achievement relation within types defined by paternal class origin

Goldthorpe paternal class	N	Correlations	Consistency			
			A	B	C	D
1	608	0.444**	0.674	0.326	0.900	0.801
2	902	0.479**	0.577	0.426	0.869	0.825
3	513	0.458**	0.522	0.478	0.825	0.820
4	313	0.536**	0.415	0.585	0.791	0.848
5	331	0.508**	0.447	0.553	0.787	0.842
6	1651	0.484**	0.460	0.544	0.778	0.824
7	954	0.500**	0.376	0.627	0.718	0.830

** Correlation is significant at the 0.01 level (2-tailed).

* Correlation is significant at the 0.05 level (2-tailed).

A: the simple measure of the degree to which ability is sufficient for achievement; B: the simple measure of the degree to which ability is necessary for achievement; C: the sophisticated measure of the degree to which ability is sufficient for achievement; D: the sophisticated measure of the degree to which ability is necessary for achievement.

social class and gender. The idea of an 'average effect' of ability on achievement (though it can be calculated) is not apparently a very useful one here. Having noted this, we can, without producing endless graphs, use the indices of consistency with sufficiency and necessity to explore the achievement/ability relation over various types of case, setting them alongside standard Pearson correlation coefficients. We will do this in a way that illustrates the zooming-in idea.

Table 6.6 focuses initially on a fairly crude typology – just considering cases by paternal class of origin. We can see that the correlations vary little by class but that the simple fuzzy inclusion measure of consistency with sufficiency varies a lot. While, at this level of specification of the typology, none of the consistency measures is close to the 1.0 that would indicate perfect sufficiency, there is a clear pattern, with class 1 being nearest to this upper limit and class 7 furthest away. A similar, though reversed, pattern characterizes the measures of quasi-necessity (unsurprisingly, given the way these two simple measures are calculated[26]). Turning to the more sophisticated measures, we see a similar monotonic pattern for sufficiency, but nothing very clear for necessity. To bring out what pattern there is, we might note that, were we to set a threshold for these sophisticated measures for quasi-sufficiency and quasi-necessity of 0.800, then ability would be quasi-sufficient for achievement in classes 1, 2 and 3 and quasi-necessary in all.

---

26   Unless there are cases on the $y = x$ line, the simple measures of sufficiency and necessity will sum to 1.

Table 6.7 The ability => achievement relation within types defined jointly by paternal class origin and sex

Sex	Goldthorpe paternal class	N	Correlations	Consistency			
				A	B	C	D
Male	1	301	0.463**	0.720	0.279	0.915	0.788
Male	2	432	0.475**	0.634	0.368	0.887	0.799
Male	3	254	0.450**	0.618	0.382	0.858	0.785
Male	4	166	0.495**	0.506	0.494	0.811	0.811
Male	5	179	0.582**	0.525	0.475	0.828	0.821
Male	6	792	0.511**	0.548	0.455	0.823	0.798
Male	7	457	0.504**	0.431	0.569	0.754	0.807
Female	1	307	0.438**	0.629	0.371	0.885	0.815
Female	2	470	0.501**	0.523	0.479	0.853	0.850
Female	3	259	0.484**	0.429	0.571	0.793	0.860
Female	4	147	0.613**	0.313	0.687	0.769	0.894
Female	5	152	0.451**	0.355	0.645	0.743	0.869
Female	6	859	0.479**	0.380	0.626	0.739	0.851
Female	7	497	0.511**	0.326	0.680	0.687	0.853

** Correlation is significant at the 0.01 level (2-tailed).

* Correlation is significant at the 0.05 level (2-tailed).

A: the simple measure of the degree to which ability is sufficient for achievement; B: the simple measure of the degree to which ability is necessary for achievement; C: the sophisticated measure of the degree to which ability is sufficient for achievement; D: the sophisticated measure of the degree to which ability is necessary for achievement.

On the assumption that there is still likely to be considerable causal heterogeneity within each of these seven categories, we next aim to reduce this further by adding additional factors to the one (father's class) that gives us our types in this table. Theoretically obvious candidates include sex and grandfathers' class. Let us start by adding sex to give types characterized by father's class and sex (Table 6.7). Once again the variability in the correlation measures is small, especially in comparison with the simple measures of consistency with sufficiency and necessity. More importantly in respect of the latter, having increased the degree of specification of our analysis, we now see both increases and decreases beyond the upper and lower limits we found when just class was included in the analysis. For males from class 1 families, the simple index of consistency with sufficiency is 0.721; for females from class 7 it is 0.326. The ranges of values for the sophisticated measures are also stretched in comparison with Table 6.6. Looking at the values over 0.800 in the final two columns of Table 6.7 gives a good impression of the way sufficiency and necessity are approached differentially over class and gender types.

The final step we will take here is to add grandfathers' class to our typology. Let us assume that having both grandfathers in RG classes I or II is likely to have provided various cultural and financial resources to the respondent, some directly, some via his or her parents. Service class fathers, for example, will differ in important ways as a function of their own class origin. We now have cases defined in terms of the factors father's class, sex and whether both grandfathers were in RG class I or II. Even with the grandparental generation treated dichotomously, this step generates a table with 28 rows[27] (Table 6.8). The problem of limited diversity is immediately apparent in Table 6.8. We would not want to draw strong conclusions from rows with very small numbers (though an in-depth examination of these unusual cases might, if possible errors of measurement or data entry could be ruled out, generate interesting insights). We now have, at this level of resolution, a row (in grey) representing the 62 cases discussed earlier (see Figure 6.9) with a consistency with sufficiency on the simple measure of 0.839. On the sophisticated measure, this becomes 0.954. For these cases – defined by class over two generations and gender – measured ability is close to being sufficient for later achievement. This particular sufficiency relation could be written, in set theoretic notation, to indicate that, for the configuration FATHER'S_CLASS_1 * GRANDFATHERS'_CLASS_RGI_ OR_RGII * MALE, ABILITY is quasi-sufficient for ACHIEVEMENT.

Inspection of the table shows other interesting relationships. In particular, several other sets of cases, of both sexes, have fairly high indices of consistency with sufficiency. It is also possible to see configurations of class and gender where ability is far from being sufficient for achievement (even though our splitting of grandfathers towards the top end of the social structure will tend to dilute such relationships). For example, for females from paternal social class 7, not having both grandfathers in RG class I or II (the final row), the index of consistency is just 0.327 on the simple measure and 0.684 on the sophisticated measure. For these cases, ability was clearly not sufficient for later achievement, though it can be seen to have approached being quasi-necessary. We could present a similar tabular analysis for other categories of the grandparental class factor but won't, for reasons of space. The crucial

---

27   Within it, of course, we would expect the rows where GFs_I_II=1 to be more homogeneous that those where GFs_I_II=0.

Table 6.8 The ability => achievement relation within types defined jointly by paternal class origin, grandfathers' class and sex

Sex	Grandfathers both in class RG I or II	Goldthorpe paternal class	N	Correlations	Consistency			
					A	B	C	D
Male	Yes	1	62	0.466**	0.839	0.161	0.954	0.742
Male	Yes	2	42	0.509**	0.691	0.310	0.924	0.798
Male	Yes	3	10	0.387	0.600	0.400	0.900	0.803
Male	Yes	4	38	0.479**	0.605	0.395	0.908	0.784
Male	Yes	5	7	-0.262	0.571	0.429	0.815	0.850
Male	Yes	6	17	0.559*	0.647	0.353	0.785	0.822
Male	Yes	7	9	0.538	0.778	0.222	0.928	0.583
Male	No	1	239	0.478**	0.690	0.310	0.905	0.801
Male	No	2	390	0.470**	0.628	0.374	0.883	0.799
Male	No	3	244	0.450**	0.619	0.381	0.856	0.785
Male	No	4	128	0.597**	0.477	0.523	0.780	0.821
Male	No	5	172	0.597**	0.523	0.477	0.829	0.819
Male	No	6	775	0.510**	0.546	0.457	0.824	0.798
Male	No	7	448	0.512**	0.424	0.576	0.751	0.814

Contd.

Table 6.8 Contd

Sex	Grandfathers both in class RG I or II	Goldthorpe paternal class	N	Correlations	Consistency			
					A	B	C	D
Female	Yes	1	61	0.343**	0.656	0.344	0.922	0.831
Female	Yes	2	58	0.505**	0.672	0.328	0.911	0.851
Female	Yes	3	12	0.588*	0.833	0.167	0.947	0.784
Female	Yes	4	37	0.390*	0.351	0.649	0.826	0.889
Female	Yes	5	3	0.822	0.667	0.333	0.982	0.722
Female	Yes	6	18	0.384	0.611	0.389	0.858	0.708
Female	Yes	7	10	0.738*	0.300	0.700	0.834	0.875
Female	No	1	246	0.438**	0.622	0.378	0.875	0.811
Female	No	2	412	0.489**	0.502	0.500	0.844	0.850
Female	No	3	247	0.465**	0.409	0.591	0.784	0.866
Female	No	4	110	0.655**	0.300	0.700	0.749	0.896
Female	No	5	149	0.459**	0.349	0.651	0.738	0.873
Female	No	6	841	0.484**	0.375	0.631	0.736	0.855
Female	No	7	487	0.504**	0.327	0.680	0.684	0.852

** Correlation is significant at the 0.01 level (2-tailed).

* Correlation is significant at the 0.05 level (2-tailed).

A: the simple measure of the degree to which ability is sufficient for achievement; B: the simple measure of the degree to which ability is necessary for achievement; C: the sophisticated measure of the degree to which ability is sufficient for achievement; D: the sophisticated measure of the degree to which ability is necessary for achievement.

point to note is that the correlation coefficients in Table 6.8 do not provide the insights provided by the set theoretic indices of sufficiency and necessity.

We should add that, in the same way as a regression equation can be written to summarize the overall patterns of relationship between a dependent variable and some 'independent' variables in a dataset, a set theoretic equation can also be written to summarize those configurations of conditions that are sufficient for some outcome (with a form similar to the example we used earlier from Mahoney and Goertz's paper; see Ragin 2000). We have no space to explain and illustrate this here, but present some examples in the next chapter (for a further worked example for the dataset analysed here, see Cooper and Glaesser 2009).

Conclusion

The debate that arose concerning Bhaskar's (1975, 1979) realist accounts of both natural and social science (e.g. Pawson 1989; Ron 2002) was, in part, focused on the perennially important issue of the role regularities play in constructing causal accounts. From the perspective of early Bhaskarian realism, regularities were neither sufficient nor necessary for the establishment of knowledge concerning causal/generative mechanisms. They are not sufficient, if only because correlations are not always causal in nature. They are not necessary, if only because complex interacting mechanisms in open systems can lead to the blocking of causal tendencies. These are sound arguments. However, it is important not to throw the baby out with the bathwater. Regularities can appear in open systems, though they may be less than perfect and may be complex in nature. They can also be made visible in closed systems, such as those artificially closed systems produced in experiments (Bhaskar 1975; Cartwright 1999). In the analysis of social survey data, they can be expected to be more readily found and more adequately described when causal heterogeneity is correctly identified and taken into account, i.e. when types of case are specified, as we have argued here. In 'establishing the phenomena', to use the useful phrase Goldthorpe (2007) borrows from Merton (1987), an approach via quasi-sufficiency and quasi-necessity seems likely to be a very useful addition to our armoury. Here, in illustration of this claim, by looking at relationships within the context of configurationally defined types, we aimed to create a set of relatively closed systems in each of which the specific form of the relationship between ability and achievement could be better discerned.

In open systems, since it is always likely that several causal processes will interact to produce the observed relationships in a dataset, the social scientist clearly needs special tools to make visible the regularities associated with any particular subset of variables. The standard technique for producing/analysing the regularities arising from the action of any particular factor, net of the effects of other factors, is regression, built on the basis of correlation. Ron (2002) has argued that realists should not, contrary to the claims of some, underestimate the usefulness of this set of techniques. We agree, especially if what is wanted is knowledge of the size of various average effects. On the other hand, the question must be asked, is regression-based modelling, built on the assumption of causally independent variables and linear algebraic correlation, likely to have a greater or lesser affinity with the complex causality that characterizes the social world than the set theoretic approach, built on the assumption of conjunctural causation and the concept of sufficient and/or necessary conditions? We are suggesting that, in some contexts, including that of the sociology of class and educational achievement, the answer may be that correlation-based regression models have a lesser affinity than set theoretic ones.

Pawson (2008) has recently stressed what is common to some uses of correlational methods (by 'sucessionists') and set theoretic methods (by 'configurationists') – a failure to focus on generative mechanisms in their search for the answers to 'why?' questions. He recommends a focus on such mechanisms, as does Goldthorpe (2007) along with many others. We are sympathetic to Pawson's position. However, we would argue that in 'establishing the phenomena' and in the development and testing of theories that are themselves formulated – or can be appropriately reformulated – in the language of INUS conditions, of complex relations of sufficiency and necessity,[28] the set theoretic approach is likely to be sometimes more useful than regression modelling for describing and/or testing empirical consequences, simply because the functional forms it employs have a greater affinity with the claims of such theories. Complex causality in the world requires appropriately complex models.[29] The

---

28 Or of quasi-sufficiency and quasi-necessity, concepts which seem to echo Goldthorpe's (2007) focus on 'probabilistic' regularities.

29 We have not, of course, considered other analytic methods capable of addressing complex relations that don't employ a set theoretic approach. Log-linear analysis is an obvious example. Here one loses the dependent/independent variable distinction but gains, over the current state of development of set theoretic models, well-understood methods for significance testing.

discussion earlier of our two examples, one invented, one real, was intended to provide some arguments and evidence for this claim.

References

Abell, P. (1971) *Model Building in Sociology,* London: Weidenfeld & Nicolson.

Abbott, A. (2001) *Time Matters,* Chicago: Chicago University Press.

Bhaskar, R. (1975) *A Realist Theory of Science,* Brighton: Harvester Press.

— (1979) *The Possibility of Naturalism,* Brighton: Harvester Press.

Boudon, R. (1974a) *Education, Opportunity and Social Inequality,* New York: Wiley.

— (1974b) *The Logic of Sociological Explanation,* Harmondsworth: Penguin Education.

Bourdieu, P. (1974) 'Cultural and social reproduction', in R. Brown (ed.) *Knowledge, Education and Cultural Change,* London: Tavistock.

Byrne, D. S. (2002) *Interpreting Quantitative Data,* London: Sage.

Cartwright, N. (1999) *The Dappled World,* Cambridge: Cambridge University Press.

Clark, W. R., Gilligan, M. J. and Golder, M. (2006) 'A simple multivariate test for asymmetric hypotheses', *Political Analysis,* 14, 3, pp. 311–31.

Cooper, B. (2005a) 'Applying Ragin's crisp and fuzzy set QCA to large datasets: social class and educational achievement in the NCDS', *Sociological Research Online.* Available at (accessed 20/04/10): < http://www.socresonline.org.uk/10/2/cooper1.html >.

— (2005b) 'Applying Ragin's crisp and fuzzy set QCA to large datasets: social class and educational achievement in the National Child Development Study', presented to the Methodology Stream of European Consortium for Political Research General Conference, Budapest. Available at (accessed 20/04/10): < http://www.essex.ac.uk/ecpr/events/generalconference/budapest/papers/20/6/cooper. pdf >.

— (2006) 'Using Ragin's Qualitative Comparative Analysis with longitudinal datasets to explore the degree of meritocracy characterising educational achievement in Britain', presented to the Annual meeting of AERA, San Francisco.

Cooper, B. and Dunne, M. (2000) *Assessing Children's Mathematical Knowledge: class, sex and problem-solving,* Buckingham: Open University Press.

Cooper B. and Glaesser, J. (2007) 'Exploring social class compositional effects on educational achievement with fuzzy set methods', presented to the Annual meeting of AERA, Chicago.

— (2008a) 'How has educational expansion changed the necessary and sufficient conditions for achieving professional, managerial and technical class positions in Britain? A configurational analysis', *Sociological Research Online.* Available at (accessed 20/04/10): < http://www.socresonline. org.uk/13/3/2.html >.

— (2008b) 'Exploring configurational causation in large datasets with QCA: possibilities and problems', ESRC Research Methods Festival, Oxford. Available at (accessed 20/04/10): < http://www.ncrm. ac.uk/RMF2008/festival/programme/mthd/ >.

— (2009) 'Contrasting variable analytic and case-based approaches to the analysis of survey datasets: the example of social class and educational achievement given to key note symposium: methodological issues in research on social class, education and social mobility', BERA Annual Conference, Manchester.

— (2010a) 'Contrasting variable-analytic and case-based approaches to the analysis of survey datasets: exploring how achievement varies by ability across configurations of social class and sex', *Methodological Innovations Online* (2010), 5, 1, pp. 4–23.

— (2010b) 'Using case-based approaches to analyse large datasets: a comparison of Ragin's fsQCA and fuzzy cluster analysis', *International Journal of Social Research Methodology*. Available at: <http://dx.doi.org/10.1080/13645579.2010.483079>.

Cooper, B. and Harries, A. V. (2009) 'Realistic contexts, mathematics assessment and social class: lessons for assessment policy from an English research programme', in Verschaffel, L., Greer, B., Van Dooren, W. and Mukhopadhyay, S. (eds) *Words and Worlds: modelling verbal descriptions of situations,* Rotterdam: Sense Publications.

Freedman, D. (1991) 'Statistical models and shoe leather', *Sociological Methodology,* 21, pp. 291–313.

George, A. L. and Bennett, A. (2005) *Case Studies and Theory Development in the Social Sciences,* Cambridge: MIT Press.

Glaesser, J. (2008) 'Just how flexible is the German selective secondary school system? A configurational analysis', *International Journal of Research and Method in Education,* 31, 2, pp. 193–209.

Glaesser, J. and Cooper, B. (2010) 'Selectivity and flexibility in the German secondary school system: a configurational analysis of recent data from the German socio-economic panel', *European Sociological Review,* DOI:10.1093/esr/jcq026. Available at: <www.esr.oxfordjournals.org>.

Goertz, G. (2006) 'Assessing the trivialness, relevance, and relative importance of necessary or sufficient conditions', *Studies in Comparative International Development,* 41, 2, pp. 88–109.

Goldstein, H. (1995) *Multilevel Statistical Models,* Second edition, London: Edward Arnold.

Goldthorpe, J. H. (2007) *On Sociology, Volume One: critique and program,* Second edition, Stanford: Stanford University Press.

Hargreaves, D. (1967) *Social Relations in a Secondary School*, London: Routledge and Kegan Paul.

Kosko, B. (1994) *Fuzzy Thinking,* London: HarperCollins.

Lacey, C. (1970) *Hightown Grammar: the school as a social system,* Manchester: Manchester University Press.

Lieberson, S. (1985) *Making it Count,* Berkeley: California University Press.

Mackie, J. L. (1980) *The Cement of the Universe,* Oxford: Oxford University Press.

Mahoney, J. (2008) 'Toward a unified theory of causality', *Comparative Political Studies,* 41, 4–5, pp. 412–36.

Mahoney, J. and Goertz, G. (2006) 'A tale of two cultures: contrasting quantitative and qualitative research', *Political Analysis,* 14, 3, pp. 227–49.

Meehl, P. M. (1970) 'Nuisance variables and the ex post facto design', in Radner, M. and Winokur, S. (eds) *Minnesota Studies in the Philosophy of Science: IV,* Minneapolis: University of Minnesota.

Merton, R. K. (1987) 'Three fragments from a sociologist's notebook: establishing the phenomena, specified ignorance and strategic research materials', *Annual Review of Sociology,* 13, pp. 1–28.

Nie, N. H., Hull, C. H., Jenkins, J. G., Steinbrenner, K. and Bent, D. H. (1975) *Statistical Package for the Social Sciences,* Second edition, New York: McGraw-Hill.

Pawson, R. (1989) *A Measure for Measures,* London: Routledge.

— (2008) *'Causality for beginners',* ESRC/NCRM Research Methods Festival. Available at (accessed 20/04/10): < http://eprints.ncrm.ac.uk/245/>.

Ragin, C. (1987) *The Comparative Method,* Berkeley: California University Press.

— (2000) *Fuzzy Set Social Science,* Chicago: Chicago University Press.

— (2006a) 'The limitations of net effects thinking', in Rihoux, B. and Grimm, H. (eds) *Innovative Comparative Methods for Political Analysis,* New York: Springer.

— (2006b) 'Set relations in social research: evaluating their consistency and coverage', *Political Analysis,* 14, 3, pp. 291–310.

— (2008) *Redesigning Social Inquiry,* Chicago: Chicago University Press.

Ron, A. (2002) 'Regression analysis and the philosophy of social sciences: a critical realist view', *Journal of Critical Realism,* 1, 1, pp. 115–36.

Seawright, J. and Gerring, J. (2008) 'Case selection techniques in case study research: a menu of qualitative and quantitative options', *Political Research Quarterly,* 61, 2, pp. 294–308.

Smithson, M. J. and Verkuilen, J. (2006) *Fuzzy Set Theory: applications in the social sciences,* Thousand Oaks: Sage.

Turner, R. H. (1948) 'Statistical logic in social research', *Sociology and Social Research,* 32, pp. 697–704.

— (1960) 'Sponsored and contest mobility and the school system', *American Sociological Review,* 25, 6, pp. 855–62.

Creating Typologies: Comparing Fuzzy Qualitative Comparative Analysis with Fuzzy Cluster Analysis

Barry Cooper and Judith Glaesser

Chapter Outline

Introduction

As we noted in the previous chapter, there has been considerable critical discussion of the assumptions underlying regression methods (Abbott 2001; Freedman 1987; Lieberson 1985; Pawson 1989; Ragin 2000). In lieu of, or in addition to, these linear algebraic methods, several sociologists have argued for a greater use of case-based approaches (Elman 2005; George and Bennett 2005; Ragin and Becker 1992). Among suggestions for particular case-based methods, Ragin and others have argued for configurational approaches based on set theory (Ragin 2000; Kvist 2007). The approach developed by Ragin (crisp and fuzzy set based Qualitative Comparative Analysis, or QCA/ fsQCA) has, thus far, been used mainly with small- to medium-sized samples, but can, as we showed in the previous chapter, be used with large datasets (Cooper 2005a, b, 2006; Cooper and Glaesser 2007, 2008; Glaesser 2008; Glaesser and Cooper 2010; Ragin 2006a). Some have seen cluster analysis (CA) as an alternative fruitful way forward in overcoming the problems with regression analysis (Byrne 2002), others sequence analysis (Abbott 2001; Wiggins et al. 2007).

Users of analytic methods should have, alongside technical knowledge, some understanding of underlying assumptions, embedded procedures, strengths and limitations. In using Ragin's methods to analyse large datasets, we have become aware of important similarities and differences between his procedures and those of cluster analysis. At root, these are the consequences of two different mathematizations of procedures for classifying cases. While both approaches work with multidimensional spaces, QCA addresses the positioning of cases in these spaces via set theoretic operations while CA relies on geometric distance measures and concepts of variance minimization.

Before turning to the task of this chapter, we should note an issue we will not address here, that of description versus explanation via typologies. Several recent papers, some referring back to Lazarsfeld and Barton's work on classification, discuss 'explanatory typologies' (e.g. Elman 2005). George and Bennett (2005), in their discussion of 'typological theorizing' argue for a combining of case-based comparative analyses with process-tracing as a route to causal explanation. We have considerable sympathy with this approach, but here, given our focus on classifying procedures and their consequences in cross-case analysis, we will operate at descriptive and/or predictive levels of analysis.[1]

We first introduce relevant features of crisp set Qualitative Comparative Analysis (csQCA), fuzzy set QCA (fsQCA) and CA. We then provide an abstract two-dimensional illustration of an important algorithmic difference between the partitioning procedures of fsQCA and CA. The consequences of this difference are the central focus of the remainder of the chapter. In the empirical section, we undertake two comparisons of classifications produced by fsQCA and FCA and compare their respective predictive power.

Crisp set QCA (csQCA)

Ragin's QCA analyses, for some given dataset, the necessary and/or sufficient conditions for some outcome to occur. These conditions are often described in the QCA literature as 'causal' conditions though QCA offers no algorithmic solution to the problem of distinguishing association from causation. What it does allow is the establishment of those complex combinations of conditions, from among those selected as potentially causal by the researcher, that are able to predict, within a set theoretic framework, and within the given dataset, some outcome. We will later use the fuzzy set version of QCA but we first introduce some key ideas not covered in the previous chapter using, initially, crisp sets.

In the previous chapter we used the crisp set Boolean equation Y= (A*B*c) + (A*C*D*E), taken from Mahoney and Goertz (2006), as an example to introduce the set theoretic approach. In this equation, Y is some outcome. A, B, C, D and E are used to represent the presence of five 'causal conditions', with the absence of any of these being indicated by the use of a lower case letter, as in the case of 'c' in A*B*c. The * indicates set intersection (logical AND) and the + indicates set union (logical OR). In the previous chapter we also explained, using some simple Venn diagrams, the basic set theoretic

---

1   Nevertheless, most readers will find it easy to fill in plausible mechanisms and processes that might lie behind the relationships we discuss in our examples.

concepts needed to build a Boolean equation of this kind. To summarize (see the previous chapter for the details of the argument, set out under 'basics of the set theoretic approach'):

- For a condition, or a combination of conditions,[2] to be sufficient for an outcome we need the condition set to be a subset of the outcome set.
- For a condition to be necessary for an outcome to occur, we need the outcome set to be a subset of the condition set.

We also showed how the ideas of quasi-sufficiency and quasi-necessity can be used to deal with non-deterministic models. However, we did not in that chapter set out in detail the procedures, involving the use of *truth tables*, that allow the analyst to determine, as a first step, which particular combinations of conditions, i.e. configurations, fulfil the criteria for quasi-sufficiency and, as a second step, to present these in a logically simplified equation of the sort we have quoted from Mahoney and Goertz. These procedures are needed to establish, for example, that the configuration A*B*c is a subset of Y, a statement that includes, implicitly, the claim that it makes no difference whether D or E are present or not.[3] We therefore present below, before moving on to the more complex case of fuzzy set QCA, a simple crisp set empirical example of the procedures applied to a truth table in order to generate Boolean equations from survey datasets.

The data in Table 7.1 are taken from the National Child Development Study (NCDS) of individuals born in one week in March 1958. The 5,800 cases are those we have used elsewhere (Cooper and Glaesser 2007). In this truth table, each row captures one type of case as a configuration of conditions, showing the number of cases with each particular combination of the absence or presence of the conditions and the proportion of these achieving an outcome (consistency). As we explained in the previous chapter, in csQCA, these proportions give us a subsethood-based test of the consistency of a relation of sufficiency for each configuration for the outcome. A value of 1.0 in the final column would indicate perfect sufficiency since, in this case, each member of

---

2 In the previous chapter we focused on whether a set X, representing some single condition, was a subset of a set Y. Here we generalize that focus, allowing X to be a complex combination such as A*B*c.

3 More formally, A*B*c includes A*B*c*D*E, A*B*c*D*e, A*B*c*d*E and A*B*c*d*e.

Table 7.1 Highest qualification better than 'Ordinary' level by class, ability and sex (Cooper and Glaesser 2007)

CLASS_S = service class origin	HIGH_ABILITY = measured ability in top 20 per cent (at age 11)	MALE	Number of cases	HQUAL = highest qualification better than 'O' level	Consistency with sufficiency
1	1	1	262	1	0.863
1	1	0	333	1	0.793
0	1	1	359	1	0.691
1	0	1	502	0	0.584
0	1	0	413	0	0.521
1	0	0	458	0	0.485
0	0	1	1676	0	0.358
0	0	0	1797	0	0.224

CLASS_S: service class origin;

the configuration set is also a member of the outcome set and therefore, by the definition of a subset, the configuration set is a subset of the outcome set. A value like that of 0.863 for the configuration 111 can be taken to indicate quasi-sufficiency.

The 1s in the table indicate, respectively, membership in the sets 'SERVICE CLASS ORIGIN', 'HIGH ABILITY' and 'MALE', with 0s indicating non-membership. The configuration 111, for example, captures those cases who are in all three of the sets 'SERVICE CLASS ORIGIN', 'HIGH ABILITY' and 'MALE', while 110 captures just those cases in the three sets 'SERVICE CLASS ORIGIN', 'HIGH ABILITY' and 'male', where the lower case 'male' indicates that these cases are female. The outcome, HQUAL, is having highest qualifications at age 33 better than GCE Ordinary level or its official vocational equivalent. In no row does the proportion with the outcome reach 100 per cent. This will surprise few readers. Social causation is complex, it is unlikely that these three conditions capture all relevant processes, and 'chance', however understood, will have played a role. Ragin's proposed solution is to work with a notion of quasi-sufficiency and quasi-necessity (Ragin 2006b; also Boudon 1974; Mahoney 2008). Here, for illustrative purposes, we set 0.67 as a minimum proportion for quasi-sufficiency. Three rows marked out by entering a 1 in the outcome column go forward to the solution:

$$HQUAL = (CLASS\_S*HIGH\_ABILITY*MALE)$$
$$(CLASS\_S*HIGH\_ABILITY*male) +$$
$$(class\_s*HIGH\_ABILITY*MALE).$$

This simplifies to[4]:

$$HQUAL = HIGH\_ABILITY*(CLASS\_S+MALE).$$

Quasi-sufficient conditions for predicting this level of qualification are being of high ability combined with either service class origin or being male (or both). The consistency of this solution is 0.774 and its coverage[5] 0.299 (the latter reflecting the large proportion of cases with the outcome that fall outside the three configurations in this solution).

Fuzzy set QCA (fsQCA)

Because we will be comparing the fuzzy set version of QCA (fsQCA) with FCA, we now discuss fuzzy sets and some operations employed in fsQCA. Fuzzy sets have the advantage of addressing the concern raised by Goldthorpe (1997) that crisp set QCA, using dichotomies, often jettisons detailed information. As we noted in the previous chapter, whereas in crisp sets there are just the two states of zero and full membership, in the fuzzy approach there can also be partial memberships. The key membership value of 0.5, for example, indicates that a case is as much in as out of some set.

Matters become more complicated when we move on to consider fuzzy set **union** (OR) and **intersection** (AND). Various candidates have been proposed for these operations in the fuzzy context (Smithson 1987). A commonly accepted pair of definitions (see Ragin 2000) defines the intersection operator as the arithmetic minimum of the scores being combined,[6] and union as the arithmetic maximum. These are the operators embedded in Ragin's current fsQCA software (Ragin et al. 2006a, b). If we wish to **negate** a set (analogous

---

4 We have '111 OR 110 OR 011'. From '111 OR 110' we can note, given the chosen threshold of 0.67, that sex makes no relevant difference, and can reduce these to 11- where the dash indicates that this third condition makes no relevant difference. From '111 OR 011' we can similarly derive -11. From '11- OR -11' we can see that 'CLASS*HIGH_ABILITY OR HIGH_ABILITY*MALE' is a simpler solution, and we can take out the common factor of HIGH_ABILITY to produce the simplest solution.

5 See the previous chapter for an account of coverage, a measure of the extent to which a condition, or a combination of conditions, 'explains' the outcome.

6 For Ragin's argument for using the minimum for fuzzy set intersection, see Ragin (2000) and also the previous chapter here.

Table 7.2 Consistency and coverage indices

Consistency	Coverage
$$\dfrac{\sum_i m_{x \cap y}}{\sum_i m_x}$$	$$\dfrac{\sum_i m_{x \cap y}}{\sum_i m_y}$$

to moving from 'HIGH_ABILITY' to 'high_ability' in the earlier crisp set context) we subtract the score from 1. Using the example of *adulthood* discussed in detail in the previous chapter, a case with membership in the set of adults of 0.9 would have membership in the set of not-adults of 0.1.

Methods for evaluating the subsethood relation required for assessing sufficiency and necessity have also been much debated (Smithson 1987). Ragin has moved through four measures of consistency while developing fsQCA (Cooper 2005b). As we explained in detail in the previous chapter, fsQCA currently works with an analogue of the 'overlap' approach employed in discussing the crisp sets in Figures 6.5 and 6.6 of that chapter. Using this approach, the 'truth table algorithm' in fsQCA (version 2.0) creates indices of consistency to assess sufficiency (and coverage) using the formulae in Table 7.2 (where m_x indicates the membership score of a case in set x, the causal configuration; m_y indicates the membership score of a case in set y, the outcome; and $m_{x \cap y}$ is the intersection of sets x and y, defined as the minimum of the two scores; and sums are taken over cases {the i} in the respective sets).

The final issue is calibration, i.e. the allocation of fuzzy membership scores to features of cases. Ragin (2000) stresses the importance of using knowledge of cases alongside theoretical and substantive knowledge in this process. Since much use of QCA has been with small- and medium-sized datasets, this has been possible and fruitful. However, we do not have detailed case knowledge of the thousands of individuals in the NCDS. Verkuilen (2005) provides a review of ways we might proceed in such situations. In the terms he employed, Cooper, in earlier work with these data, employed a method of 'direct assignment' based on theoretical and substantive expertise to allocate fuzzy scores to class and qualification categories.[7] We initially use those calibrations in this chapter (see Cooper 2005a, for details) because we wish to

---

7   Cooper (2006) explored a method not fully dependent on such expertise, derived from Cheli and Lemmi's (1995) work.

Table 7.3 Fuzzy memberships in A and B and derived sets

Case id	A	B	a	b	AB	Ab	aB	ab
1	1.00	0.00	0.00	1.00	0.00	**1.00**	0.00	0.00
2	1.00	0.51	0.00	0.49	**0.51**	0.49	0.00	0.00
3	0.55	0.45	0.45	0.55	0.45	**0.55**	0.45	0.45
4	0.65	0.55	0.35	0.45	**0.55**	0.45	0.35	0.35
5	0.20	0.45	0.80	0.55	0.20	0.20	0.45	**0.55**
6	0.20	0.51	0.80	0.49	0.20	0.20	**0.51**	0.49

explore the use of CA with previously analysed calibrated data.[8] However, we then vary one of the calibrations in order to explore the effect of this on our initial findings. In this chapter, both QCA and cluster analysis are applied to these fuzzy measures.

When using fuzzy sets, because cases can have non-zero membership in more than one configuration, a special procedure is needed to create a truth table analogous to Table 7.1, where cases are uniquely in one configuration. The truth table algorithm employed in the current version of fsQCA achieves this. We can illustrate this via a simple invented example with two causal conditions, A and B, for each case and where cases have been allocated fuzzy membership in sets A and B. Columns 2–5 of Table 7.3 show the fuzzy set membership values of A, B and their negations (calculated by subtracting these values from 1). Columns 6–9 show the degree of membership in the four possible intersections[9] of the sets A, B and the negations a, b. Crucially, some cases have non-zero membership in more than one of the configurations AB, Ab, aB and ab.

For each case we have also shown in bold the largest of the four values among the four possible intersections. In each row, given we have no values of A or B equal to 0.5, we have just one value greater than 0.5, i.e. greater than the crossover value for being more in than out of a fuzzy set. In his 'truth table algorithm' Ragin uses this particular value to locate each case in one 'corner' of the property space (and therefore the truth table) comprising the four sets AB, Ab, aB and ab. This move, effectively removing the problems caused by each case potentially having non-zero membership in all four intersections,

---

8 It also ensures that we use, during CA, only variables scaled to have the same range of values (0–1).

9 Calculated by taking the minimum value of each pair.

allows cases to be allocated to just one row of a truth table. *It is the key move in fsQCA, given prior calibration, in allocating cases to the theoretically defined types which together populate the multidimensional space.* Each case is allocated to the one set, i.e. the one row in a truth table, in which it has a membership greater than 0.5. We will return to some other features of fsQCA later, but now turn to CA.

Cluster analysis

Since cluster analysis is better known than fsQCA, we describe it only briefly. Conventional (crisp, hard) cluster analysis comes in many forms (Bailey 1994). What they have in common is the goal of dividing some set of cases into subgroups whose members are potentially of similar kinds or types.[10] Cases are seen as distributed in a multidimensional space, candidate cluster centres are represented by particular coordinates in this space, each case is allocated to just one cluster, and minimizing the sum of some measure of the distances of cases from their cluster centres is the typical procedure used to determine, iteratively, the final cluster structure and the allocation of cases to it. Some algorithms (agglomerative) begin by assuming that each case is a cluster and gradually merge these small clusters to form larger ones; others (divisive) begin by allocating all cases to one cluster and then gradually divide this to form some smaller number of final clusters (Bailey 1994). In the less well-known fuzzy cluster analysis (FCA), CA can also be used to allocate cases non-uniquely to clusters. Here cases can have fractional degrees of membership, analogous to fuzzy set memberships, in several clusters, with these memberships, in the basic so-called probabilistic variant of FCA, constrained to add to 1[11] (de Oliveira and Pedrycz 2007; Kruse et al. 2007). In all these variants of

---

10 The 'potentially' is important here. CA can report a cluster structure even where no real kinds exist. Of course, the relation of the configurations in QCA to any real types will be only as good as the choice of factors and calibrations.

11 In fuzzy clustering, partitions of cases produced under this constraint can be misleading (Kruse et al. 2007: 10) given some distributions of cases in multidimensional space. The cluster analysis method we employ, k-means CA, is divisive. For our data, we know that crisp k-means CA and probabilistic c-means fuzzy CA produce very similar classifications. This gives us confidence that the 'sharing' of memberships produced by probabilistic FCA is not greatly compromising the 'typicality' aspect here (on these features of membership, see Kruse et al. (2007)).

CA, the cluster structure found depends partly on the particular sample analysed, given an iterative procedure is used to generate the clusters.[12]

While there has been much energy expended trying to mechanize the choice of an optimal number of clusters in a given analysis, this choice is still often presented as involving judgement based on whether theoretical or substantive sense can be made of the clusters found (Lattin et al. 2003). Here, we constrain the number of clusters to match the number of configurations in our fsQCA analyses.

Having introduced these two classificatory approaches, we present, before employing real data, a simple illustration of a key difference between fsQCA and crisp CA that also applies to FCA.

fsQCA versus CA: a two-dimensional non-empirical illustration

While fsQCA uses an explicit (set theoretic) argument to justify its partitioning of a dataset, forms of cluster analysis depend, most commonly, on distance-based measures of similarity or dissimilarity. Looking at Figure 7.1 – and thinking in terms of four clusters to match the number of configurations generated by a truth table analysis involving two conditions A and B – we can see that, given the distribution of the twelve cases across the two-dimensional space, a clustering algorithm based on minimizing distances between the cases and the geometric centres of the unique cluster to which they belong, would be expected, if set to find four clusters, to produce the four groupings represented by different shapes. We can also see that fsQCA using the minimization rule for set intersection, coupled with its rule of allocating cases to the set (or configuration) in which they have a membership greater than 0.5, would produce the same partitioning of this population (see discussion of Table 7.3).

---

12 With QCA, the situation is different. QCA, via its truth table, lists all the logically possible configurations. As long as there is at least one case to go in each row, they all 'exist'. With CA, the distribution of cases can be such that, given the iterative procedure that is used to generate the clusters, some logically possible clusters may, depending on the sample, be found 'not to exist'. However, it is the case that, when using QCA with small samples (or even large samples with particular distributions of cases), there may be no cases found to represent some configurations but, nevertheless, the configurations still exist in the sense that they are given, deductively, once the dimensions of the analysis are set.

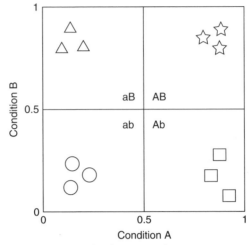

Figure 7.1 12 invented cases with membership in A and B

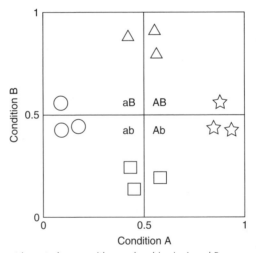

Figure 7.2 12 different invented cases with memberships in A and B

Now consider the distribution of cases in Figure 7.2. Here, using any obvious distance measure to produce four clusters, we will obtain via CA the four groupings shown differentiated by shape. The fsQCA partition will however be different, given the critical role of the 0.5 membership score. Here, employing fsQCA's truth table rule for allocating cases to a unique set, the left-most triangle goes to aB, but its two cluster companions to AB. We obtain two different partitions, reflecting the algorithm employed. This exercise sets up a potential competition between the two approaches. Which of the two partitionings might better account for some outcome?

One message to take from this comparison is that the extent of the difference in the partitionings produced by the two approaches will be affected by the distribution of the cases across the two-dimensional space (and, more generally, across n-dimensional spaces). In datasets where the density of cases is greatest near the 0.5 fuzzy membership scores, differences between the two partitionings will tend to be greater.

We move now to a three-dimensional space, using real data from the NCDS. We employ fuzzy measures of class origin, ability and the binary, non-fuzzy, measure of sex, with highest qualification achieved by age 33 as our outcome. We have two reasons for including the binary condition of sex. First, we wanted to apply CA to the sorts of mix of crisp and fuzzy factors that have appeared in published work using fsQCA and, second, given the way CA treats the binary factor, we can use 2-d figures to make our discussion of the 3-d case clearer. The differences we discuss between fsQCA and CA are not, however, dependent on this decision to include a binary factor.

fsQCA versus FCA: a first three-dimensional empirical illustration

We address a three-dimensional space on the conditions side (fuzzy class, fuzzy ability, sex) and employ fuzzy highest qualifications as our outcome. We need briefly to describe the measures/calibrations we use in this first comparison, some of which were also used in the previous chapter. Given space constraints, we will not set out the rationale for these calibrations (see Cooper 2005a). Our purpose in our first comparison is to compare the ways fsQCA and FCA treat a set of already calibrated measures. Sex is a crisp set, with a score of 1 indicating full membership in the set MALE. Class origin, labelled CLASS_F, is allocated the fuzzy scores shown in Table 7.4. A score of 1 here indicates membership of the upper service class and the other scores indicate partial or zero membership in CLASS_F, a set then for which full membership is *defined* to be membership of the upper service class. The fuzzy outcome measure we label HQUAL_F (Table 7.5). The calibration of ability (measured via testing at age 11) is shown in Figure 7.3. This reflects its origin in Cooper (2005a) where having high ability was defined as having a score

Table 7.4 Class scheme employed (Erikson and Goldthorpe 1993) and fuzzy scores

Class	Label	CLASS_F: fuzzy score
1	Upper service	1.000
2	Lower service	0.830
3	Routine non-manual	0.583
4	Petty bourgeoisie	0.583
5	Supervisors etc.	0.417
6	Skilled manual	0.170
7	Semi- and unskilled manual	0.000

Table 7.5 Fuzzy scores for highest qualification at age 33

Highest qualification gained at age 33	HQUAL_F: fuzzy score
Degree or higher NVQ5, 6	1.00
Higher qualification NVQ4	0.83
A Level/equivalent to NVQ3	0.67
O Level/equivalent to NVQ2	0.42
CSE 2-5/equivalent to NVQ1	0.17
No qualification	0.00

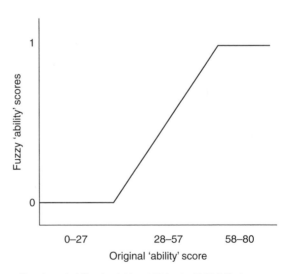

Figure 7.3 Fuzzy calibration of ability (variable *n*920 in the NCDS files)

in the top 20 per cent of the cohort distribution. We label this fuzzy version ABILITY_F. A considerable number of cases have been given scores of 1 or 0, though the majority have partial scores. A score of 1 in ABILITY_F therefore indicates having high ability as defined.

Three conditions generate $2^3 = 8$ rows in an fsQCA truth table. We use fuzzy clustering to produce eight clusters to explore the match with these eight fsQCA configurations. We crosstabulate the fsQCA and FCA partitions, then discuss some cases that fall off the main diagonal. We then focus on accounting for our outcome, HQUAL_F. We employ again the 5,800 cases from the NCDS with no missing data on these and some other variables we have used elsewhere (Cooper and Glaesser 2007).

Recall that probabilistic FCA, instead of allocating cases to just one cluster, allows cases to have partial membership in several, with the total of the memberships for any case set at 1 (Pedrycz 2005).[13] We employ the commonly used fuzzy c-means algorithm (a fuzzy relative of crisp k-means) in the software Fuzzy Grouping 2 (Pisces Conservation 2005) to produce our eight clusters.[14] Given the iterative nature of this procedure and its dependence on random starting seeding of candidate cluster centres, we have checked that our solution is relatively stable under repetitions of the procedure with and without reordering of the cases in the data spreadsheet.

Table 7.6 gives the cluster centres for the resulting eight clusters. Allowing for small perturbations introduced, we assume, by the iterative procedure, we can see that sex is preserved as a crisp feature by FCA. Apart from this, though less clearly for cluster 7, the cluster centres are distinguished by the various possible combinations of high and low scores on CLASS_F and ABILITY_F.

---

13 We had initially, in a longer earlier version of this chapter, begun by using crisp clustering procedures, with each case being allocated to just one cluster. However, we had then also to employ, in a second stage, fuzzy clustering procedures, where each case can have partial membership in several clusters, in order to be able to undertake a set theoretic comparison with fsQCA of the predictive power of QCA and CA. For our sample, a crosstabulation of membership in the crisp k-means clusters with membership in the FCA cluster in which a case has its maximum membership as 98.16 per cent of cases on the leading diagonal. In comparing, therefore, 'best' FCA cluster membership with membership in fsQCA configurations we are working with nearly the same crosstabulation structure as we had when employing crisp k-means, but we are able, in addition, to make use of partial cluster memberships.

14 We use the normally recommended setting of the 'fuzziness coefficient'.

Table 7.6 Cluster centres from FCA

	Cluster							
	1	2	3	4	5	6	7	8
CLASS_F	0.848	0.743	0.143	0.828	0.117	0.141	0.644	0.113
ABILITY_F	0.940	0.288	0.834	0.928	0.113	0.863	0.420	0.097
MALE	0.003	0.992	0.996	0.997	0.003	0.003	0.008	0.997
QCA lookalike	110	101	011	111	000	010	100	001

Table 7.7 The fsQCA configurations by best FCA cluster (number of cases)

	FCA cluster where each case has its maximum membership							
fsQCA configuration (Class, Ability, Male)	4	1	2	7	3	6	8	5
111	742	0	60	0	0	0	0	0
110	0	784	0	155	0	0	0	0
101	0	0	400	0	0	0	0	0
100	0	0	0	306	0	0	0	0
011	0	0	3	0	705	0	0	0
010	0	0	0	22	0	848	0	0
001	0	0	33	0	29	0	827	0
000	0	0	0	30	0	0	0	856

The final row shows the QCA 'lookalike' configuration to which each cluster is most similar.

Table 7.7 crosstabulates membership in the fsQCA configurations with membership in the cluster in which each case has the largest membership. 94.28 per cent of cases fall on the leading diagonal, and no cells mix sexes. If we repeat this exercise, but only using cases from the FCA solution who have a degree of membership over 0.5 (to simulate the way the fsQCA truth table algorithm locates cases in a unique configuration), then 97.46 per cent of 4,652 cases fall on the leading diagonal.

The cluster centres from the FCA, four for each sex, seem to represent four ideal typical cases that cover the same high/high, low/low, high/low and low/high combinations of class and ability as does fsQCA. There are, however, some fairly large groups off the diagonal (e.g. the 155 cases comprising configuration 110 by cluster 7). Who are they? Why are they off the diagonal?

Since it's the largest absolute mismatch, let's take the cell with 155 cases as an example. For QCA, these are cases in the set/configuration 110,

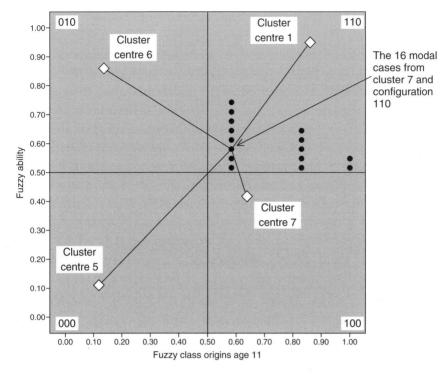

Figure 7.4 The 155 cases in both configuration 110 and with maximum membership in fuzzy cluster 7 (with 4 cluster centres for females)

i.e. females with membership above 0.5 in both CLASS_F and ABILITY_F. We find, as would be expected from our earlier 2-d illustration, that at least one of the fuzzy scores for class or ability is near the 0.5 boundary. These cases are females, either in Goldthorpe's class 3 or they are in the service class (1 or 2) but with ability scores close to 0.5. Holding sex to female, i.e. taking a 2-d slice through the 3-d space, the 155 cases are shown in Figure 7.4, which also shows the 4 cluster centres for females. The 155 cases hug at least one of the 0.5 boundaries. We have here an empirical example of the problem we described in Figure 7.2.

Turning to FCA, we need to look at cluster '7', of which these 155 cases are members. The cluster centre for this cluster is at 0.64, 0.42 and 0 for class, ability and sex. The prototypical member of this cluster (0.64, 0.42, 0) would not be allocated, under fsQCA, to the configuration 110 since ability is not above 0.5. Most cases in cluster 7 are, in fact, in the fsQCA configuration 100. These 155 members of cluster 7, however, have a fuzzy class score above

0.5, as well as fuzzy ability scores above 0.5 and a MALE score of zero and so go to 110.

We can take, for further illustration, the modal cases, of which there are 16, from among the 155; they have scores of 0.58, 0.58, 0 (Figure 7.4). Notwithstanding their membership in the configuration 110, their distance from the centre of cluster 7 is smaller, as expected, than their distance from any of the other clusters containing females. They are nearer this cluster centre than the one that appears most like QCA's 110 (which is cluster 1 with centre 0.85, 0.94, 0). The nearness of these 16 cases to two 0.5 boundaries is the basis of this difference in classification. Although they are in 110, they are only just more in than out of CLASS_F and ABILITY_F.

Comparing fsQCA and FCA: prediction using a conventional approach

We now look at the extent to which the two classifications predict HQUAL_F. We begin with a conventional approach. We compare the size of the contingency coefficient for, first, the relation between the cases' memberships in fuzzy highest qualification (Table 7.5) and in their fsQCA configuration, and, second, for the relation between their membership in fuzzy highest qualification and their membership in the fuzzy cluster in which each case has maximum membership. The two contingency coefficients are 0.487 (for fsQCA) and 0.492 (for FCA). Both classifications explain very similar amounts of variation. However, as we saw in the previous chapter such summary correlational measures may not provide a great deal of insight into possible set theoretic relationships, to which we now turn.

Comparing fsQCA and FCA: prediction using a set theoretic approach

We now compare fsQCA and FCA-based prediction using a set theoretic approach. Here, we compare fsQCA and FCA on fsQCA's own ground. We attempt a comparison of the predictive power of two classifications based on CLASS_F, ABILITY_F and MALE using quasi-sufficiency in place of variance explained. First, we describe the set theoretic solution of the model HQUAL_F = Function (CLASS_F, ABILITY_F, MALE). In doing this, we introduce a feature of the truth table algorithm in fsQCA that will be seen to have motivated our use of fuzzy CA. This additional complicating feature is that the truth table algorithm in fsQCA, although it allocates cases to a unique row of the truth table on the basis of their having a score of over 0.5 in just one configuration, actually calculates the consistency and coverage indices for each configuration for all cases with non-zero membership, not just these strongest ones (Ragin 2004).[15] Ragin's argument is that the number of cases in each row can be used as an indicator of the *existence* or otherwise of strong exemplars of each configuration but that the *relation* between the sets represented by the configurations and the outcome should be tested using all non-zero memberships in the configurations.

The truth table, from the fsQCA software, for the outcome HQUAL_F and the conditions CLASS_F, ABILITY_F and MALE is part of Table 7.8. One additional column has been added to indicate the number of the FCA cluster that is nearest in shared membership to each configuration. Another provides row coverage figures. For an illustrative solution, we take the three highest consistency levels as indicating consistency with quasi-sufficiency. Doing this allows three configurations into the solution (111, 110, 011). The simplified solution becomes:

(CLASS_F*ABILITY_F)+(ABILITY_F*MALE) or, simplifying further,
ABILITY_F*(CLASS_F+MALE).

---

15 Because of this decision, the main consequence of varying the distribution of cases around the 0.5 boundary (e.g. by choosing particular calibrations of conditions) will be on the classification of cases into configurations. Since this classification is used in the calculation of the contingency coefficients for conventional prediction, the distribution of cases will matter for this. For set theoretic prediction using the fsQCA software, on the other hand, the distribution of cases *across the categories* of the classification is not directly relevant to the calculation of the consistency measures, though varying a calibration will affect consistency measures via changing the membership scores entered into the formulae in Table 7.2. In addition, with smaller datasets, a situation could arise, as a classificatory consequence of a calibration decision, in which the number of cases allocated by the truth table algorithm to a configuration becomes too low for us to want to use the consistency result, even if it is high enough, as the basis for entering the configuration into the subsequent minimization process.

Table 7.8 HQUAL_F = Function (CLASS_F, ABILITY_F, MALE): the resulting truth table

Most similar FCA cluster	CLASS_F	ABILITY_F	MALE	number	HQUAL_F	Consistency (from fsQCA software)	Coverage (from Excel calculation)
4	1	1	1	802	1	0.876	0.248
1	1	1	0	939	1	0.830	0.268
3	0	1	1	708	1	0.791	0.233
2	1	0	1	400	0	0.750	0.133
6	0	1	0	870	0	0.721	0.252
7	1	0	0	306	0	0.721	0.118
8	0	0	1	889	0	0.560	0.183
5	0	0	0	886	0	0.496	0.163

The software calculates the overall consistency and coverage for this solution. To do this, cases' memberships in ABILITY_F*(CLASS_F+MALE), calculated using the individual scores for the three conditions, become the m_x in the formulae in Table 7.2 (and cases' scores on HQUAL_F supply the m_y). Overall consistency is 0.789 and overall coverage is 0.653.

As explained, the consistencies with quasi-sufficiency in the penultimate column of Table 7.8 are calculated using all cases with non-zero membership. To simulate this using cluster analysis we must use FCA rather than the more straightforward crisp k-means CA, where cases have membership in only one cluster. We now turn to the analysis of quasi-sufficiency, with HQUAL_F as the outcome, treating the FCA clusters as sets in which cases have the partial memberships allocated by FCA. Here we simulate the approach used in fsQCA's truth table algorithm, i.e. we allow all cases with non-zero membership in a cluster to contribute to the calculation of consistency and coverage. Table 7.9 is the

Table 7.9 HQUAL_F as outcome, using FCA clusters as the rows

fsQCA 'lookalike' configuration	FCA cluster	Consistency	Coverage
111	4	0.874	0.208
110	1	0.840	0.218
011	3	0.771	0.190
101	2	0.756	0.132
100	7	0.745	0.137
010	6	0.702	0.198
001	8	0.522	0.145
000	5	0.457	0.126

resulting truth table giving consistency and coverage figures for each cluster. It includes the fsQCA configurations that are the 'lookalikes' for FCA clusters. The cluster rows are ordered by descending consistency. Given the approximate mapping of configurations onto clusters, the orderings of consistency are almost the same in Tables 7.8 and 7.9. Row coverage figures are also similar. A three-row solution of this table comprises FCA clusters 4, 1 and 3. A glance at the 'lookalike' configurations for these clusters shows this to be the parallel solution to the one derived using fsQCA. Using FCA, we have, in our simulated set theoretic analysis, produced results structurally similar to those of fsQCA.

We now calculate the overall consistency and coverage for this FCA solution, as we did for the parallel one produced by fsQCA. We noted, in producing overall consistency and coverage for fsQCA, that we needed to use the individual fuzzy values of CLASS_F, ABILITY_F and MALE to calculate the membership of a case in the illustrated solution, ABILITY_F*(CLASS_F+MALE). Now, we don't have such a tidy simplified Boolean expression for our FCA-based solution. We rather have CLUSTER_4+CLUSTER_1+CLUSTER_3, analogous to the configurations 111, 110 and 011. A case's membership in this can be calculated by applying the maximum rule for fuzzy set union (logical OR) to the three partial cluster memberships.[16] Doing this, we obtain, for the three-cluster solution, an overall consistency of 0.812 and a coverage of 0.516. The consistency figure can be seen to be very close to the 0.789 in the fsQCA solution. The coverage figures are less close (0.516 v. 0.653) but we have, in simulating fsQCA via FCA, produced similar results.

An important question arises. We have already noted that the distribution of cases' membership scores on the various conditions entering any analysis will affect the degree to which fsQCA and FCA produce similar results. We

---

16 Because of paradoxes in the fuzzy set context (Ragin 2000: 241) the results obtained by plugging in fuzzy membership scores to the simplified solution ABILITY_F*(CLASS_F +MALE) and, alternatively, to (CLASS_F*ABILITY_F*MALE)+(CLASS_F*ABILITY_F*male)+(class_f *ABILITY_F* MALE) can be different, while they would be the same in a crisp set context. For an example, consider the triplet CLASS_F=0.55, ABILITY_F=0.6, MALE=1. Indeed, while the overall consistency of our fsQCA solution using the simplified solution (the choice made in the fsQCA software) is 0.789, it would become 0.814 if we were to take the maximum of 111, 110 and 011. The comparable coverage figures are, respectively, 0.653 and 0.630. In the FCA context, we are constrained to use the approach that takes the maximum of the three-cluster memberships.

must therefore consider to what extent the calibrations we have employed thus far, given that, in conjunction with the real features of cases and any measurement error, they generate these distributions, limit the generalizability of our findings up to this point.

The consequences of recalibrating ability: a second 3-d empirical illustration

So far, we have discussed some of the underlying procedures involved in fsQCA and shown where they differ from those of cluster analysis. We have undertaken a substantive comparison of a QCA and an FCA, applying these analytic procedures to a previously calibrated dataset. We have found that the two approaches have produced similar results in respect of both classification and prediction.

Given that fsQCA, via the truth table algorithm, builds its classification of cases on the basis of the assumption that the boundaries set by fuzzy scores of 0.5 should determine, in conjunction with a particular definition of set intersection, where cases belong, while FCA employs an iterative approach based on minimizing some distance-based function, it is perhaps surprising that, thus far, we have found these methods producing such similar results. This applies to both the classifying stage of the work and the subsequent stage of 'explaining' an outcome in both conventional and set theoretic ways. There is, however, an important point to make at this stage of the chapter concerning the likely generalizability of these results.

We employed a particular existing set of fuzzy calibrations. Given that we have shown that it is cases with fuzzy scores near 0.5 that are likely to be differently classified by fsQCA and FCA, it is easy to see that the distributions of fuzzy scores will play a role in determining the proportion of cases that fall off the leading diagonal in any comparison of the two classificatory approaches. Of our two non-binary conditions, one, ABILITY_F, has a large proportion of cases with scores of 1 or 0, far from the key 0.5 boundary. About a quarter of the scores for CLASS_F are also 1 or 0. Distributions of scores with a higher proportion of cases near the 0.5 boundary than ours will tend to produce greater differences in classification. Inevitably, the researcher using fsQCA needs to create fuzzy calibrations of factors prior to undertaking any truth table-based analysis. In general, different calibrations will produce different degrees of classificatory mismatch between fsQCA and CA, simply as a consequence of cases being moved nearer to or further from 0.5 membership scores. Only therefore in some cases, we can anticipate, will comparisons come out like the one we have undertaken earlier.

To illustrate the importance of calibration for classification, we will now present a comparison of QCA and FCA in which the calibration of ability is changed. In place of the calibration employed so far in this chapter (that derived from Cooper 2005a: see Figure 7.3 here), we will employ in this second empirical comparison the simple calibration used in the previous chapter. Ability will be calibrated, for illustrative purposes, by transforming the original measure running from 0 to 80 by a simple linear transformation to a fuzzy set measure running from 0 to 1.[17] The calibration of the other factors will remain unchanged, enabling us to focus on the effect of the change in the calibration of this single factor. The crucial difference in the calibration is, of course, that the fuzzy scores of zero and one in the calibration of ability used so far in this chapter are replaced by a range of values (see Figure 7.5). We have termed this calibration of ability, **ABILITY_F_ALTERNATE**.

As before we have undertaken a number of fuzzy cluster analyses. First, we created four versions of the new dataset in which the cases were randomly ordered. In addition, given our use of random seeds to get the iterations started in the Fuzzy Grouping software, we also ran two analyses for each of these four random orderings, generating eight sets of results. As before, to facilitate our comparison with QCA, we constrained the FCA to produce eight clusters.

The results are less stable across random orderings and iterations than we found for the FCA employing the earlier 2005 calibration of ability. However, four of our eight fuzzy clusterings produced the same cluster structure, i.e. they had identical cluster centroids, and we will therefore use

---

17 The use of this second calibration of ability, because it includes some cases with a fuzzy membership score of 0.5, will lead to the loss of some cases from the QCA analysis (for the reason, see the earlier discussion of Table 7.3). We should also add that, since undertaking the analyses presented earlier in this chapter (taken from Cooper and Glaesser 2011a), we have made a decision to remove eight cases from the dataset of 5,800 who have reported ability scores of zero. We have rerun the FCA analyses with this new set of 5,972 cases, and have found the most commonly reported cluster centroids to be almost identical to those we found for the 5,800, only varying in the third decimal place.

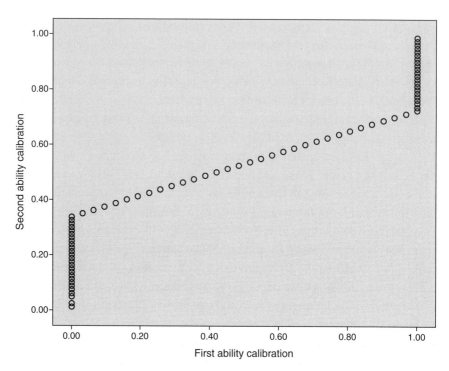

Figure 7.5 The two calibrations of ability compared

this most frequent result in our comparison here.[18] The cluster centroids are shown in Table 7.10.

The first thing to note in comparison with Table 7.6, showing the results when the earlier calibration of ability was employed, is that the eight QCA lookalikes do not map one-to-one onto the eight rows of the relevant QCA truth table. The lookalike configuration 111 appears twice, as does 110. The configurations 101 and 100 are absent. An effect of moving a large proportion of the fuzzy ability scores away from values of 0 and 1 towards 0.5 while allowing them to become more differentiated, is clearly visible. Using this second set of calibrated factors, we find that FCA does not produce the eight possible configurations that comprise the truth table for a three-factor QCA.

---

18 It is also the case that the remaining four results did not, unlike one we have chosen to use here, produce 2 groups of 4 clusters with, respectively, 4 values of 0 and 4 of 1 for male as part of the cluster centroids. Of these remaining four, two were almost identical to one another. The other two were very similar to one another.

Table 7.10 The chosen cluster centroids using the second calibration of ability

				Cluster				
FCA cluster	**3**	**8**	**5**	**7**	**2**	**1**	**4**	**6**
N	805	747	788	700	753	648	600	751
CLASS_F	0.114	0.110	0.132	0.132	0.892	0.580	0.580	0.891
ABILITY_F_ ALTERNATE	0.369	0.342	0.670	0.649	0.708	0.593	0.585	0.662
MALE	0.001	0.999	0.001	0.999	0.002	0.002	0.997	0.998
QCA lookalike	000	001	010	011	110	110	111	111

Table 7.11 Best FCA cluster by QCA configurations (using ABILITY_F_ALTERNATE)

				Cluster					
	6	**4**	**2**	**1**	**7**	**5**	**8**	**3**	**Total**
No config.	17	12	9	10	26	0	14	28	116
000	0	0	0	35	0	0	0	727	762
001	0	49	0	0	0	0	733	0	782
010	0	0	0	118	0	788	0	50	956
011	0	98	0	0	674	0	0	0	772
100	0	0	86	152	0	0	0	0	238
101	169	144	0	0	0	0	0	0	313
110	0	0	658	333	0	0	0	0	991
111	565	297	0	0	0	0	0	0	862
Total	751	600	753	648	700	788	747	805	5792

We can anticipate therefore that a crosstabulation of these clusters with the parallel configurations produced by an fsQCA[19] incorporating the new ability calibration will produce more cases off the main diagonal than we found in our earlier illustration. Table 7.11, which allocates cases to the FCA cluster in which they have the greatest membership, bears this out. The picture is clearer in Table 7.12 where we have collapsed the lookalike clusters 6 and 4, and 2 and 1.

---

19 The change in calibration produces only small changes in fsQCA configuration membership. If the two distributions of configuration membership are crosstabulated (with the *n* falling from 5,792 to 5,676 because 116 cases do not have a unique membership score above 0.5), 95.38 per cent of the cases fall on the leading diagonal. The 262 cases changing configuration as a consequence of the change in the calibration of ability have ability scores in the centre of the distribution. Looking, for example, at the fuzzy scores for the second ability calibration, their fuzzy ability scores range from 0.51 to 0.53.

Table 7.12 Best FCA cluster by QCA configurations (using ABILITY_F_ALTERNATE)

	Cluster						
	6 or 4	2 or 1	7	5	8	3	Total
000	0	35	0	0	0	**727**	762
001	49	0	0	0	**733**	0	782
010	0	118	0	**788**	0	50	956
011	98	0	**674**	0	0	0	772
100	0	238	0	0	0	0	238
101	313	0	0	0	0	0	313
110	0	**991**	0	0	0	0	991
111	**862**	0	0	0	0	0	862
Total	1322	1382	674	788	733	777	5676

Here, 84.13 per cent of the 5,676 cases[20] fall into one of the six cells marked in bold. The comparable figure for the earlier analysis was 94.28 per cent.[21] The set of 313 off diagonal cases (QCA 101 v. FCA lookalike 111), the set of 238 (100 v. 110), the set of 118 (010 v. 110) and the set of 98 (011 v. 111) are the four largest contributors to this mismatching. Since the 169 who are in QCA configuration 101 but FCA cluster 6 (lookalike 111) are the biggest single group of mismatched cases, we will say a little more about these. These cases are all male. Their distribution by fuzzy class origin and the new fuzzy ability calibration is shown in Figure 7.6. It can be seen that while, as males, they meet the criteria for membership in the QCA configuration 101 since their scores for class are above 0.5 but those for ability below 0.5, FCA has allocated them to cluster 6 located in the QCA lookalike quadrant 111. It remains to compare the predictive power of the new classifications.

Comparing fsQCA and FCA with ability recalibrated: conventional prediction

Again, we begin with the conventional approach, comparing the size of the contingency coefficient for the relation between the cases' memberships in

---

20   As we noted in an earlier footnote, some cases (116) with values of 0.5 on the new fuzzy ability score are lost as a result of the way the truth table algorithm in fsQCA creates its truth table. Our 5,792 cases become 5,676.

21   We can, as we did in the case of our first comparison, look just at cases whose membership score in their best FCA cluster is over 0.5. The percentage failing on the leading diagonal rises to 91.63 (n = 4983). For our first fsQCA/FCA comparison, it was 97.46 per cent (n = 4652).

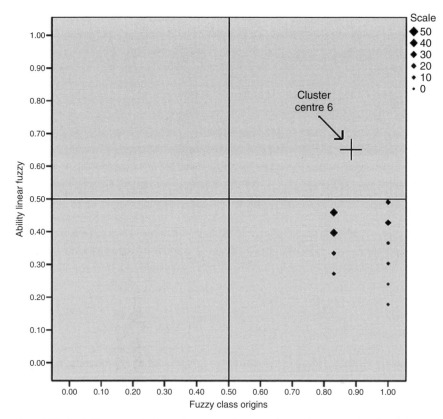

Figure 7.6 The 169 males in both configuration 101 and with maximum membership in fuzzy cluster 6 (lookalike 111)

fuzzy highest qualification and in their fsQCA configuration, and, second, for the relation between their membership in fuzzy highest qualification and their membership in the fuzzy cluster in which each case has maximum membership. The two contingency coefficients are 0.492 (for fsQCA) and 0.459 (for FCA).[22] Both classifications explain similar amounts of variation, but with fsQCA having the better predictive power.

Comparing fsQCA and FCA with ability recalibrated: set theoretic prediction

We now compare fsQCA and FCA-based prediction using a set theoretic approach. The fsQCA truth table, with rows ordered by consistency with

---

22   The 116 cases not classified by fsQCA are omitted, giving $n = 5676$.

Table 7.13 HQUAL_F = Function (CLASS_F, ABILITY_F_ALTERNATE, MALE): the resulting truth table

CLASS_F	ABILITY_F_ALTERNATE	MALE	Number	HQUAL_F	Consistency
1	1	1	862	1	0.874
1	0	1	313	1	0.832
1	1	0	991	1	0.829
1	0	0	238	1	0.817
0	1	1	772	1	0.789
0	1	0	956	0	0.715
0	0	1	782	0	0.682
0	0	0	762	0	0.635

sufficiency, is shown in Table 7.13. Here we will look at a solution involving the first five rows, given the relatively large gap in the consistency measure between the configurations 011 and 010. The minimized solution, with overall consistency with sufficiency of 0.744 and coverage of 0.746 is:

CLASS_F + ABILITY_F_ALTERNATE*MALE.

The change in the calibration of ability has produced a substantially different solution to the one we found when analysing Table 7.8. Class alone is sufficient. Here ABILITY_F_ALTERNATE does not appear as a factor in all the elements of the solution. Since the second row of Table 7.13 is the configuration 101, i.e., CLASS* ability_f_alternate *MALE, this would remain the case were we to use just the first three rows, as we did in our earlier truth table analysis employing the initial calibration of ability.[23]

Now we turn to set theoretic prediction using the FCA clusters. Clearly, we would have a difficulty here in following the same procedure we used to undertake the set theoretic analysis using the set of FCA clusters derived when the first calibration of ability was employed. As Table 7.14 shows (ordered by consistency), we are missing two lookalike configurations and, for two other lookalike configurations, we have two entries. This new fsQCA/FCA comparison, unlike the first one we undertook, points to some limits on the extent to which FCA produces similar results to fsQCA. Nevertheless, if we

---

23 The three row solution is CLASS_F*ABILITY_F_ALTERNATE + CLASS_F*MALE, or CLASS_F*(ABILITY_F_ALTERNATE+MALE). In practice, we would not want to treat the difference in consistency between the third and fourth configuration (0.829 v. 0.817) as a sound basis for choosing to present a three-row solution.

Table 7.14 HQUAL_F as outcome, using new FCA clusters

fsQCA 'lookalike' configuration	FCA cluster	Consistency	Coverage
111	6	0.839	0.189
110	2	0.817	0.192
111	4	0.788	0.159
011	7	0.734	0.186
110	1	0.713	0.153
010	5	0.673	0.190
001	8	0.551	0.140
000	3	0.484	0.130
101	–	–	–
100	–	–	–

compare this table with Table 7.9, we can see that the first three rows of that table cover the same configurations as the first five rows of this new table. ABILITY is a component of all three configurations appearing in these five rows, as it was for the three highest consistency configurations in Table 7.9. The FCA solutions seem to be more stable across the change of calibration of ability than the fsQCA solution.

Conclusion

We have employed FCA, a technique not well-known in mainstream social science. Our experience tells us that the only way to understand the affordances and limitations of complex analytic techniques is to work through them in the sort of detail we have here. Having first shown, via a non-empirical example, that we could expect fsQCA and CA to produce different classifications as a function of the way fuzzy measures are constructed, specifically near the 0.5 boundaries representing those cases who are as much in as out of sets, we explored the consequences of this via two extended empirical examples. In the first case, we found that in respect of both classification and prediction, whether treated in a traditional fashion or via a set theoretic approach, the two methods produced similar results. In the second case, using a revised calibration of one of our factors, we found much less similarity. Indeed, here, FCA did not provide the simple analogue of the fsQCA truth table that it had in our first empirical example. As we noted in an earlier paper (Cooper and Glaesser 2011a), it is important not to generalize too readily from any particular comparison of fsQCA with CA.

There is an additional important point that we have not yet explicitly discussed. The configurational categories that enter into any fsQCA analysis of the achievement of an outcome are given once the choice of factors has been made.[24] Membership in them is determined by allocation of the fuzzy scores, via some calibration procedure, to these features of cases (such as CLASS_F and ABILITY_F here). The approach is explicitly theoretical in this particular sense rather than inductive (though some may be tempted to finesse calibrations in an ad hoc manner in order to raise consistency and/or coverage figures). The key point is that the distribution of fuzzy scores over the cases does not determine the classification itself, only membership in the configurations comprising it. CA is quite different. Cluster structure and membership are produced together, iteratively. The cluster structure is usually determined by some sort of distance minimizing procedure and it is partly dependent on the particular sample employed (Lattin et al. 2003). In FCA, alongside the cluster structure, the fractional cluster memberships will also change with sample.[25] Readers should bear this in mind; again, other comparisons may not come out like either of ours.

We should also note that we have put a restriction on FCA in forcing it to produce a number of clusters that match the number of configurations in our fsQCA truth tables. Although other work we have done does not suggest that FCA with a greater number of clusters would have had much more predictive power than that we have reported, this is an important point to bear in mind. On the other hand, an advocate of fsQCA might point out, in the interests of a fair comparison, that the predictive power of fsQCA itself might have been greater given a different calibration of the factors.

In this chapter we have compared the classifications produced by different methods partly by crosstabulating classifications and partly by assessing the predictive power of classifications. In so far as we have relied on the latter, we have implicitly taken the view that the types comprising a classification, in so far as they capture real types in the social world, might be expected to have varying causal powers and, as we argued at the end of the previous

---

24 Some of these may not have any empirical members, either for logical reasons or because of the limited diversity that characterizes social data (Ragin 2000).

25 If distribution-dependent methods are used as part of the calibration procedure in fsQCA applications (see, for example, Cheli and Lemmi 1995), fuzzy memberships will also become partly dependent on sample. However, this sample-dependence is not a necessary feature of fsQCA, as it is in CA.

chapter, these might be expected to be reflected in various forms of (less than perfect) regularities. We have not attempted to assess the validity of each classification by comparing it with some independent source of evidence on the nature of such real types. If there were such real types, and if they were adequately captured by the limited number of dimensions we have analysed in this chapter, then it might be asked whether they were characteristic of a particular society during a particular period, or of some type of society, or, indeed, had a more universal existence, though the latter would seem unlikely. As Lieberson has pointed out in discussing regression analyses, the equations summarizing some sociological analysis are often descriptions of relationships existing at some particular time rather than accounts of basic causal processes (Lieberson 1985: 192). In our case, if the basic causal processes partly concern conflict between social classes over the distribution of educational opportunities, as seems likely, then, as the social and economic contexts for this conflict change – partly as a consequence of the conflict itself – we can expect that the nature of the cases tending to experience success and failure will also change.

Finally, we have observed the tendency, deplored by some, for the ready availability of software such as SPSS to lead to uncritical application of analytic techniques to data (Uprichard et al. 2008). We do not want to see this happening to the exciting research tool, constantly being developed by Charles Ragin and colleagues, embodied in the fsQCA software. Ragin himself has, especially in *Fuzzy Set Social Science* (2000) but also, more recently, in *Redesigning Social Inquiry* (2008), provided plenty of detail about the complexities and paradoxes of the fuzzy set approach (see also Cooper and Glaesser 2011b). Researchers should not, in our opinion, employ fsQCA without an understanding of these. We hope our contribution in this chapter will also act as an additional aid for those embarking on the mode of configurational analysis made easier by fsQCA and for those who have wondered about its relation to other ways of classifying cases, such as cluster analysis.

References

Abbott, A. (2001) *Time Matters,* London and Chicago: Chicago University Press.

Bailey, K. D. (1994) *Typologies and Taxonomies,* Thousand Oaks: Sage.

Boudon, R. (1974) *The Logic of Sociological Explanation,* Harmondsworth: Penguin.

Byrne, D. (2002) *Analysing Quantitative Data,* London: Sage.

Cheli, B. and Lemmi, A. (1995) 'A "totally fuzzy and relative" approach to the measurement of poverty', *Economic Notes,* 94, 1, pp. 115–34.

Cooper, B. (2005a) 'Applying Ragin's crisp and fuzzy set QCA to large datasets: social class and educational achievement in the National Child Development Study', *Sociological Research Online*, 10, 2.

— (2005b) 'On applying Ragin's crisp and fuzzy set QCA to large datasets', *European Consortium for Political Research* conference, Budapest. Retrieved 15 September 2009 from http://www.essex.ac.uk/ecpr/events/generalconference/budapest/papers/20/6/cooper.pdf

— (2006) 'Using Ragin's *Qualitative Comparative Analysis* with longitudinal datasets to explore the degree of meritocracy characterising educational achievement in Britain', Annual Meeting of the *American Educational Research Association*, San Francisco.

Cooper, B. and Glaesser, J. (2007) 'Exploring social class compositional effects on educational achievement with fuzzy set methods: a British study', Annual Meeting of the *American Educational Research Association*, Chicago.

— (2008) 'How has educational expansion changed the necessary and sufficient conditions for achieving professional, managerial and technical class positions in Britain? A configurational analysis', *Sociological Research Online*, 13, 3.

— (2011a) 'Using case-based approaches to analyse large datasets: a comparison of Ragin's fsQCA and fuzzy cluster analysis', *International Journal of Social Research Methodology*, 14, 1, pp. 31–48.

— (2011b) 'Paradoxes and pitfalls in using fuzzy set QCA: illustrations from a critical review of a study of educational inequality', *Sociological Research Online*, 16, 3.

de Oliveira, J. V. and Pedrycz, W. (eds) (2007) *Advances in Fuzzy Clustering and its Applications*, New York: Wiley.

Elman, C. (2005) 'Explanatory typologies in qualitative studies of international politics', *International Organization*, 59, pp. 293–326.

Erikson, R. and Goldthorpe, J. H. (1993) *The Constant Flux*, Oxford: Clarendon Press.

Freedman, D. A. (1987) 'As others see us: a case study in path analysis', *Journal of Educational Statistics*, 12, 2, pp. 101–28.

George, A. L. and Bennett, A. (2005) *Case Studies and Theory Development in the Social Sciences*. Cambridge, Mass.: MIT Press.

Glaesser, J. (2008) 'Just how flexible is the German selective secondary school system? A configurational analysis', *International Journal of Research and Method in Education*, 312, pp. 193–209.

Glaesser, J. and Cooper, B. (2010) 'Selectivity and flexibility in the German secondary school system: a configurational analysis of recent data from the German socio-economic panel', *European Sociological Review*, DOI:10.1093/esr/jcq026. Available at: <www.esr.oxfordjournals.org>.

Goldthorpe, J. H. (1997) 'Current issues in comparative macrosociology: a debate on methodological issues', *Comparative Social Research*, 16, pp. 1–26.

Kruse, R., Doring, C. and Lesot, M.-J. (2007) 'Fundamentals of fuzzy clustering', in de Oliveira, J. V. and Pedrycz, W. (eds) *Advances in Fuzzy Clustering and its Applications*, New York: Wiley, pp. 3–30.

Kvist, J. (2007) 'Fuzzy set ideal type analysis', *Journal of Business Research*, 60, pp. 474–81.

Lattin, J. M., Carroll, J. D. and Green, P. E. (2003) *Analyzing multivariate data*, Pacific Grove CA: Thomson Brooks.

Lieberson, S. (1985) *Making it Count*, Berkeley: University of California Press.

Mahoney, J. (2008) 'Toward a unified theory of causality', *Comparative Political Studies*, 41, 4/5, pp. 412–36.

Mahoney, J. and Goertz, G. (2006) 'A tale of two cultures: contrasting quantitative and qualitative research', *Political Analysis*, 14, 3, pp. 227–49.

Pawson, R. (1989) *A Measure for Measures*, London: Routledge.

Pedrycz, W. (2005) *Knowledge-Based Clustering*, New York: Wiley.

Pisces Conservation Ltd (2005) *Fuzzy Grouping 2: Manual*, Lymington, UK: Pisces Conservation Ltd.

Ragin, C. (2000) *Fuzzy Set Social Science*, Chicago: Chicago University Press.

— (2004) 'From fuzzy sets to crisp truth tables'. Retrieved 13 August 2005 from http://www.compasss. org/files/wpfiles/Raginfztt_April05.pdf.

— (2006a) 'The limitations of net-effects thinking', in Rihoux, B. and Grimm, H. (eds) *Innovative Comparative Methods for Policy analysis*, New York: Springer, pp. 13–41.

— (2006b) 'Set relations in social research: evaluating their consistency and coverage', *Political Analysis*, 14, pp. 291–310.

— (2008) *Redesigning Social Inquiry*, Chicago: University of Chicago Press.

Ragin, C. and Becker, H. S. (1992) *What is a Case?* Cambridge: Cambridge University Press.

Ragin, C., Drass, K. A. and Davey, S. (2006a) *Fuzzy-Set/Qualitative Comparative Analysis 2.0*. Tucson, Arizona: Department of Sociology, University of Arizona.

Ragin, C., Rubinson, C., Schaefer, D., Anderson, S., Williams, E. and Giesel, H. (2006b) *User's Guide to Fuzzy-Set/Qualitative Comparative Analysis 2.0*. Tucson, Arizona: Department of Sociology, University of Arizona.

Smithson, M. J. (1987) *Fuzzy Set Analysis for Behavioral and Social Sciences*, New York: Springer-Verlag.

Uprichard, E., Burrows, R. and Byrne, D. (2008) 'SPSS as an "inscription device": from causality to description?', *The Sociological Review*, 56, 4, pp. 606–22.

Verkuilen, J. (2005) 'Assigning membership in a fuzzy set analysis', *Sociological Methods and Research*, 33, 4, pp. 462–96.

Wiggins, R. D., Erzberger, C., Hyde, M., Higgs, P. and Blane, D. (2007) 'Optimal matching analysis using ideal types to describe the lifecourse: an illustration of how histories of work, partnerships and housing relate to quality of life in early old age', *International Journal of Social Research Methodology*, 10, 4, pp. 259–78.

Conclusion

Chapter Outline

The divide between quantitative and qualitative approaches to social science is as wide today as it has ever been, despite growing interest in 'mixing' methods from across this divide (see Cresswell and Plano Clark 2007 and Teddlie and Tashakkori 2009). While there have been some attempts to identify a 'common logic' in social science methodology, these have usually taken quantitative method as the model, or at least this has been the perception of qualitative researchers (see, for example, King et al. 1994 and Brady and Collier 2004). Moreover, many on the qualitative side would deny any continuity between their work and quantitative method, because they regard the latter as ontologically, epistemologically and/or politically inappropriate in studying human social action; or, at least, because they believe that it represents an incommensurable paradigm standing over against their own (see, for example, Smith 1989). Some also reject the idea that there could be a *logic* of inquiry, viewing research instead as a form of art or bricolage (Denzin and Lincoln 2005).

In the Introduction, we argued that this institutionalization of the qualitative–quantitative distinction needs to be challenged. We suggested that the various issues that have been identified as distinguishing qualitative from quantitative work, and as differentiating particular kinds of qualitative research from one another, vary sharply in character. Some currently influential positions on some of these issues – especially among qualitative researchers – undermine the very possibility of enquiry, in the ordinary sense of that term, or amount to attempts to turn it into a different activity – such as politics or art. By contrast, other issues implicated in the qualitative–quantitative divide are genuine and difficult problems that need to be approached by comparing the assumptions and products of different research strategies, and reflecting on concrete examples of research. Our book has been devoted to exploring issues of the latter kind, in particular those relating to causal analysis.

We began by establishing that there are quite severe problems with currently influential approaches to social science explanation, whether quantitative or qualitative. The frequentist or correlational approach that dominates quantitative work, relying upon the general linear model, has been subjected to increasing criticism, not least by some quantitative methodologists: for example for being unable to exercise the sort of control over confounding variables it claims; for failing to take account of the complexity of social causation, including how factors combine together and operate differently over time according to sequence and duration; for failing to give adequate emphasis to the task of theory-building; and so on (Lieberson 1985; Freedman 1987; Pawson 1989; Ragin 2000: 198–9 and *passim*; Abbott 2001; Berk 2004; Kent 2009). In Chapter 2, we also noted a tendency to rely upon speculative models of the processes generating outcomes, in areas of research such as social mobility. If we turn to qualitative inquiry, we find that many of its exponents today deny that their task is explanation, in the sense of causal analysis – emphasizing, instead, the role of 'thick' description and the interpretation of meaning or discourse (Hammersley 2008a and b, and Chapter 3). Yet, in practice, they usually produce what are actually candidate causal explanations, albeit employing strategies that are generally weak and ineffective as means for testing the validity of these hypotheses. They also sometimes draw general conclusions about the causal mechanisms generating aggregate patterns that are subject to serious threats to validity (see Chapter 4).

There are, of course, some approaches to qualitative work that have been directly concerned with causal analysis. As we saw, an influential approach within US sociology in the first half of the twentieth century, analytic induction (AI), was presented by its advocates as superior in pursuing this task to 'statistical method'. Furthermore, grounded theorizing (GT), which currently remains very popular, was also originally directed towards the task of causal analysis (Glaser and Strauss 1967), even though some current advocates seek to distance themselves from its early 'positivism' (Charmaz 2006; Bryant and Charmaz 2007: 36–41). Furthermore, in some areas of social research today, notably political science, there are sophisticated rationales and strategies for pursuing causal analysis via qualitative case studies, involving within-case and/or cross-case investigation, one example being Qualitative Comparative Analysis (QCA).

In this book we have explored these various approaches, and compared them with the model of correlational quantitative research. We drew a distinction between aggregate-focused and case-focused analytic strategies, this mapping only partially on to the qualitative–quantitative distinction: not all quantitative work is aggregate-focused, and not all qualitative analysis is case-focused. We examined some of the philosophical assumptions and methodological problems associated with case-focused modes of analysis and also explored the results of applying configurational and correlational approaches, as well as *different kinds of* configurational approach, to the same data. In the course of this, we discovered that the category 'case-focused analysis' is quite diverse, not just in the sense that there are versions that would conventionally be assigned to opposite sides of the qualitative–quantitative divide, but also that there are important differences among those that are generally treated as qualitative, for example between AI and QCA. Moreover, these differences themselves raise troublesome methodological issues, notably regarding assumptions about the nature of social causation upon which they rely.

Taking stock

So, it is clear that in this book we have been examining a multiplex field, structured by several potentially independent dichotomies or dimensions relating to variations in investigative and analytic strategy, few of which are neatly aligned with the qualitative–quantitative divide. They are worth enumerating:

1. *Cases treated as objects existing in the world versus cases treated as instances of categories.*
   This first distinction is quite closely related to the contrast between a nomothetic and an idiographic orientation, mentioned in the Introduction. There are some advocates of case-study work who prioritize the study of cases that have intrinsic interest – whether communities, organizations, people, or innovatory educational or social programmes of one sort or another. For example, Stake (1995, 2005) contrasts intrinsic with instrumental case studies, giving priority to the former. Other

commentators, however, insist that a case is always *a case of* something (Ragin 1992). And the implication of this is that what is treated as a case within the scope of any investigation is never an object in the world *in itself* (whatever that might mean) but includes only those aspects of it that are relevant to membership of the category or categories that are the focus of enquiry (Hammersley and Gomm 2000).

Sometimes, as with Stake, this distinction is used as a basis for differentiating forms of case study, but it is quite common for case studies to be systematically ambiguous in this respect: seeking both to document the features of some particular phenomenon *and* to draw conclusions about a general category to which it belongs, and therefore to make claims about the other phenomena also coming under that heading. Yet this is to conflate two quite different goals – idiographic and nomothetic – and probably thereby to pursue neither of them very effectively.

A similar tension is to be found within much survey research. Here there is often intrinsic interest in the particular population that is the target, so that in the first instance the conclusions drawn relate to this. However, there is a common tendency, implicit or explicit, to draw wider conclusions about cases beyond that population, perhaps claiming that the causal relationship discovered applies universally. Indeed, in some sense this is necessarily implied if a causal relationship has been identified, but what is crucial and often neglected is to identify the scope conditions under which it occurs (Walker and Cohen 1985).

There does seem to be an important dichotomy here, but our view is that both kinds of investigation can be of value.

2. *Developmental versus simultaneous modes of investigation.*
Both AI and GT involve what we referred to in Chapter 5 as a developmental approach, in that causal theories are initially developed through investigation of a small set of cases, and then tested and further developed through iterative waves of investigation of more cases, in ways that are shaped by the emerging theory. By contrast, much QCA work, in line with most quantitative and qualitative surveys, employs what might be called a simultaneous approach, whereby all the data to be used are acquired, and all are analysed, more or less at the same time.

There is much to be said in favour of a developmental approach, not least that the theory is being tested in the context of new cases, not the ones where it was initially developed, thereby providing a more rigorous testing process. This may force crucial rethinking of either the hypothesis or the definition of the phenomenon being explained. Indeed, we should note that it is difficult in simultaneous approaches to redefine the explanandum, since the data have already been collected on the basis of the original definition. A developmental approach is especially valuable when combined with strategic selection of cases (see below).

At the same time, a developmental approach makes what we refer to below as *systematic* analysis of the effects of all configurations of the factors examined more difficult. This would have to be done at the end of the developmental process, or periodically during its course, and there may be questions about whether this is feasible or worthwhile.[1] A developmental approach also causes problems for any attempt to draw inferences from the sample of cases investigated to some wider empirical population. There are also logistical reasons why a simultaneous approach may be adopted: studies often rely upon secondary data, or necessitate large-scale surveys that must be carried out in one sweep. This suggests that there may be a tension between a developmental approach and the number of cases studied.

3. *Systematic versus ad hoc analysis.*

QCA involves a systematic approach in the sense that it specifically sets out to explore all combinations of causal factors within a dataset in terms of their relationship to the occurrence of the outcome to be explained. By contrast, AI does not do this: new variables or features of cases are added at various points in the developmental process, while some of those previously built into early hypotheses are dropped. There is no systematic exploration of all combinations of the factors that have been considered. As a result, it may be that only *some* of the combinations of factors producing the outcome have been discovered.[2]

Like 'developmental', the word 'systematic' has positive overtones, and it does seem clear that it is desirable to be systematic in this sense, wherever possible. However, as already noted, there are issues about whether this can be combined with a developmental approach. There is also a danger that use of the techniques for systematic assessment introduced by QCA will be treated as a substitute for theoretical thinking, rather than as an aid to it. We should also note that systematic comparison generally occurs only *within* the set of cases and factors about which data have been collected, so that its value is heavily dependent upon prior sampling and data collection decisions.

4. *Number of cases studied.*

While it is conventional to contrast survey research with case study in terms of the number of cases for which data are collected and analysed, this is clearly a matter of degree – it is not a dichotomy. Furthermore, if we look at the various studies discussed in this book we find considerable variation in the number of cases investigated. While some of the studies referred to in Chapter 4 effectively focused on a single case, even while seeking to draw conclusions about national patterns, the classic examples of analytic induction carried out by Lindesmith (1937, 1968) and Cressey (1971) involved

---

1 For an approximation to the combination of these two approaches, see Athens 2010. A developmental approach also causes problems for any attempt to draw inferences from the sample of cases investigated to some wider empirical population.

2 If more than one combination leading to the same outcome *were* discovered, AI would demand a reformulation of the original outcome so as to recognize distinct, causally homogeneous types.

60 to several hundred cases. Furthermore, in Chapters 6 and 7 it was shown that case-focused analysis can be applied to even larger datasets, consisting of thousands of cases. It is also true that correlational modes of analysis can be, and have been, applied in studies investigating relatively small numbers of cases.

There are, of course, always pragmatic constraints involved in deciding how many cases to investigate. At any given level of resource, the more cases investigated, generally speaking, the less information can be collected and analysed about each one, and the less checking there can be of the reliability of this information (Hammersley 1992: ch11). It is important to emphasize, however, that these constraints do not necessarily prevent investigation of an adequate number of cases at an adequate level of 'depth'. Neither depth nor breadth are of value in themselves, a fact that can easily be forgotten – with qualitative researchers tending to exaggerate the value of the former, and quantitative researchers the latter. In each investigation, judgement must be made about how much depth and breadth are required in order to answer the research questions being addressed. There are obviously key questions to be considered about how this should be decided; as well as about how studies investigating different numbers of cases might be designed to complement one another.

5. *How cases are selected.*
Sometimes cases seem to be selected primarily in terms of convenience. For cost reasons, there may be reliance upon whatever relevant data are already available, within official statistics or secondary data banks. This may provide access to far more cases, and perhaps better data, than it would be feasible for an individual researcher to collect her or himself. Where data are to be collected by the researcher, there may be few criteria for choosing cases at the start of the investigation. This is true in some qualitative research, where the research focus is broad and uncertain at that point. As a result, a single case, or a few cases, may be selected simply because they seem likely to exemplify the phenomenon of interest. In the case of surveys, haphazard or snowball sampling may be employed, so that once again little or no strategic intent is involved. Even where strategic selection *is* applied, the sample may be restricted to a particular region, even though a wider area is the target population. In Chapter 3, we noted how Reay et al. (2005) had drawn their sample from London, but seemed to generalize their findings beyond this, perhaps to the UK as a whole or even wider. This is also by no means uncommon in quantitative surveys.

The most commonly mentioned strategic basis for selecting cases in social science is random sampling, of one sort or another. This promises to maximize the chances of achieving a representative sample of some specific population, and allows some assessment of how likely it is that this has been achieved. While, as we noted in Chapter 1, this approach by no means guarantees to deliver what it promises, notably because of the problem of non-response, it is nevertheless of great value. Qualitative researchers also sometimes aim at generalizations that are designed to be representative of a wider population, even though they do not usually rely upon statistical analysis. They may seek to select cases that are typical in relevant respects of the population concerned, or choose cases that map what are taken to be the key dimensions of variation within the population, though as we noted in Chapter 4 the need to do this, and the problems associated with doing it, are frequently overlooked.

However, not all selection of cases is aimed at identifying representative or typical cases, or at providing a basis for judging the range of variation within an extant population. Within the literature on case study, there is often reference to the investigation of 'critical' or 'deviant' cases, the purpose of this often being to test theories (see Eckstein 1992; Seawright and Gerring 2008), and there has also been some attention to this in the survey analysis and statistics literature (Kendall and Wolff 1949; Tukey 1977). A classic example of this strategy is the decision of Goldthorpe et al. (1969) to study car workers in the UK, as an instance of 'affluent workers', in order to determine whether they tend to adopt middle-class attitudes towards work and society, and therefore whether an embourgeoisement of the working class is taking place in Western societies.[3] Another classic example, this time more qualitative and micro-focused in character, is Cicourel and Kitsuse's (1973) selection of a school in which a counselling system was highly developed, as a basis for drawing conclusions about the likely future form schooling would take in the US.

The various kinds of case-focused analysis we have examined differ somewhat as regards selection of cases. There does not seem to be any requirement in the use of QCA to select cases in a strategic fashion, though there is sometimes an emphasis on maximizing diversity (Ragin 1994: ch5). The selection of cases in the classic studies using AI seems to have been largely non-strategic, even though later on in the research, in the case of Lindesmith (1937, 1968) and Cressey (1971), there was some selection of cases strategically to test the causal hypothesis that had been developed. In addition, Lindesmith sought cases from other countries than the US, in order to check whether his hypothesis applied universally across societies.

The case of GT is somewhat different, here the strategic selection of cases is specifically required, though it is directed at the *development*, rather than testing, of theory. As we saw in Chapter 3, Glaser and Strauss (1967) were rather ambiguous about whether or not the cases selected also entailed testing the emerging theory, and this ambiguity has persisted in later discussions. The extent to which testing occurs may vary across particular studies.

6. *Number of variables, or features of cases, included in the investigation.*
One aspect of what is meant by qualitative researchers when they refer to 'depth' of investigation is the number of features of each case – in effect, the number of

---

3 It is worth noting that the particular enterprise investigated, at Luton in the UK, was selected at least partly on grounds of convenience for travel.

variables – given attention. As we noted earlier, there is no value *per se* in maximizing the number of variables included in a causal analysis, and there must be judgement about what are and are not likely to be relevant variables.

Correlational studies usually, though by no means always, involve a relatively small number of variables, and these are treated singly, either assessing their relative contribution to the likelihood of the outcome and/or treating some as potentially confounding variables that need to be controlled through comparative analysis.[4] AI and QCA studies tend to include more variables than is common in many correlational studies, though this is not always the case. GT tends to encourage inclusion of a relatively large number of variables through a concern with producing broad theories (see Chapter 3) and perhaps also in order to produce a 'dense' analysis.

As already noted, there are, of course, two sorts of ground for inclusion of variables. One concerns which variables might combine with one another to generate the type(s) of outcome to be explained. The second relates to variables that are not of direct concern in the investigation but that could operate as important mediating or confounding factors.

A preoccupation with confounding variables is, of course, central in survey analysis, where the usual focus is on assessing the net contribution of each individual causal factor. This concern is also central in experimental analysis, where it is assumed that factors external to the causal system being investigated might interfere with or obscure the operation of that system – hence the need for random allocation to groups. Curiously, despite the fact that AI represents, in many respects, an application of this experimental logic to case study, there is little attention given by studies using this approach to confounding factors. Indeed, the insistence that a single negative case should force reformulation of the causal hypothesis, or of the definition of the explanandum, actually neglects the role of such factors. Furthermore, in the absence of the sort of physical control of background variables that random allocation provides in experimental research, it seems unlikely that any causal hypothesis will be found to have no exceptions (Robinson 1951). In the case of QCA, the assumption seems to be that, if all relevant factors are included in the investigation, the search for which combinations produce the outcome circumvents any need to allow for confounding factors. This may be true, though there is the problem of how the range of relevant factors is to be determined effectively. This necessarily relies upon theoretical ideas about what causes what, and it is always possible that relevant factors will be overlooked. Equally, what factors are included may be constrained by the information available about cases. Much the same points could be made about GT or survey analysis.

---

4 Of course, what is a confounding factor in the light of one research focus can be a central variable in another.

7. *Synchronic versus diachronic techniques of analysis: a concern with the correlation or configuration of features across or within cases versus investigation of temporal sequences and/or durations of features within cases.*

While implicated in much discussion of case study versus survey analysis, this dimension in fact cross-cuts that between aggregate-focused and case-focused analysis. It is important to emphasize that what we are referring to here are techniques for constructing and searching datasets to discover patterns that might indicate causal processes, not theoretical understandings of those processes: any theoretical analysis must assume a diachronic dimension, at the very least that causes precede their effects.[5]

Most survey analysis is 'cross-sectional', in the sense that, in effect, it studies the impact of various factors notionally occurring at a single point in time, while much case-study research is explicitly concerned with tracing *processes* over time within particular cases (George and Bennett 2005; Gerring 2006). The most developed form of this is, of course, historical analysis, in which different types of causal factor are identified according to their mode of diachronic operation, for example distinguishing between background and trigger factors (Roberts 1996). However, survey researchers sometimes seek to investigate what happens over time within cases through panel studies or other longitudinal designs. And there is much qualitative research – including much of that committed to employing AI, GT, QCA or qualitative survey – that does not specifically investigate temporal processes within cases, even if it makes assumptions about these.

In this book we have been primarily concerned with the contrast between various forms of synchronic analysis: correlational versus configurational, as well as different versions of configurational analysis. Given this, it is perhaps worth illustrating in a little more detail what is involved in diachronic analysis. A classic example from the substantive field that has been our main focus is Lacey's (1970) study of *Hightown Grammar*. This examined key aspects of change in an English secondary school and its relationship with its environment over several decades. However, Lacey was primarily concerned with a more detailed examination of a particular causal process investigated over the time period in which the research was carried out. This concerned the effects of differentiation of the students by teachers in terms of academic ability and behavioural compliance, notably through the streaming (tracking) system. Lacey argued that this led to a polarization in attitudes on the part of the students, with those assigned to top streams remaining committed to academic success while those in bottom streams often came to reject it. Identifying this causal

---

5 There has been some dispute in the literature on causation about whether this temporal sequence is always required. See, for example, the article by J. Faye on 'Backward Causation' in the *Stanford Encyclopedia of Philosophy*, at (accessed 1.3.11): http://plato.stanford.edu/entries/causation-backwards/ However, it is not a key issue in social science, as far as we can tell, even though intentional and functional explanations are sometimes wrongly taken to assume it (Lessnoff 1974: 118–30).

process involved charting changes in differentiation and polarization, at the level of the school, the classroom, and the individual student, over a two-year period.

Sometimes it seems to be assumed that, through this sort of diachronic analysis, causal processes can be directly observed and documented. However, this questionable assumption need not be made. Rather, the task is to show not just that candidate causes and effects are in the right sequence(s), with 'cause(s)' preceding 'effect(s)', but also to document more complex temporal patterns among causal factors, and among potentially mediating features that occur between causes and effects. This both fills out the causal account (generating hypotheses about or evidence for particular causal mechanisms) but also provides evidence for the claim that the cause-effect relation claimed is operating in the case studied (Roberts 1996). One stimulus for this kind of work has been notions of path dependency, and interest in complexity theory, concerned with how quite minor changes in conditions can lead to very different trajectories (Mahoney 2000; Byrne 2005).

As much of the literature on case-study methodology in political science emphasizes, one of the strengths of this sort of work is the *combining* of synchronic with diachronic analysis. However, what is involved here is a range of analytic options, there is no single 'best strategy': both synchronic and diachronic techniques are of value, as well as attempts to combine them to various degrees and in different ways. Furthermore, all of them must be seen as complementing, rather than substituting for, theoretical thinking.

8. *Searching for deterministic or probabilistic patterns in the data.*
   This dimension also cross-cuts the qualitative/quantitative and case-focused/aggregate-focused distinctions. While AI contrasts with correlational research in this respect, GT is also satisfied with probabilistic patterns – it is not concerned with identifying necessary and jointly sufficient conditions for the occurrence of types of phenomena. QCA is a more complex case. It is frequently concerned with identifying necessary *or* sufficient conditions; furthermore, it also allows for more probabilistic patterns (Ragin 2000, 2006; Goertz 2006).

   This dimension is of some importance in methodological terms. As we saw in Chapter 5, a major rationale for seeking deterministic patterns put forward by advocates of AI is that this facilitates drawing conclusions from investigations of a small number of cases, since a single exception forces recasting of the theory. If probabilistic patterns are allowed, this no longer applies (see Lieberson 1992). Instead the researcher has to make judgements about whether exceptions count against the theory concerned or are merely outliers to a probabilistic trend. Furthermore, large numbers of cases would probably need to be studied in order to identify such trends.

These, then, are some of the issues that arise out of our discussions in earlier chapters. Each requires much greater consideration than we are able to offer here.

So, rather than social scientists being faced with a set of dichotomies that are isomorphic with one another, many of the issues we have listed involve dimensions, and these do not map on to one another so as to form a small set of alternative approaches, certainly not just two. While there are some constraints operating – for example between how many cases are investigated and the depth in which each can be studied – there is in practice considerable leeway in the decisions made as regards each of these issues. Furthermore, the considerations that need to be taken into account in making judgements about them are, for the most part, what we might call pragmatic rather than philosophical ones. In other words, they are not determined by epistemological or ontological commitments, but are more strategic in character; and, often, the various strategies can be usefully combined.

This is not to deny, however, that there are some difficult, unresolved philosophical issues facing causal analysis in social science. Indeed, there are many of these. We will focus here on just a few interrelated ones. The first concerns the question of whether the sort of theory pursued by some of the approaches we have discussed is a viable or worthwhile enterprise. The aim of these has been to produce a theory that captures a relatively closed system of causal relationships generating a particular type of outcome wherever it occurs, assuming certain background conditions. In its most extreme and single-minded form, found in AI, what is to be discovered is in effect an entirely closed system, in that the task is to find a set of factors that *always* produces a specific type of outcome, and is *the only* set that does so. In other words, causation is conceptualized in terms of a set of necessary and jointly sufficient conditions. The other approaches we have discussed are less stringent in their requirements, focusing on sufficient or on necessary conditions, or even on factors that simply contribute to an increased likelihood that a particular type of outcome will occur.

There are serious questions about whether the model employed by AI can be applied in the social world. Some commentators argue that closed causal systems can only be identified at the psychological level (Homans 1967), others that they cannot even be found there but only at the levels of phenomena dealt with by modern physics (Ellis 2008, 2009). Something like this position was adopted by Mill in the nineteenth century. He specifically denied that the methods of agreement and difference, which he identified as the core of scientific method, and which form the basis for the sorts of analysis we have been discussing, could be applied in sociology. The reason for this was the sheer number of variables involved in the causation of social phenomena. Other commentators, notably Blumer (1969), have emphasized the contingent character of human action, since it involves processes in which actors interpret the situations they face and decide on what strategies to adopt in dealing with them. It is rather surprising, in this respect, that AI developed in the same context as Blumer's symbolic interactionism.[6] The issues here concern the ontology of the social world. But how are we to determine the nature of social causation? Can this be done independently of social science, or only *through* social science? Can it be done at all?

A second issue is highlighted by an ambiguity we detected in Ragin's discussion of QCA – between the idea that it produces a general theory and the notion that it facilitates our development of explanations in particular cases. We might wonder whether we should not focus exclusively on the second of these options, adopting what we referred to earlier as an idiographic orientation. Is producing information about particular cases not the most important goal of social science? This is the position taken by Max Weber, albeit not on ontological but rather on praxiological grounds (Turner and Factor 1984; Ringer 1997). Note that this includes seeking to identify causal processes operating within particular extant populations, in the manner explored in Chapters 4, 6 and 7.

A further question relates to whether our explanations for particular phenomena necessarily rely upon tested theories. Or, to put the issue another way: do the various theoretical ideas about causal processes that are already available to us need to be tested to see whether they apply generally? Does doing this improve their value as resources in explaining what occurred in particular circumstances? After all, however effectively they have been tested in general terms, we would still need to determine whether they apply in each case (Hammersley 2011).

These are interesting, important and difficult questions. And they clearly have major practical implications. However, there are also limits to their relevance for social science: they must not be allowed to block the road of inquiry.

Final thoughts

The central message of our book is that the qualitative–quantitative distinction must not be accepted as the framework within which we think about social research. While it picks out some important kinds of variation in orientation, these differ sharply in character. Given this, we need to focus on

---

6 Blumer was one of Lindesmith's teachers.

specific issues rather than global contrasts. We are faced with a complex field not a simple divide. Moreover, while some of the criticisms directed across the qualitative–quantitative border, from both sides, are misdirected, many do point to important limitations that need to be recognized. In this book we have tried to engage in detail with some of the methodological problems facing social science, so as to identify productive strategies for causal analysis. We hope, at the very least, to have provided some clarification of these, and thereby to have facilitated further work by others.

References

Abbott, A. (2001) *Time Matters*, Chicago: University of Chicago Press.

Athens, L. (2010) 'Naturalistic inquiry in theory and practice', *Journal of Contemporary Ethnography*, 39, 1, pp. 87–125.

Berk, R. A. (2004) *Regression Analysis: a constructive critique*, Thousand Oaks CA: Sage.

Blumer, H. (1969) *Symbolic Interactionism: perspective and method*, Englewood Cliffs NJ: Prentice-Hall. [Reprinted by University of California Press, Berkeley, 1998.]

Brady, H. E. and Collier, D. (eds) (2004) *Rethinking Social Inquiry: diverse tools, shared standards*, Lanham MD: Rowman and Littlefield.

Bryant, A. and Charmaz, K. (eds) (2007) *The Sage Handbook of Grounded Theory*, London: Sage.

Byrne, D. S. (2005) 'Complexity, configuration and cases', *Theory, Culture & Society*, 22, 5, pp. 95–111.

Charmaz, K. (2000) 'Grounded Theory: objectivist and constructivist methods', in Denzin, N. and Lincoln, Y. (eds) *Handbook of Qualitative Research*, Second edition, Thousand Oaks CA: Sage, pp. 509–35.

Cicourel, A. and Kitsuse, J. (1963) *The Educational Decision-Makers*, Indianapolis IND: Bobbs-Merrill.

Cressey, D. (1971) *Other People's Money*, Second edition, Belmont CA: Wadsworth.

Cresswell, J. W. and Plano Clark, V. L. (2007) *Designing and Conducting Mixed Methods Research*, Thousand Oaks CA: Sage.

Denzin, N. and Lincoln, Y. (eds) (2005) *Handbook of Qualitative Research*, Thousand Oaks CA: Sage.

Eckstein, H. (1992) 'Case study and theory in political science', *Regarding Politics*, Berkeley CA: University of California Press.

Ellis, B. (2008) 'Essentialism and natural kinds', in Psillos, S. and Curd, M. (eds) *The Routledge Companion to Philosophy of Science*, London: Routledge.

— (2009) *The Metaphysics of Scientific Realism*, Durham: Acumen.

Freedman, D. A. (1987) 'As others see us: a case study in path analysis' (with discussion), *Journal of Educational Statistics*, 12, pp. 101–223.

George, A. and Bennett (2005) *Case Studies and Theory Development in the Social Sciences*, Cambridge MS: MIT Press.

Gerring, J. (2006) *Case Study Research: principles and practices*, Cambridge: Cambridge University Press.

Glaser, B. and Strauss, A. (1967) *The Discovery of Grounded Theory*, Chicago: Aldine.

Goertz, G. (2006) 'Assessing the trivialness, relevance, and relative importance of necessary or sufficient conditions in social science', *Studies in Comparative International Development*, 41, 2, pp. 88–109.

Goldthorpe, J., Lockwood, D., Bechhofer, F. and Platt, J. (1969) *The Affluent Worker in the Class Structure*, Cambridge: Cambridge University Press.

Gomm, R., Hammersley, M. and Foster, P. (eds) (2000) *Case Study Method*, London: Sage.

Hammersley, M. (1992) *What's Wrong with Ethnography?*, London: Routledge.

— (2008a) 'Causality as conundrum: the case of qualitative inquiry', *Methodological Innovations Online*, 2, 3. Available at (accessed 7.12.10): http://erdt.plymouth.ac.uk/mionline/public_html/viewarticle.php?id=63&layout=html

— (2008b) *Questioning Qualitative Inquiry*, London: Sage.

— (2011) 'Theorising and explaining in social science', unpublished paper.

Hammersley, M. and Gomm, R. (2000) Introduction, in Gomm et al. (eds).

Homans, G. C. (1967) *The Nature of Social Science*, New York: Harcourt.

Kendall, P. and Wolff, K. (1949) 'Analysis of deviant cases in communications research', in Lazarsfeld, P. and Stanton, F. (eds) *Communications Research, 1948–9*, New York, Harper and Bros. Reprinted as 'The two purposes of deviant case analysis', in Lazarsfeld, P. and Rosenberg, M. (eds) *The Language of Social Research*, Glencoe ILL: Free Press.

Kent, R. (2009) 'Case-centred methods and quantitative analysis', in Byrne, D. and Ragin, C. (eds) *The Sage Handbook of Case-Based Methods*, London: Sage.

King, G., Keohane, R. O. and Verba, S. (1994) *Designing Social Inquiry*, Princeton: Princeton University Press.

Lacey, C. (1970) *Hightown Grammar*, Manchester: Manchester University Press.

Lessnoff, M. (1974) *The Structure of Social Science*, London: Allen and Unwin.

Lieberson, S. (1985) *Making it Count: the improvement of social research and theory*, Berkeley: University of California Press.

— (1992) 'Small N's and big conclusions: an examination of the reasoning in comparative studies based on a small number of cases', in Ragin, C. and Becker, H. S. (eds) *What is a Case?*, Cambridge: Cambridge University Press.

Lindesmith, A. (1937) *The Nature of Opiate Addiction*, Chicago: University of Chicago Libraries.

— (1968) *Addiction and Opiates*, Chicago: Aldine.

Mahoney, J. (2000) 'Path dependence in historical sociology', *Theory and Society*, 29, 4, pp. 507-48.

Mill, J. S. (1843–72) *A System of Logic Ratiocinative and Inductive*. (Edition used: Volumes VII and VIII of *Collected Works of John Stuart Mill*, Toronto: University of Toronto Press, 1974.)

Pawson, R. (1989) *A Measure for Measures: a manifesto for empirical sociology*, London: Routledge.

Ragin, C. (1992) ' "Casing" and the process of social inquiry', in Ragin, C. and Becker, H. S. (eds) *What is a Case?*, Cambridge: Cambridge University Press.

— (1994) *Constructing Social Research: the unity and diversity of method*, Thousand Oaks CA: Pine Forge Press.

— (2000) *Fuzzy-Set Social Science*, Chicago: University of Chicago Press.

— (2006) 'The limitations of net-effects thinking', in B. Rihoux and Grimm, H. (eds), *Innovative Comparative Methods for Policy Analysis* , New York: Springer, pp. 13–41.

Reay, D., David, M. and Ball, S. (2005) *Degrees of Choice: social class, race and gender in higher education*, Stoke on Trent: Trentham Books.

Ringer, F. (1997) *Max Weber's Methodology*, Cambridge MS: Harvard University Press.

Roberts, C. (1996) *The Logic of Historical Explanation*, University Park PA: Pennsylvania State University Press.

Robinson, W. S. (1951) 'The logical structure of analytic induction', *American Sociological Review*, 16, 6, pp. 812–18. (Responses from Lindesmith and Weinberg, and reply by Robinson, in *American Sociological Review*, 17, pp. 492–4.)

Seawright, J. and Gerring, J. (2008) 'Case selection techniques in case study research: a menu of qualitative and quantitative options', *Political Research Quarterly*, 61, 2, pp. 294–308.

Smith, J. K. (1989) *The Nature of Social and Educational Inquiry*, Norwood NJ: Ablex.

Stake, R. (1995) *The Art of Case Study Research*, Thousand Oaks CA: Sage.

Stake, R. (2005) 'Qualitative case studies', in Denzin and Lincoln (eds)

Teddlie, C. and Tashakkori, A. (2009) *Foundations of Mixed Methods Research*, Thousand Oaks CA: Sage.

Tukey, J. W. (1977) *Exploratory Data Analysis*, Reading MS: Addison-Wesley.

Turner, S. P. and Factor, R. A. (1984) *Max Weber and the Dispute over Reason and Value*, London: Routledge and Kegan Paul.

Walker, H. A. and Cohen, B. P. (1985) 'Scope statements: imperatives for evaluating theory', *American Sociological Review*, 50, pp. 288–301.

Author Index

Subject Index